# LORNA ]

## A Romance of Exmoor.

By R. D. BLACKMORE,

AUTHOR OF 'CRADOCK NOWELL,' ETC.

Μή μοι γᾶν Πέλοπος, μή μοι χρύσεια τάλαντα
Εἴη ἔχειν, μηδὲ πρόσθε θέειν ἀνέμων·
'Αλλ' ὑπὸ τᾷ πέτρᾳ τᾷδ' ᾀσομαι, ἀγκὰς ἔχων τυ,
Σύννομα μᾶλ' ἐσορῶν τὰν Σικελὰν ἐς ἅλα.

### IN THREE VOLUMES.

#### VOL. III.

### LONDON:
### SAMPSON LOW, SON, & MARSTON,
CROWN BUILDINGS, 188, FLEET STREET.
1869.

LONDON: PRINTED BY W. CLOWES & SONS, STAMFORD STREET AND CHARING CROSS.

# CONTENTS OF VOL. III.

| Chapter | | Page |
|---|---|---|
| I. | Jeremy finds out Something | 1 |
| II. | Mutual Discomfiture | 18 |
| III. | Getting into Chancery | 36 |
| IV. | John becomes too Popular | 49 |
| V. | Lorna knows her Nurse | 69 |
| VI. | Master Huckaback's Secret | 92 |
| VII. | Lorna gone away | 109 |
| VIII. | Annie Luckier than John | 128 |
| IX. | Therefore he seeks Comfort | 140 |
| X. | The King must not be prayed for | 152 |
| XI. | John is worsted by the Women | 169 |
| XII. | Slaughter in the Marshes | 183 |
| XIII. | Falling among Lambs | 196 |
| XIV. | Suitable Devotion | 210 |
| XV. | Lorna still is Lorna | 226 |
| XVI. | John is John no longer | 239 |
| XVII. | Not to be put up with | 257 |
| XVIII. | Compelled to Volunteer | 270 |

| CHAPTER | | PAGE |
|---|---|---|
| XIX. A Long Account Settled.. .. .. .. .. | | 284 |
| XX. The Counsellor and the Carver .. .. .. | | 294 |
| XXI. How to get out of Chancery .. .. .. | | 307 |
| XXII. Driven beyond Endurance .. .. .. .. | | 316 |
| XXIII. Life and Lorna come again .. .. .. .. | | 328 |

# LORNA DOONE:

## A ROMANCE OF EXMOOR.

## CHAPTER I.

" You know, my son," said Jeremy Stickles, with a good pull at his pipe, because he was going to talk so much, and putting his legs well along in the settle; " it has been my duty, for a wearier time than I care to think of (and which would have been unbearable, except for your great kindness), to search this neighbourhood narrowly, and learn every thing about every body. Now the neighbourhood itself is queer; and people have different ways of thinking from what we are used to in London. For instance now, among your folk, when any piece of news is told, or any man's conduct spoken of, the very first question that arises in your minds is this—'was this action kind and good?' Long after that, you say to yourselves, 'does the law enjoin, or forbid this thing?' Now here is your fundamental error: for among all truly civilized people, the fore-

most of all questions is, 'how stands the law herein?'
And if the law approve, no need for any further ques-
tioning. That this is so, you may take my word : for
I know the law pretty thoroughly.

"Very well; I need not say any more about that,
for I have shown that you are all quite wrong. I
only speak of this savage tendency, because it explains
so many things which have puzzled me among you,
and most of all your kindness to men whom you never
saw before; which is an utterly illegal thing. It also
explains your toleration of these outlaw Doones so
long. If your views of law had been correct, and law
an element of your lives, these robbers could never
have been indulged for so many years, amongst you:
but you must have abated the nuisance."

"Now, Stickles," I cried, "this is too bad !" he was
delivering himself so grandly. "Why you yourself
have been amongst us, as the balance, and sceptre, and
sword of law, for nigh upon a twelvemonth; and have
you abated the nuisance, or even cared to do it, until
they began to shoot at you ? "

"My son," he replied; "your argument is quite
beside the purpose, and only tends to prove more
clearly that which I have said of you. However, if
you wish to hear my story, no more interruptions. I
may not have a chance to tell you, perhaps for weeks,
or I know not when, if once those yellows and reds
arrive, and be blessed to them, the lubbers ! Well, it
may be six months ago, or it may be seven, at any rate
a good while before that cursed frost began, the mere

name of which sends a shiver down every bone of my
body; when I was riding one afternoon from Dulverton
to Watchett "——

"Dulverton to Watchett!" I cried. "Now what
does that remind me of? I am sure, I remember
something "——

"Remember this, John, if anything—that another
word from thee, and thou hast no more of mine. Well,
I was a little weary perhaps, having been plagued at
Dulverton with the grossness of the people. For they
would tell me nothing at all about their fellow-towns-
man, your worthy Uncle Huckaback, except that he
was a God-fearing man, and they only wished I was
like him. I blessed myself for a stupid fool, in thinking to have pumped them; for by this time, I might
have known that, through your Western homeliness,
every man in his own country is something more than
a prophet. And I felt, of course, that I had done
more harm than good by questioning; inasmuch as
every soul in the place would run straightway and
inform him that the King's man from the other side
of the forest had been sifting out his ways and works."

"Ah," I cried, for I could not help it; "you begin
to understand at last, that we are not quite such a set
of oafs, as you at first believed us."

"I was riding on from Dulverton," he resumed with
great severity; yet threatening me no more, which
checked me more than fifty threats: "and it was late
in the afternoon, and I was growing weary. The road
(if road it could be called) turned suddenly down from

the higher land to the very brink of the sea; and
rounding a little jut of cliff I met the roar of the
breakers.  My horse was scared, and leaped aside;
for a northerly wind was piping, and driving hunks of
foam across, as children scatter snow-balls.  But he
only sank to his fetlocks in the dry sand, piled with
pop-weed; and I tried to make him face the waves;
and then I looked about me.

"Watchett town was not to be seen, on account of a
little foreland, a mile or more upon my course, and
standing to the right of me.  There was room enough
below the cliffs (which are nothing there to yours,
John) for horse and man to get along, although the
tide was running high with a northerly gale to back it.
But close at hand, and in the corner, drawn above the
yellow sands and long eyebrows of wrack-weed, as
snug a little house blinked on me as ever I saw, or
wished to see.

" You know that I am not luxurious, neither in any
way given to the common lusts of the flesh, John.  My
father never allowed his hair to grow a fourth part of
an inch in length, and he was a thoroughly godly man;
and I try to follow in his footsteps, whenever I think
about it.  Nevertheless I do assure you that my view
of that little house, and the way the lights were
twinkling, so different from the cold and darkness of
the rolling sea, moved the ancient Adam in me, if he
could be found to move.  I love not a house with too
many windows: being out of house and doors, some
three-quarters of my time, when I get inside a house,

I like to feel the difference. Air and light are good for people who have any lack of them; and if a man once talks about them, 'tis enough to prove his need of them. But, as you well know, John Ridd, the horse who has been at work all day, with the sunshine on his eyes, sleeps better in dark stable, and needs no moon to help him.

"Seeing therefore that this same inn had four windows, and no more, I thought to myself how snug it was, and how beautifully I could sleep there. And so I made the old horse draw hand, which he was only too glad to do, and we clomb above the spring-tide mark, and over a little piece of turf, and struck the door of the hostelry. Some one came, and peeped at me through the lattice overhead, which was full of bulls' eyes; and then the bolt was drawn back, and a woman met me very courteously. A dark and foreign-looking woman, very hot of blood, I doubt, but not altogether a bad one. And she waited for me to be first to speak; which an Englishwoman would not have done.

" 'Can I rest here for the night?' I asked, with a lift of my hat to her; for she was no provincial dame, who would stare at me for the courtesy: 'my horse is weary from the sloughs, and myself but little better: beside that, we both are famished.'

" 'Yes, sir, you can rest and welcome. But of food, I fear, there is but little, unless of the common order. Our fishers would have drawn the nets, but the waves were violent. However we have—what you call it? I

never can remember; it is so hard to say—the flesh of
the hog salted.'

" 'Bacon!' said I: 'what can be better? And
half-a-dozen of eggs with it, and a quart of fresh-drawn
ale. You make me rage with hunger, madam. Is it
cruelty, or hospitality?'

" 'Ah, good!' she replied, with a merry smile, full
of southern sunshine: 'you are not of the men round
here: you can think, and you can laugh!'

" 'And most of all, I can eat, good madam. In that
way I shall astonish you; even more than by my
intellect.'

" She laughed aloud, and swung her shoulders, as
your natives cannot do; and then she called a little
maid to lead my horse to stable. However I preferred
to see that matter done myself, and told her to send
the little maid for the frying-pan and the egg-box.

" Whether it were my natural wit and elegance of
manner; or whether it were my London freedom and
knowledge of the world; or (which is perhaps the
most probable, because the least pleasing supposition)
my ready and permanent appetite, and appreciation of
garlic—I leave you to decide, John: but perhaps all
three combined to recommend me to the graces of my
charming hostess. When I say 'charming,' I mean of
course by manners and by intelligence, and most of all
by cooking; for as regards external charms (most
fleeting and fallacious) hers had ceased to cause
distress, for I cannot say how many years. She said
that it was the climate—for even upon that subject,

she requested my opinion—and I answered, 'if there be a change; let madam blame the seasons."

"However, not to dwell too much upon our little pleasantries (for I always get on with these foreign women, better than with your Molls and Pegs), I became, not inquisitive, but reasonably desirous to know, by what strange hap or hazard, a clever and a handsome woman, as she must have been some day, a woman moreover with great contempt for the rustic minds around her, could have settled here in this lonely inn, with only the waves for company, and a boorish husband who slaved all day in turning a potter's wheel at Watchett. And what was the meaning of the emblem set above her doorway, a very unattractive cat sitting in a ruined tree?

"However I had not very long to strain my curiosity; for when she found out who I was, and how I held the King's commission, and might be called an officer, her desire to tell me all was more than equal to mine of hearing it. Many and many a day, she had longed for some one both skilful and trustworthy, most of all for some one bearing warrant from a court of justice. But the magistrates of the neighbourhood would have nothing whatever to say to her, declaring that she was a crack-brained woman, and a wicked, and even a foreign one.

"With many grimaces she·assured me, that never by her own free will would she have lived so many years in that hateful country, where the sky for half the year was fog, and rain for nearly the other half.

It was so, the very night when first her evil fortune
brought her there; and so no doubt it would be, long
after it had killed her. But if I wished to know the
reason of her being there, she would tell me in few
words, which I will repeat as briefly.

"By birth she was an Italian, from the mountains of
Apulia, who had gone to Rome to seek her fortunes,
after being badly treated in some love-affair. Her
Christian name was Benita; as for her surname, that
could make no difference to any one. Being a quick
and active girl, and resolved to work down her troubles,
she found employment in a large hotel; and rising
gradually, began to send money to her parents. And
here she might have thriven well, and married well
under sunny skies, and been a happy woman; but that
some black day sent thither a rich and noble English
family, eager to behold the Pope. It was not however
their fervent longing for the Holy Father, which had
brought them to St. Peter's roof; but rather their own
bad luck in making their home too hot to hold them.
For although in the main good Catholics, and pleasant
receivers of anything; one of their number had given
offence, by the folly of trying to think for himself.
Some bitter feud had been among them, Benita knew
not how it was; and the sister of the nobleman who
had died quite lately was married to the rival claimant,
whom they all detested. It was something about
dividing land; Benita knew not what it was.

"But this Benita did know, that they were all great
people, and rich, and very liberal; so that when they

offered to take her, to attend to the children, and to speak the language for them, and to comfort the lady, she was only too glad to go, little foreseeing the end of it. Moreover she loved the children so, from their pretty ways and that, and the things they gave her, and the style of their dresses; that it would have broken her heart almost never to see the dears again.

"And so, in a very evil hour, she accepted the service of the noble Englishman, and sent her father an old shoe filled to the tongue with money, and trusted herself to fortune. But even before she went, she knew that it could not turn out well; for the laurel leaf which she threw on the fire would not crackle even once, and the horn of the goat came wrong in the twist, and the heel of her foot was shining. This made her sigh at the starting-time; and after that what could you hope for?

"However, at first all things went well. My Lord was as gay as gay could be; and never would come inside the carriage, when a decent horse could be got to ride. He would gallop in front, at a reckless pace, without a weapon of any kind, delighted with the pure blue air, and throwing his heart around him. Benita had never seen any man so admirable, and so childish. As innocent as an infant; and not only contented, but noisily happy with anything. Only other people must share his joy; and the shadow of sorrow scattered it; though it were but the shade of poverty.

"Here Benita wept a little; and I liked her none

the less, and believed her ten times more; in virtue
of a tear or two.

"And so they travelled through Northern Italy, and
throughout the south of France, making their way
anyhow; sometimes in coaches, sometimes in carts,
sometimes upon mule-back, sometimes even a-foot and
weary; but always as happy as could be. The children laughed, and grew, and throve (especially the
young lady, the elder of the two), and Benita began
to think that omens must not be relied upon. But
suddenly, her faith in omens was confirmed for ever.

"My Lord, who was quite a young man still, and
laughed at English arrogance, rode on in front of his
wife and friends, to catch the first of a famous view, on
the French side of the Pyrenee hills. He kissed his
hand to his wife, and said that he would save her the
trouble of coming. For those two were so one in one,
that they could make each other know whatever he or
she had felt. And so my Lord went round the corner,
with a fine young horse leaping up at the steps.

"They waited for him, long and long; but he never
came again; and within a week, his mangled body lay
in a little chapel-yard; and if the priests only said
a quarter of the prayers they took the money for,
God knows they can have no throats left; only a
relaxation.

"My Lady dwelled for six months more—it is a
melancholy tale (what true tale is not so?)—scarcely
able to believe that all her fright was not a dream.
She would not wear a piece or shape of any mourning-

clothes, she would not have a person cry, or any
sorrow among us. She simply disbelieved the thing,
and trusted God to right it. The Protestants, who
have no faith, cannot understand this feeling. Enough
that so it was, and so my Lady went to heaven.

"For when the snow came down in autumn on the
roots of the Pyrenees, and the chapel-yard was white
with it, many people told the lady that it was time for
her to go. And the strongest plea of all was this, that
now she bore another hope of repeating her husband's
virtues. So at the end of October, when wolves came
down to the farm-lands, the little English family went
home towards their England.

"They landed somewhere on the Devonshire coast,
ten or eleven years agone, and stayed some days at
Exeter; and set out thence in a hired coach, without
any proper attendance, for Watchett, in the north of
Somerset. For the lady owned a quiet mansion in the
neighbourhood of that town, and her one desire was to
find refuge there, and to meet her lord, who was sure
to come (she said) when he heard of his new infant.
Therefore with only two serving-men and two maids
(including Benita) the party set forth from Exeter;
and lay the first night at Bampton.

"On the following morn they started bravely, with
earnest hope of arriving at their journey's end by daylight. But the roads were soft and very deep, and the
sloughs were out in places; and the heavy coach broke
down in the axle, and needed mending at Dulverton;
and so they lost three hours or more, and would have

been wiser to sleep there. But her ladyship would not
hear of it: she must be home that night she said, and
her husband would be waiting. How could she keep
him waiting now, after such a long, long time?

" Therefore, although it was afternoon, and the year
now come to December, the horses were put to again,
and the heavy coach went up the hill, with the lady,
and her two children, and Benita, sitting inside of it;
the other maid, and two serving-men (each man with a
great blunderbuss) mounted upon the outside; and
upon the horses three Exeter postilions. Much had
been said at Dulverton, and even back at Bampton,
about some great freebooters; to whom all Exmoor
owed suit and service, and paid them very punctually.
Both the serving-men were scared, even over their
ale, by this. But the lady only said, 'Drive on;
I know a little of highwaymen: they never rob a
lady.'

" Through the fog, and through the muck, the coach
went on, as best it might; sometimes foundered in a
slough, with half of the horses splashing it, and sometimes knuckled up on a bank, and straining across the
middle, while all the horses kicked at it. However
they went on till dark as well as might be expected.
But when they came, all thanking God, to the pitch
and slope of the sea-bank, leading on towards Watchett
town, and where my horse had shyed so; there the
little boy jumped up, and clapped his hands at the
water; and there (as Benita said) they met their fate,
and could not fly it.

"Although it was past the dusk of day, the silver light from the sea flowed in, and showed the cliffs, and the grey sand-line, and the drifts of wreck, and wrack-weed. It showed them also a troop of horsemen, waiting under a rock hard by, and ready to dash upon them. The postilions lashed towards the sea, and the horses strove in the depth of sand, and the serving-men cocked their blunderbusses, and cowered away behind them; but the lady stood up in the carriage bravely, and neither screamed nor spoke, but hid her son behind her. Meanwhile the drivers drove into the sea, till the leading horses were swimming.

"But before the waves came into the coach, a score of fierce men were round it. They cursed the postilions for mad cowards, and cut the traces, and seized the wheel-horses, all wild with dismay in the wet and the dark. Then, while the carriage was heeling over, and well-nigh upset in the water, the lady exclaimed, 'I know that man! He is our ancient enemy:' and Benita (foreseeing that all their boxes would be turned inside out, or carried away) snatched the most valuable of the jewels, a magnificent necklace of diamonds, and cast it over the little girl's head, and buried it under her travelling-cloak, hoping so to save it. Then a great wave, crested with foam, rolled in, and the coach was thrown on its side, and the sea rushed in at the top and the windows, upon shrieking, and clashing, and fainting away.

"What followed Benita knew not, as one might well

suppose, herself being stunned by a blow on the head, beside being palsied with terror. 'See, I have the mark now,' she said, 'where the jamb of the door came down on me!' But when she recovered her senses, she found herself lying upon the sand, the robbers were out of sight, and one of the serving-men was bathing her forehead with sea-water. For this she rated him well, having taken already too much of that article; and then she arose and ran to her mistress, who was sitting upright on a little rock, with her dead boy's face to her bosom, sometimes gazing upon him, and sometimes questing round for the other one.

"Although there were torches and links around, and she looked at her child by the light of them; no one dared to approach the lady, or speak, or try to help her. Each man whispered his fellow to go, but each hung back himself, and muttered that it was too awful to meddle with. And there she would have sate all night, with the fine little fellow stone dead in her arms, and her tearless eyes dwelling upon him, and her heart but not her mind thinking; only that the Italian woman stole up softly to her side, and whispered, 'It is the will of God.'

"'So it always seems to be,' were all the words the mother answered; and then she fell on Benita's neck; and the men were ashamed to be near her weeping; and a sailor lay down and bellowed. Surely these men are the best.

"Before the light of the morning came along the tide to Watchett, my lady had met her husband. They

took her into the town that night, but not to her own
castle; and so the power of womanhood (which is itself
maternity) came over swiftly upon her. The lady
whom all people loved (though at certain times, particular) lies in Watchett little churchyard, with son
and heir at her right hand, and a little babe, of sex
unknown, sleeping on her bosom.

"This is a miserable tale," said Jeremy Stickles
brightly; "hand me over the schnapps, my boy.
What fools we are to spoil our eyes for other people's
troubles! Enough of our own to keep them clean,
although we all were chimney-sweeps. There is nothing like good hollands, when a man becomes too
sensitive. Restore the action of the glands; that is
my rule, after weeping. Let me make you another,
John. You are quite low-spirited."

But although Master Jeremy carried on so (as
became his manhood), and laughed at the sailor's
bellowing; bless his heart, I knew as well that tears
were in his brave keen eyes, as if I had dared to look
for them, or to show mine own.

"And what was the lady's name?" I asked; "and
what became of the little girl? And why did the
woman stay there?"

"Well!" cried Jeremy Stickles, only too glad to be
cheerful again: "talk of a woman, after that! As we
used to say at school—'Who dragged whom, how
many times, in what manner, round the wall of what?'
But to begin, last first, my John (as becomes a woman):
Benita stayed in that blessed place, because she could

not get away from it. The Doones—if Doones indeed
they were, about which you of course know best—took
every stiver out of the carriage; wet or dry, they took
it. And Benita could never get her wages: for the
whole affair is in Chancery; and they have appointed
a receiver."

"Whew!" said I, knowing something of London,
and sorry for Benita's chance.

"So the poor thing was compelled to drop all
thought of Apulia, and settle down on the brink of
Exmoor, where you get all its evils, without the good
to balance them. She married a man, who turned a
wheel, for making the blue Watchett ware; partly
because he could give her a house, and partly because
he proved himself a good soul towards my lady.
There they are, and have three children; and there
you may go and visit them."

"I understand all that, Jeremy; though you do tell
things too quickly; and I would rather have John Fry's
style, for he leaves one time for his words to melt.
Now, for my second question. What became of the
little maid?"

"You great oaf!" cried Jeremy Stickles: "you
are rather more likely to know, I should think, than
any one else in all the kingdoms."

"If I knew, I should not ask you. Jeremy Stickles,
do try to be neither conceited, nor thick-headed."

"I will, when you are neither," answered Master
Jeremy; "but you occupy all the room, John. No
one else can get in, with you there."

"Very well, then let me out. Take me down in both ways."

"If ever you were taken down; you must have your double joints ready now. And yet in other ways, you will be as proud and set up as Lucifer. As certain sure as I stand here, that little maid is Lorna Doone."

## CHAPTER II.

IT must not be supposed that I was altogether so thick-headed as Jeremy would have made me out. But it is part of my character that I like other people to think me slow, and to labour hard to enlighten me, while all the time I can say to myself, " This man is shallower than I am ; it is pleasant to see his shoals come up, while he is sounding mine so !" Not that I would so behave, God forbid, with anybody (be it man or woman) who in simple heart approached me, with no gauge of intellect. But when the upper hand is taken, upon the faith of one's patience, by a man of even smaller wits (not that Jeremy was that, neither could he have lived to be thought so), why, it naturally happens, that we knuckle under, with an ounce of indignation.

Jeremy's tale would have moved me greatly both with sorrow and anger, even without my guess at first, and now my firm belief, that the child of those unlucky parents was indeed my Lorna. And as I thought of the lady's troubles, and her faith in Providence, and her cruel childless death, and then imagined how my

darling would be overcome to hear it, you may well
believe that my quick replies to Jeremy Stickles'
banter were but as the flourish of a drum to cover
the sounds of pain.

For when he described the heavy coach and the
persons in and upon it, and the breaking down at
Dulverton, and the place of their destination, as well
as the time and the weather, and the season of the
year, my heart began to burn within me, and my mind
replaced the pictures, first of the foreign lady's-maid by
the pump caressing me, and then of the coach strug-
gling up the hill, and the beautiful dame, and the fine
little boy, with the white cockade in his hat; but most
of all the little girl, dark-haired and very lovely, and
having even in those days the rich soft look of Lorna.

But when he spoke of the necklace thrown over the
head of the little maiden, and of her disappearance,
before my eyes arose at once the flashing of the beacon-
fire, the lonely moors embrowned with light, the tramp
of the outlaw cavalcade, and the helpless child head-
downward lying across the robber's saddle-bow. Then
I remembered my own mad shout of boyish indignation,
and marvelled at the strange long way by which the
events of life come round. And while I thought of my
own return, and childish attempt to hide myself from
sorrow in the sawpit, and the agony of my mother's
tears, it did not fail to strike me as a thing of omen,
that the selfsame day should be, both to my darling
and myself, the blackest and most miserable of all
,youthful days.

The King's Commissioner thought it wise, for some
good reason of his own, to conceal from me, for the
present, the name of the poor lady supposed to be
Lorna's mother; and knowing that I could easily now
discover it, without him, I let that question abide
awhile. Indeed I was half afraid to hear it, remembering that the nobler and the wealthier she proved to
be, the smaller was my chance of winning such a wife
for plain John Ridd. Not that she would give me up:
that I never dreamed of. But that others would interfere; or indeed I myself might find it only honest to
relinquish her. That last thought was a dreadful blow,
and took my breath away from me.

Jeremy Stickles was quite decided—and of course
the discovery being his, he had a right to be so—that
not a word of all these things must be imparted to
Lorna herself, or even to my mother, or any one whatever. "Keep it tight as wax, my lad," he cried, with
a wink of great expression; "this belongs to me, mind;
and the credit, ay, and the premium, and the right of
discount, are altogether mine. It would have taken
you fifty years to put two and two together so, as I
did, like a clap of thunder. Ah, God has given some
men brains; and others have good farms and money,
and a certain skill in the lower beasts. Each must
use his special talent. You work your farm: I work
my brains. In the end, my lad, I shall beat you."

"Then, Jeremy, what a fool you must be, if you
cudgel your brains to make money of this, to open the
barn-door to me, and show me all your threshing."

"Not a whit, my son. Quite the opposite. Two men always thresh better than one. And here I have you bound to use your flail, one two, with mine, and yet in strictest honour bound not to bushel up, till I tell you."

"But," said I, being much amused by a Londoner's brave, yet uncertain, use of simplest rural metaphors, for he had wholly forgotten the winnowing: "surely if I bushel up, even when you tell me, I must take half-measure."

"So, you shall, my boy," he answered; "if we can only cheat those confounded knaves of Equity. You shall take the beauty, my son, and the elegance, and the love, and all that—and my boy, I will take the money."

This he said in a way so dry, and yet so richly unctuous, that being gifted somehow by God, with a kind of sense of queerness, I fell back in my chair, and laughed, though the underside of my laugh was tears.

"Now, Jeremy, how if I refuse to keep this half as tight as wax? You bound me to no such partnership, before you told the story; and I am not sure, by any means, of your right to do so afterwards."

"Tush!" he replied: "I know you too well, to look for meanness in you. If from pure good-will, John Ridd, and anxiety to relieve you, I made no condition precedent, you are not the man to take advantage, as a lawyer might. I do not even want your promise. As sure as I hold this glass, and drink your health and love in another drop (forced on me by pathetic words), so surely will you be bound to me, until I do release you. Tush! I know men well by this time: a mere look of trust from one is worth another's ten thousand oaths."

"Jeremy, you are right," I answered; "at least as regards the issue. Although perhaps you were not right in leading me into a bargan like this, without my own consent or knowledge. But supposing that we should both be shot in this grand attack on the valley (for I mean to go with you now, heart and soul), is Lorna to remain untold of that which changes all her life?"

"Both shot!" cried Jeremy Stickles: "my goodness, boy, talk not like that! And those Doones are cursed good shots too. Nay, nay, the yellows shall go in front; we attack on the Somerset side, I think. I from a hill will reconnoitre, as behoves a general, you shall stick behind a tree, if we can only find one big enough to hide you. You and I to be shot, John Ridd, with all this inferior food for powder anxious to be devoured!"

I laughed, for I knew his cool hardihood, and never flinching courage; and sooth to say no coward would have dared to talk like that.

"But when one comes to think of it," he continued, smiling at himself; "some provision should be made for even that unpleasant chance. I will leave the whole in writing, with orders to be opened, &c., &c.—Now no more of that, my boy; a cigarro after schnapps, and go to meet my yellow boys."

His "yellow boys," as he called the Somersetshire trained bands, were even now coming down the valley

from the " London-road," as every one since I went up
to town, grandly entitled the lane to the moors. There
was one good point about these men, that having no
discipline at all, they made pretence to none whatever.
Nay, rather they ridiculed the thing, as below men of
any spirit. On the other hand Master Stickles' troopers
looked down on these native fellows, from a height
which I hope they may never tumble, for it would
break the necks of all of them.

Now these fine natives came along, singing, for their
very lives, a song the like of which set down here
would oust my book from modest people, and make
everybody say, " this man never can have loved Lorna."
Therefore, the less of that the better ; only I thought,
" what a difference from the goodly psalms of the
alehouse."

Having finished their canticle, which contained more
mirth than melody, they drew themselves up, in a sort
of way supposed by them to be military, each man
with heel and elbow struck into those of his neighbour, and saluted the King's Commissioner. " Why,
where are your officers ? " asked Master Stickles ;
" how is it that you have no officers ? " Upon this
there arose a general grin, and a knowing look passed
along their faces, even up to the man by the gatepost.
" Are you going to tell me, or not," said Jeremy,
" what is become of your officers ? "

" Plaise zur," said one little fellow at last, being
nodded at by the rest to speak, in right of his known
eloquence ; " hus tould Harfizers, as a wor no nade of

un, now King's man hiszell wor coom, a puppose vor
to command us laike."

"And do you mean to say, you villains," cried
Jeremy, scarce knowing whether to laugh, or to swear,
or what to do; "that your officers took their dismissal
thus, and let you come on without them."

"What could 'em do?" asked the little man, with
reason certainly on his side: "hus zent 'em about
their business, and they was glad enough to goo."

"Well!" said poor Jeremy, turning to me; "a
pretty state of things, John! Three score cobblers,
and farming men, plasterers, tailors, and kettles-to-
mend; and not a man to keep order among them,
except my blessed self, John! And I trow there is
not one among them could hit a barn-door flying. The
Doones will make riddles of all of us."

"However he had better hopes, when the sons of
Devon appeared, as they did in about an hour's time;
fine fellows and eager to prove themselves. These
had not discarded their officers, but marched in good
obedience to them, and were quite prepared to fight
the men of Somerset (if need be) in addition to the
Doones. And there was scarcely a man among them
but could have trounced three of the yellow men, and
would have done it gladly too, in honour of the red
facings.

"Do you mean to suppose, Master Jeremy Stickles,"
said I, looking on with amazement, beholding also all
our maidens at the upstair windows wondering; "that
we, my mother a widow woman, and I a young man of

small estate, can keep and support all these precious fellows, both yellow ones, and red ones, until they have taken the Doone Glen?"

"God forbid it, my son!" he replied, laying a finger upon his lip: "Nay, nay, I am not of the shabby order, when I have the strings of government. Kill your sheep at famine prices, and knead your bread at a figure expressing the rigours of last winter. Let Annie make out the bill every day, and I at night will double it. You may take my word for it, Master John, this spring-harvest shall bring you in three times as much as last autumn's did. If they cheated you in town, my lad, you shall have your change in the country. Take thy bill, and write down quickly."

However this did not meet my views of what an honest man should do; and I went to consult my mother about it, as all the accounts would be made in her name.

Dear mother thought that if the King paid only half again as much as other people would have to pay, it would be perhaps the proper thing; the half being due for loyalty: and here she quoted an ancient saying,—

> "The King, and his staff
> Be a man and a half;"

which, according to her judgment, ruled beyond dispute the law of the present question. To argue with her after that (which she brought up with such triumph) would have been worse than useless. Therefore I just told Annie to make the bills at a third below the current market prices; so that the upshot would be fair. She promised me honestly that she would; but with a twinkle in her bright blue eyes, which she must have caught from Tom Faggus. It always has appeared to me that stern and downright honesty upon money-matters is a thing not understood of women; be they as good as good can be.

The yellows and the reds together numbered a hundred and twenty men, most of whom slept in our barns and stacks; and besides these we had fifteen troopers of the regular army. You may suppose that all the country was turned upside down about it; and the folk who came to see them drill—by no means a needless exercise—were a greater plague than the soldiers. The officers too of the Devonshire band were such a torment to us, that we almost wished their men had dismissed them, as the Somerset troop had done with theirs. For we could not keep them out of our house, being all young men of good family, and therefore not to be met with bars. And having now three lovely maidens (for even Lizzy might be called so, when she cared to please), mother and I were at wit's ends, on account of those blessed officers. I never got a wink of sleep; they came whistling under the window so; and directly I went out to chase them, there was nothing but a cat to see.

Therefore all of us were right glad (except perhaps Farmer Snowe, from whom we had bought some victuals at rare price) when Jeremy Stickles gave orders to march, and we began to try to do it. A good deal of boasting went overhead, as our men defiled along the

lane; and the thick broad patins of pennywort jutted
out between the stones, ready to heal their bruises.
The parish choir came part of the way, and the singing-
loft from Countisbury; and they kept our soldiers'
spirits up with some of the most pugnacious Psalms.
Parson Bowden marched ahead, leading all our van
and file, as against the Papists; and promising to go
with us, till we came to bullet distance. Therefore we
marched bravely on, and children came to look at us.
And I wondered where Uncle Reuben was, who ought
to have led the culverins (whereof we had no less than
three) if Stickles could only have found him: and then
I thought of little Ruth; and without any fault on my
part, my heart went down within me.

The culverins were laid on bark; and all our horses
pulling them, and looking round every now and then,
with their ears curved up like a squirrel'd nut, and their
noses tossing anxiously, to know what sort of plough
it was man had been pleased to put behind them—man,
whose endless whims and wildness they could never
understand, any more than they could satisfy. However they pulled their very best—as all our horses
always do—and the culverins went up the hill, without
smack of whip, or swearing. It had been arranged,
very justly no doubt, and quite in keeping with the
spirit of the Constitution, but as it proved not too wisely,
that either body of men should act in its own county
only. So when we reached the top of the hill, the
sons of Devon marched on, and across the track leading into Doone-gate, so as to fetch round the western

side, and attack with their culverin from the cliffs,
whence the sentry had challenged me on the night of
my passing the entrance.   Meanwhile the yellow lads
were to stay upon the eastern highland, whence Uncle
Reuben and myself had reconnoitred so long ago ; and
whence I had leaped into the valley at the time of the
great snowdrifts.   And here they were not to show
themselves ; but keep their culverin in the woods, until
their cousins of Devon appeared on the opposite parapet
of the glen.

The third culverin was entrusted to the fifteen
troopers ; who with ten picked soldiers from either
trained band, making in all five-and-thirty men, were
to assault the Doone-gate itself, while the outlaws
were placed between two fires from the eastern cliff
and the western.   And with this force went Jeremy
Stickles, and with it went myself, as knowing more
about the passage than any other stranger did.   Therefore, if I have put it clearly, as I strive to do, you will
see that the Doones must repulse at once three simul-
taneous attacks, from an army numbering in the whole
one hundred and thirty-five men, not including the
Devonshire officers ; fifty men on each side I mean,
and thirty-five at the head of the valley.

The tactics of this grand campaign appeared to me
so clever, and beautifully ordered, that I commended
" Colonel Stickles," as everybody now called him, for
his great ability and mastery of the art of war.   He
admitted that he deserved high praise ; but said that
he was not by any means equally certain of success, so

large a proportion of his forces being only a raw militia,
brave enough no doubt for anything, when they saw
their way to it; but knowing little of gunnery, and
wholly unused to be shot at. Whereas all the Doones
were practised marksmen, being compelled when lads
(like the Balearic slingers) to strike down their meals
before tasting them. And then Colonel Stickles asked
me, whether I myself could stand fire; he knew that I
was not a coward, but this was a different question. I
told him that I had been shot at, once or twice before;
but nevertheless disliked it, as much as almost anything. Upon that, he said that I would do; for that
when a man got over the first blush of diffidence, he
soon began to look upon it as a puff of destiny.

I wish I could only tell what happened, in the battle
of that day, especially as nearly all of the people round
these parts, who never saw gun-fire in it, have gotten
the tale so much amiss; and some of them will even
stand in front of my own hearth, and contradict me to
the teeth; although at the time they were not born,
nor their fathers put into breeches. But, in truth, I
cannot tell, exactly, even the part in which I helped;
how then can I be expected, time by time, to lay before
you, all the little ins and outs of places, where I myself
was not? Only I can contradict things, which I know
could not have been: and what I plainly saw should not
be controverted in my own house.

Now we five-and-thirty men lay back, a little way
round the corner, in the hollow of the track which
leads to the strong Doone-gate. Our culverin was in

amongst us, loaded now to the muzzle, and it was not comfortable to know that it might go off at any time. Although the yeomanry were not come (according to arrangement), some of us had horses there; besides the horses who dragged the cannon, and now were sniffing at it. And there were plenty of spectators to mind these horses for us, so soon as we should charge; inasmuch as all our friends and neighbours, who had so keenly prepared for the battle, now resolved to take no part, but look on, and praise the winners.

At last, we heard the loud bang-bang, which proved that Devon and Somerset were pouring their indignation hot into the den of malefactors, or at least so we supposed; therefore at double quick march we advanced round the bend of the cliff which had hidden us, hoping to find the gate undefended, and to blow down all barriers with the fire of our cannon. And indeed it seemed likely at first to be so, for the wild and mountainous gorge of rock appeared to be all in pure loneliness, except where the coloured coats of our soldiers, and their metal trappings, shone with the sun behind them. Therefore we shouted a loud hurrah, as for an easy victory.

But while the sound of our cheer rang back among the crags above us, a shrill clear whistle cleft the air for a single moment, and then a dozen carbines bellowed, and all among us flew murderous lead. Several of our men rolled over, but the rest rushed on like Britons, Jeremy and myself in front, while we heard the horses plunging at the loaded gun behind us.

"Now, my lads," cried Jeremy; "one dash, and we are beyond them!" For he saw that the foe was overhead in the gallery of brushwood.

Our men with a brave shout answered him, for his courage was fine example; and we leaped in under the feet of the foe, before they could load their guns again. But here, when the foremost among us were past, an awful crash rang behind us, with the shrieks of men, and the din of metal, and the horrible screaming of horses. The trunk of the tree had been launched overhead, and crashed into the very midst of us. Our cannon was under it, so were two men, and a horse with his poor back broken. Another horse vainly struggled to rise, with his thigh-bone smashed and protruding.

Now I lost all my presence of mind at this, for I loved both those good horses, and shouting for any to follow me, dashed headlong into the cavern. Some five or six men came after me, the foremost of whom was Jeremy, when a storm of shot whistled and pattered around me, with a blaze of light and a thunderous roar. On I leaped, like a madman, and pounced on one gunner, and hurled him across his culverin; but the others had fled, and a heavy oak door fell to, with a bang, behind them. So utterly were my senses gone, and nought but strength remaining, that I caught up the cannon with both hands, and dashed it, breech-first, at the doorway. The solid oak burst with the blow, and the gun stuck fast, like a builder's putlog.

But here I looked round in vain for any to come and follow up my success. The scanty light showed me no figure moving through the length of the tunnel behind me; only a heavy groan or two went to my heart, and chilled it. So I hurried back to seek Jeremy, fearing that he must be smitten down.

And so indeed I found him, as well as three other poor fellows, struck by the charge of the culverin, which had passed so close beside me. Two of the four were as dead as stones, and growing cold already, but Jeremy and the other could manage to groan, just now and then. So I turned my attention to them, and thought no more of fighting.

Having so many wounded men, and so many dead among us, we loitered at the cavern's mouth, and looked at one another, wishing only for somebody to come and take command of us. But no one came; and I was grieved so much about poor Jeremy, besides being wholly unused to any violence of bloodshed, that I could only keep his head up, and try to stop him from bleeding. And he looked up at me pitifully, being perhaps in a haze of thought, as a calf looks at a butcher.

The shot had taken him in the mouth; about that no doubt could be, for two of his teeth were in his beard, and one of his lips was wanting. I laid his shattered face on my breast, and nursed him, as a woman might. But he looked at me with a jerk at this; and I saw that he wanted coolness.

While here we stayed, quite out of danger (for the fellows from the gallery could by no means shoot us, even if they remained there, and the oaken door whence the others fled was blocked up by the culverin), a boy who had no business there (being in fact our clerk's apprentice to the art of shoe-making) came round the corner upon us, in the manner which boys, and only boys, can use with grace and freedom ; that is to say, with a sudden rush, and a sidelong step, and an impudence.

" Got the worst of it !" cried the boy : "better be off all of you. Zomerzett and Devon a vighting; and the Doones have drashed 'em both. Maister Ridd, even thee be drashed."

We few, who yet remained of the force which was to have won the Doone-gate, gazed at one another, like so many fools, and nothing more. For we still had some faint hopes of winning the day, and recovering our reputation, by means of what the other men might have done without us. And we could not understand at all how Devonshire and Somerset, being embarked in the same cause, should be fighting with one another.

Finding nothing more to be done, in the way of carrying on the war, we laid poor Master Stickles and two more of the wounded upon the carriage of bark and hurdles, whereon our gun had lain; and we rolled the gun into the river, and harnessed the horses yet alive, and put the others out of their pain, and sadly wended homewards, feeling ourselves to be thoroughly beaten, yet ready to maintain that it was no fault of ours whatever. And in this opinion the women joined, being only too glad and thankful to see us come home alive again.

Now, this enterprise having failed so, I prefer not to dwell too long upon it; only just to show the mischief which lay at the root of the failure. And this mischief was the vile jealousy betwixt red and yellow uniform. Now I try to speak impartially, belonging no more to Somerset than I do to Devonshire, living upon the borders, and born of either county. The tale was told me by one side first; and then quite to a different tune by the other; and then by both together, with very hot words of reviling, and a desire to fight it out again. And putting this with that, the truth appears to be as follows.

The men of Devon, who bore red facings, had a long way to go round the hills, before they could get into due position on the western side of the Doone Glen. And knowing that their cousins in yellow would claim the whole of the glory, if allowed to be first with the firing, these worthy fellows waited not to take good aim with their cannon, seeing the others about to shoot; but fettled it any how on the slope, pointing in a general direction; and trusting in God for aimworthiness, laid the rope to the breech, and fired. Now as Providence ordained it, the shot, which was a casual mixture of anything considered hard— for instance jug-bottoms and 'knobs of doors—the whole of this pernicious dose came scattering and shattering among the unfortunate yellow men upon the opposite cliff; killing one and wounding two.

Now what did the men of Somerset do, but instead of waiting for their friends to send round and beg pardon, train their gun full mouth upon them, and

with a vicious meaning shoot? Nor only this, but
they loudly cheered, when they saw four or five red
coats lie low; for which savage feeling not even the
remarks of the Devonshire men concerning their coats
could entirely excuse them. Now I need not tell the
rest of it; for the tale makes a man discontented.
Enough that both sides waxed hotter and hotter with
the fire of destruction. And but that the gorge of
the cliffs lay between, very few would have lived to
tell of it: for our western blood becomes stiff and firm,
when churned with the sense of wrong in it.

At last the Doones (who must have laughed at the
thunder passing over head) recalling their men from
the gallery, issued out of Gwenny's gate (which had
been wholly overlooked) and fell on the rear of the
Somerset men, and slew four beside their cannon.
Then while the survivors ran away, the outlaws took
the hot culverin, and rolled it down into their valley.
Thus of the three guns set forth that morning, only
one ever came home again, and that was the gun of
the Devonshire men; who dragged it home themselves,
with the view of making a boast about it.

This was a melancholy end of our brave setting out:
and every body blamed every one else; and several of
us wanted to have the whole thing over again, as then
we must have righted it. But upon one point all agreed,
by some reasoning not clear to me, that the root of the
evil was to be found in the way Parson Bowden went
up the hill, with his hat on, and no cassock.

## CHAPTER III.

Two of the Devonshire officers (Captains Pyke and Dallan) now took command of the men who were left, and ordered all to go home again, commending much the bravery which had been displayed on all sides, and the loyalty to the King, and the English Constitution. This last word always seems to me to settle everything when said, because nobody understands it, and yet all can puzzle their neighbours. So the Devonshire men, having beans to sow (which they ought to have done on Good Friday) went home; and our Somerset friends only stayed for two days more to backbite them.

To me the whole thing was purely grievous; not from any sense of defeat (though that was bad enough), but from the pain and anguish caused by death, and wounds, and mourning. "Surely we have woes enough," I used to think of an evening, when the poor fellows could not sleep, or rest, or let others rest around them; "surely all this smell of wounds is not incense men should pay to the God who made them. Death, when it comes and is done with, may be a bliss to any one;

but the doubt of life or death, when a man lies, as it were, like a trunk upon the saw-pit, and a grisly head looks up at him, and the groans of pain are cleaving him, this would be beyond all bearing, but for Nature's sap—sweet hope."

Jeremy Stickles lay and tossed, and thrust up his feet in agony, and bit with his lipless mouth the clothes, and was proud to see blood upon them. He looked at us, ever so many times, as much as to say, "fools, let me die; then I shall have some comfort:" but we nodded at him sagely, especially the women, trying to convey to him, on no account to die yet. And then we talked to one another (on purpose for him to hear us) how brave he was, and not the man to knock under in a hurry, and how he should have the victory yet; and how well he looked, considering.

These things cheered him, a little now, and a little more next time; and every time we went on so, he took it with less impatience. Then once when he had been very quiet, and not even tried to frown at us, Annie leaned over, and kissed his forehead, and spread the pillows and sheet, with a curve as delicate as his own white ears; and then he feebly lifted hands, and prayed to God to bless her. And after that he came round gently; though never to the man he had been, and never to speak loud again. For a time (as I may have implied before) Master Stickles' authority, and manner of levying duties, had not been taken kindly by the people round our neighbourhood. The manors of East Lynn, and West Lynn, and even that of Woolhanger—

although just then all three were at issue about some
rights of wreck, and the hanging of a sheep-stealer (a
man of no great eminence, yet claimed by each, for the
sake of his clothes)—these three, having their rights
impugned, or even superseded, as they declared, by the
quartering of soldiers in their neighbourhood, united
very kindly to oppose the King's Commissioner. However Jeremy had contrived to conciliate the whole of
them, not so much by anything engaging in his deport-
ment, or delicate address, as by holding out bright
hopes that the plunder of the Doone Glen might become divisible among the adjoining manors. Now I
have never discovered a thing which the lords of
manors (at least in our part of the world) do not
believe to belong to themselves, if only they could get
their rights. And it did seem natural enough that if
the Doones were ousted, and a nice collection of prey
remained, this should be parted among the people
having ancient rights of plunder. Nevertheless Master
Jeremy knew that the soldiers would have the first of
it, and the King what they could not carry.

And perhaps he was punished justly for language so
misleading, by the general indignation of the people all
around us, not at his failure, but at himself, for that
which he could in no wise prevent. And the stewards
of the manors rode up to our house, on purpose to
reproach him, and were greatly vexed with all of us,
because he was too ill to see them.

To myself (though by rights the last to be thought
of, among so much pain and trouble) Jeremy's wound

was a great misfortune, in more ways than one. In the
first place, it deferred my chance of imparting either to
my mother or to Mistress Lorna, my firm belief that
the maid I loved was not sprung from the race which
had slain my father; neither could he in any way have
offended against her family. And this discovery I was
yearning more, and more, to declare to them; being
forced to see (even in the midst of all our warlike
troubles) that a certain difference was growing betwixt
them both, and betwixt them and me. For although
the words of the Counsellor had seemed to fail among
us, being bravely met and scattered; yet our courage
was but as wind flinging wide the tare-seeds, when the
sower casts them from his bag. The crop may not
come evenly; many places may long lie bare, and the
field be all in patches. Yet almost every vetch will
spring, and tiller out, and stretch across the scatterings
where the wind puffed.

And so dear mother, and darling Lorna now had
been for many a day, thinking, worrying, and wearing,
about the matter between us. Neither liked to look
at the other, as they used to do; with mother admiring
Lorna's eyes, and grace, and form of breeding; and
Lorna loving mother's goodness, softness, and simplicity. And the saddest and most hurtful thing was that
neither could ask the other of the shadow falling
between them. And so it went on, and deepened.

In the next place Colonel Stickles' illness was a
grievous thing to us, in that we had no one now to
command the troopers. Ten of these were still alive,

and so well approved to us, that they could never
fancy aught, whether for dinner or supper, without its
being forthcoming.  If they wanted trout they should
have it; if colloped venison, or broiled ham, or salmon
from Lynmouth and Trentisoe, or truffles from the
woodside; all these were at the warriors' service, until
they lusted for something else.  Even the wounded
men ate nobly; all except poor Jeremy, who was
forced to have a young elder shoot, with the pith
drawn, for to feed him.  And once, when they wanted
pickled loach (from my description of it), I took up my
boyish sport again, and pronged them a good jarful.
Therefore none of them could complain: and yet they
were not satisfied; perhaps for want of complaining.

Be that as it might, we knew that if they once
resolved to go (as they might do at any time, with only
a corporal over them), all our house, and all our goods,
ay, and our own precious lives, would and must be at
the mercy of embittered enemies.  For now the Doones,
having driven back, as every one said, five hundred
men—though not thirty had ever fought with them—
were in such feather all round the country, that nothing
was too good for them.  Offerings poured in at the
Doone-gate, faster than Doones could away with them;
and the smpathy both of Devon and Somerset became
almost oppressive.  And perhaps this wealth of con-
gratulation, and mutual good feeling between plunderer
and victim, saved us from any piece of spite; kindliness having won the day, and every one loving every
one.

But yet another cause arose, and this the strongest
one of all, to prove the need of Stickles' aid, and
calamity of his illness. And this came to our knowledge first, without much time to think of it. For two
men appeared at our gate one day, stripped to their
shirts, and void of horses, and looking very sorrowful.
Now having some fear of attack from the Doones, and
scarce knowing what their tricks might be, we received
these strangers cautiously, desiring to know who they
were, before we let them see all our premises.

However it soon became plain to us that although
they might not be honest fellows, at any rate they
were not Doones; and so we took them in, and fed,
and left them to tell their business. And this they
were glad enough to do; as men who have been
maltreated almost always are. And it was not for
us to contradict them, lest our victuals should go
amiss.

These two very worthy fellows—nay, more than that
by their own account, being downright martyrs—were
come, for the publick benefit, from the Court of Chancery, sitting for everybody's good, and boldly redressing
evil. This Court has a power of scent unknown to the
Common-law practitioners, and slowly yet surely tracks
its game; even as the great lumbering dogs, now
introduced from Spain, and called by some people
"pointers," differ from the swift gaze-hound, who sees
his prey and runs him down, in the manner of the
common lawyers. If a man's ill fate should drive him
to make choice between these two, let him rather be

chased by the hounds of law, than the tracking dogs
of Equity.

Now, as it fell in a very black day (for all except the
lawyers) His Majesty's Court of Chancery, if that be
what it called itself, gained scent of poor Lorna's life,
and of all that might be made of it. Whether through
that brave young lord who ran into such peril, or
through any of his friends; or whether through that
deep old Counsellor, whose game none might penetrate;
or through any disclosures of the Italian woman, or
even of Jeremy himself; none just now could tell us:
only this truth was too clear—Chancery had heard of
Lorna, and then had seen how rich she was; and never
delaying in one thing, had opened mouth, and swal-
lowed her.

The Doones, with a share of that dry humour which
was in them hereditary, had welcomed the two appa-
ritors (if that be the proper name for them) and led
them kindly down the valley, and told them then to
serve their writ. Misliking the look of things, these
poor men began to fumble among their clothes; upon
which the Doones cried, "Off with them! Let us see
if your message be on your skins." And with no more
manners than that, they stripped, and lashed them out
of the valley; only bidding them come to us, if they
wanted Lorna Doone: and to us they came accordingly.
Neither were they sure at first but that we should treat
them so; for they had no knowledge of west country,
and thought it quite a godless place, wherein no writs
were holy.

We however comforted and cheered them so considerably, that in gratitude they showed their writs, to which they had stuck, like leeches. And these were twofold ; one addressed to Mistress Lorna Doone, so called, and bidding her keep in readiness to travel whenever called upon, and commit herself to nobody, except the accredited messengers of the right honourable Court; while the other was addressed to all subjects of His Majesty, having custody of Lorna Doone, or any power over her. And this last both threatened, and exhorted, and held out hopes of recompense; if she were rendered truly. My mother and I held consultation over both these documents, with a mixture of some wrath and fear, and a fork of great sorrow to stir them. And now having Jeremy Stickles' leave, which he gave with a nod when I told him all, and at last made him understand it, I laid bare to my mother as well what I knew, as what I merely surmised, or guessed, concerning Lorna's parentage. All this she received with great tears, and wonder, and fervent thanks to God, and still more fervent praise of her son, who had nothing whatever to do with it. However, now the question was, how to act about these writs. And herein it was most unlucky that we could not have Master Stickles, with his knowledge of the world and especially of the law-courts, to advise us what to do, and to help in doing it. And firstly of the first I said, " We have rogues to deal with: but try we not to rogue them."

To this, in some measure, dear mother agreed;

though she could not see the justice of it; yet thought
that it might be wiser, because of our want of practice.
And then I said, "Now, we are bound to tell Lorna,
and to serve her citation upon her, which these good
fellows have given us."

"Then go, and do it thyself, my son;" mother
replied with a mournful smile, misdoubting what the
end might be. So I took the slip of brown parchment,
and went to seek my darling.

Lorna was in her favourite place, the little garden,
which she tended with such care and diligence. Seeing
how the maiden loved it, and was happy there, I had
laboured hard to fence it from the dangers of the wood.
And here she had corrected me, with better taste, and
sense of pleasure, and the joys of musing. For I meant
to shut out the brook, and build my fence inside of it:
but Lorna said no; if we must have a fence, which
could not but be injury, at any rate leave the stream
inside, and a pleasant bank beyond it. And soon I
perceived that she was right, though not so much as
afterwards; for the fairest of all things in a garden,
and in summer-time most useful, is a brook of crystal
water; where a man may come and meditate, and the
flowers may lean and see themselves, and the rays of
the sun are purfled. Now partly with her own white
hands, and partly with Gwenny's red ones, Lorna had
made of this sunny spot a haven of beauty to dwell in.
It was not only that colours lay in the harmony we
would seek of them; neither was it the height of plants,
sloping to one another; nor even the delicate tone of

foliage following suit, and neighbouring. Even the
breathing of the wind, soft and gentle in and out,
moving things that need not move, and passing longer-
stalked ones, even this was not enough among the flush
of fragrance, to tell a man the reason of his quiet satisfaction. But so it shall for ever be. As the river we
float upon (with wine, and flowers, and music) is nothing
at the well-spring but a bubble without reason.

Feeling many things, but thinking without much to
guide me, over the grass-plats laid between, I went up
to Lorna. She in a shower of damask roses, raised her
eyes, and looked at me. And even now, in those sweet
eyes, so deep with loving-kindness, and soft maiden
dreamings, there seemed to be a slight unwilling, half-
confessed withdrawal; overcome by love and duty, yet
a painful thing to see.

"Darling," I said, "are your spirits good? Are
you strong enough to-day, to bear a tale of cruel sorrow;
but which perhaps, when your tears are shed, will leave
you all the happier?"

"What can you mean?" she answered trembling,
not having been very strong of late, and now surprised at my manner: "are you come to give me up,
John?"

"Not very likely," I replied; "neither do I hope such
a thing would leave you all the happier. Oh Lorna, if
you can think that so quickly as you seem to have done;
now you have every prospect, and strong temptation to
it. You are far, far above me in the world; and I
have no right to claim you. Perhaps, when you have

heard these tidings, you will say, 'John Ridd begone; you life and mine are parted.'"

"Will I?" cried Lorna, with all the brightness of her playful ways returning: "you very foolish and jealous, John, how shall I punish you for this? Am I to forsake every flower I have, and not even know that the world goes round, while I look up at you, the whole day long, and say, 'John, I love, love, love you?'"

During these words, she leaned upon me, half in gay imitation of what I so often made her do, and half in depth of earnestness; as the thrice-repeated word grew stronger, and grew warmer, with and to her heart. And as she looked up at the finish, saying, "you," so musically, I was much inclined to clasp her round; but remembering who she was, forbore; at which she seemed surprised with me.

"Mistress Lorna," I replied, with I know not what temptation, making little of her caresses, though more than all my heart to me; "Mistress Lorna, you must keep your rank, and proper dignity. You must never look at me with anything but pity now."

"I shall look at you with pity, John," said Lorna, trying to laugh it off, yet not knowing what to make of me: "if you talk any more of this nonsense, knowing me as you ought to do. I shall even begin to think that you, and your friends, are weary of me, and of so long supporting me; and are only seeking cause to send me back to my old misery. If it be so, I will go. My life matters little to any one." Here the great bright tears arose; but the maiden was too proud to sob.

"Sweetest of all sweet loves," I cried, for the sign of a tear defeated me; "what possibility could make me ever give up Lorna?"

"Dearest of all dears," she answered; "if you dearly love me, what possibility could make me ever give you up, dear?"

Upon that there was no more forbearing; but I kissed and clasped her, whether she were Countess, or whether Queen of England; mine she was, at least in heart; and mine she should be wholly. And she being of the same opinion, nothing was said between us.

"Now, Lorna," said I, as she hung on my arm, willing to trust me anywhere, "come to your little plant-house, and hear my moving story."

"No story can move me much, dear," she answered rather faintly, for any excitement stayed with her; "since I know your strength of kindness, scarcely any tale can move me, unless it be of yourself, love; or of my poor mother."

"It is of your poor mother, darling. Can you bear to hear it?" And yet I wondered why she did not say as much of her father.

"Yes, I can hear anything. But although I cannot see her, and have long forgotten, I could not bear to hear ill of her."

"There is no ill to hear, sweet child, except of evil done to her. Lorna, you are of an ill-starred race."

"Better that than a wicked race," she answered with

her usual quickness, leaping at conclusion: "tell me I am not a Doone, and I will—but I cannot love you more."

"You are not a Doone, my Lorna: for that, at least, I can answer; though I know not what your name is."

"And my father—your father—what I mean is"——

"Your father and mine never met one another. Your father was killed by an accident in the Pyrenean mountains, and your mother by the Doones; or at least they caused her death, and carried you away from her."

All this, coming as in one breath upon the sensitive maiden, was more than she could bear all at once; as any but a fool like me must of course have known. She lay back on the garden bench, with her black hair shed on the oaken bark, while her colour went and came; and only by that, and her quivering breast, could any one say that she lived and thought. And yet she pressed my hand with hers, that now I might tell her all of it.

## CHAPTER IV.

No flower that I have ever seen, either in shifting of light and shade, or in the pearly morning, may vie with a fair young woman's face when tender thought and quick emotion vary, enrich, and beautify it. Thus my Lorna hearkened softly, almost without word or gesture, yet with sighs and glances telling, and the pressure of my hand, how each word was moving her.

When at last my tale was done, she turned away, and wept bitterly for the sad fate of her parents. But to my surprise she spoke not even a word of wrath or rancour. She seemed to take it all as fate.

"Lorna, darling," I said at length; for men are more impatient in trials of time than women are; "do you not even wish to know what your proper name is?"

"How can it matter to me, John?" she answered with a depth of grief which made me seem a trifler. "It can never matter now, when there are none to share it."

"Poor little soul!" was all I said, in a tone of purest pity; and to my surprise she turned upon me, caught me in her arms, and loved me as she never had done before.

"Dearest, I have you," she cried; "you, and only you, love. Having you I want no other. All my life is one with yours. Oh, John, how can I treat you so?"

Blushing through the wet of weeping, and the gloom of pondering, yet she would not hide her eyes, but folded me, and dwelled on me.

"I cannot believe," in the pride of my joy, I whispered into one little ear, "that you could ever so love me, beauty, as to give up the world for me."

"Would you give up your farm for me, John?" cried Lorna, leaping back and looking, with her wondrous power of light, at me; "would you give up your mother, your sisters, your home, and all that you have in the world, and every hope of your life, John?"

"Of course I would. Without two thoughts. You know it; you know it, Lorna."

"It is true that I do," she answered, in a tone of deepest sadness; "and it is this power of your love which has made me love you so. No good can come of it; no good. God's face is set against selfishness."

As she spoke in that low tone I gazed at the clear lines of her face (where every curve was perfect), not with love and wonder only, but with a strange, new sense of awe.

"Darling," I said, "come nearer to me. Give me surety against that. For God's sake never frighten me with the thought that He would part us."

"Does it, then, so frighten you?" she whispered,

coming close to me; "I know it, dear; I have known it long; but it never frightens me. It makes me sad, and very lonely, till I can remember."

"Till you can remember what?" I asked with a long, deep shudder; for we are so superstitious.

"Until I do remember, love, that you will soon come back to me, and be my own for ever. This is what I always think of; this is what I hope for."

Although her eyes were so glorious, and beaming with eternity, this distant sort of beatitude was not much to my liking. I wanted to have my love, on earth; and my dear wife, in my own home; and children in good time, if God should please to send us any. And then I would be to them exactly what my father was to me. And beside all this, I doubted much about being fit for heaven; where no ploughs are, and no cattle; unless sacrificed bulls went thither.

Therefore I said, "Now kiss me, Lorna; and don't talk any nonsense." And the darling came, and did it; being kindly obedient; as the other world often makes us.

"You sweet love," I said at this, being slave to her soft obedience; "do you suppose I should be content to leave you until Elysium?"

"How on earth can I tell, dear John, what you will be content with?"

"You, and only you," said I; "the whole of it lies in a syllable. Now you know my entire want: and want must be my comfort."

"But surely if I have money, sir, and birth, and

E 2

rank, and all sorts of grandeur, you would never dare
to think of me."

She drew herself up with an air of pride, as she
gravely pronounced these words, and gave me a scornful glance, or tried; and turned away as if to enter
some grand coach or palace; while I was so amazed
and grieved in my raw simplicity, especially after the
way in which she had first received my news (so loving
and warm-hearted) that I never said a word, but stared,
and thought, "How does she mean it?"

She saw the pain upon my forehead, and the wonder
in my eyes, and leaving coach and palace too, back she
flew to me in a moment, as simple as simplest milkmaid.

"Oh you fearfully stupid John, you inexpressibly
stupid John," she cried with both arms round my neck,
and her lips upon my forehead; "you have called
yourself thick-headed, John; and I never would believe it. But now I do with all my heart. Will you
never know what I am, love?"

"No, Lorna, that I never shall. I can understand
my mother well, and one at least of my sisters, and
both the Snowe girls very easily: but you I never
understand; only love you all the more for it."

"Then never try to understand me, if the result is
that, dear John. And yet I am the very simplest of
all foolish simple creatures. Nay, I am wrong; therein
I yield the palm to you, my dear. To think that I can
act so! No wonder they want me in London, as an
ornament for the stage, John."

Now in after days, when I heard of Lorna as the

richest, and noblest, and loveliest lady to be found in London, I often remembered that little scene, and recalled every word and gesture, wondering what lay under it. Even now, while it was quite impossible once to doubt those clear deep eyes, and the bright lips trembling so; nevertheless I felt how much the world would have to do with it; and that the best and truest people cannot shake themselves quite free. However, for the moment, I was very proud, and showed it.

And herein differs fact from fancy, things as they befall us from things as we would have them, human ends from human hopes, that the first are moved by a thousand, and the last on two wheels only, which (being named) are desire and fear. Hope of course is nothing more than desire with a telescope, magnifying distant matters, overlooking near ones; opening one eye on the objects, closing the other to all objections. And if hope be the future tense of desire, the future of fear is religion—at least with too many of us.

Whether I am right or wrong in these small moralities, one thing is sure enough, to wit, that hope is the fastest traveller, at any rate in the time of youth. And so I hoped that Lorna might be proved of blameless family, and honourable rank and fortune; and yet none the less for that, love me and belong to me. So I led her into the house, and she fell into my mother's arms; and I left them to have a good cry of it, with Annie ready to help them.

If Master Stickles should not mend enough to gain his speech a little, and declare to us all he knew, I was to set out for Watchett, riding upon horseback, and there to hire a cart with wheels, such as we had not begun, as yet, to use on Exmoor. For all our work went on broad wood, with runners and with earth-boards ; and many of us still looked upon wheels (though mentioned in the Bible) as the invention of the evil one, and Pharaoh's especial property.

Now instead of getting better, Colonel Stickles grew worse and worse, in spite of all our tendance of him, with simples and with nourishment, and no poisonous medicines, such as doctors would have given him. And the fault of this lay not with us, but purely with himself and his unquiet constitution. For he roused himself up to a perfect fever, when through Lizzie's giddiness he learned the very thing which mother and Annie were hiding from him, with the utmost care: namely, that Serjeant Bloxham had taken upon himself to send direct to London, by the Chancery officers, a full report of what had happened, and of the illness of his chief, together with an urgent prayer for a full battalion of King's troops, and a plenary commander.

This Serjeant Bloxham, being senior of the surviving soldiers, and a very worthy man in his way, but a trifle over zealous, had succeeded to the captaincy, upon his master's disablement. Then, with desire to serve his country, and show his education, he sate up most part of three nights, and wrote this wonderful report by the aid of our stable lanthorn. It was a very fine piece of work, as three men to whom he read it (but only one at a time) pronounced, being under seal of secresy. And all might have gone well with it, if the author could only have held his tongue, when near the ears of women. But this was beyond his sense, as it seems, although so good a writer.  For having heard that our Lizzie was a famous judge of literature (as indeed she told almost every one) he could not contain himself, but must have her opinion upon his work.

Lizzie sate on a log of wood, and listened with all her ears up, having made proviso that no one else should be there to interrupt her.   And she put in a syllable here and there, and many a time she took out one (for the Serjeant over-loaded his gun, more often than under-charged it; like a liberal man of letters) and then she declared the result so good, and the style to be so elegant, so chaste, and yet so fervent, that the Serjeant broke his pipe in three, and fell in love with her on the spot.   Now this has led me out of my way; as things are always doing, partly through their own perverseness, partly through my kind desire to give fair turn to all of them, and to all the people who do them.   If any one expects of me a strict and well-drilled story, standing " at attention " all the time, with hands at the side like two wens on my trunk, and eyes going neither right nor left; I trow that man has been disappointed many a page ago, and has left me to my evil ways; and if not, I love his charity.   Therefore let me seek his grace, and get back, and just begin again.

That great despatch was sent to London by the Chancery officers, whom we fitted up with clothes, and for three days fattened them; which in strict justice they needed much, as well as in point of equity. They were kind enough to be pleased with us, and accepted my new shirts generously: and urgent as their business was, another week (as they both declared) could do no harm to nobody, and might set them upon their legs again. And knowing, although they were London-men, that fish do live in water, these two fellows went fishing all day, but never landed anything. However their holiday was cut short; for the Serjeant, having finished now his narrative of proceedings, was not the man to let it hang fire, and be quenched perhaps by Stickles.

Therefore, having done their business, and served both citations, these two good men had a pannier of victuals put up by dear Annie, and borrowing two of our horses, rode to Dunster; where they left them, and hired on towards London. We had not time to like them much; and so we did not miss them; especially in our great anxiety about poor Master Stickles.

Jeremy lay between life and death, for at least a fortnight. If the link of chain had flown upwards (for half-a-link of chain it was which took him in the mouth so) even one inch upwards, the poor man could have needed no one except Parson Bowden; for the bottom of his skull, which holds the brain as in an egg-cup, must have clean gone from him. But striking him horizontally, and a little upon the skew, the metal came out at the back of his neck, and (the powder not being strong, I suppose) it lodged in his leather collar.

Now the rust of this iron hung in the wound, or at least we thought so; though since I have talked with a man of medicine, I am not so sure of it. And our chief aim was to purge this rust; when rather we should have stopped the hole, and let the oxide do its worst, with a plug of new flesh on both sides of it.

At last I prevailed upon him, by argument, that he must get better, to save himself from being ignobly and unjustly superseded; and hereupon I reviled Serjeant Bloxham more fiercely than Jeremy's self could have done, and indeed to such a pitch that Jeremy almost forgave him, and became much milder. And after that his fever, and the inflammation of his wound, diminished very rapidly.

However, not knowing what might happen, or even how soon poor Lorna might be taken from our power, and falling into lawyers' hands, have cause to wish herself most heartily back among the robbers, I set forth one day for Watchett, taking advantage of the visit of some troopers from an out-post, who would make our house quite safe. I rode alone, being fully primed, and having no misgivings. For it was said that even the Doones had begun to fear me, since I cast their culverin through the door, as above related; and they could not but believe, from my being still untouched (although so large an object) in the thickest of their fire, both of gun and cannon, that I must bear a charmed life, proof against ball and bullet. However, I knew that Carver Doone was not a likely man to hold any superstitious opinions; and of him I

had an instinctive dread, although quite ready to face
him.

Riding along, I meditated upon Lorna's history;
how many things were now beginning to unfold themselves, which had been obscure and dark! For instance, Sir Ensor Doone's consent, or to say the least
his indifference, to her marriage with a yeoman; which
in a man so proud (though dying) had greatly puzzled
both of us. But now, if she not only proved to be no
grandchild of the Doone, but even descended from his
enemy, it was natural enough that he should feel no
great repugnance to her humiliation. And that
Lorna's father had been a foe to the house of Doone,
I gathered from her mother's cry, when she beheld
their leader. Moreover that fact would supply their
motive in carrying off the unfortunate little creature,
and rearing her among them, and as one of their own
family; yet hiding her true birth from her. She was
a "great card;" as we say, when playing All-fours at
Christmas-time: and if one of them could marry her,
before she learned of right and wrong; vast property,
enough to buy pardons for a thousand Doones, would be
at their mercy. And since I was come to know Lorna
better, and she to know me thoroughly—many things
had been outspoken, which her early bashfulness had
kept covered from me. Attempts I mean to pledge her
love to this one, or that other; some of which perhaps
might have been successful; if there had not been too
many.

And then, as her beauty grew richer and brighter,

Carver Doone was smitten strongly, and would hear of
no one else as a suitor for her; and by the terror of his
claim drove off all the others. Here too lay the expla-
nation of a thing which seemed to be against the laws
of human nature; and upon which I longed, but dared
not, to cross-question Lorna. How could such a lovely
girl, although so young, and brave, and distant, have
escaped the vile affections of a lawless company?

But now it was as clear as need be. For any proven
violence would have utterly vitiated all claim upon her
grand estates; at least as those claims must be urged
before a court of equity. And therefore all the elders
(with views upon her real estate) kept strict watch on the
youngers, who confined their views to her personalty.

Now I do not mean to say that all this, or the hundred other things which came, crowding consideration,
were half as plain to me at the time, as I have set them
down above. Far be it from me to deceive you so.
No doubt my thoughts were then dark and hazy, like
an oil-lamp full of fungus; and I have trimmed them,
as when they burned, with scissors sharpened long
afterwards. All I mean to say is this, that jogging
along to a certain tune of the horse's feet, which we
call "three half-pence and two pence," I saw my way
a little into some things which had puzzled me.

When I knocked at the little door, whose sill was
gritty and grimed with sand, no one came for a very
long time to answer me, or to let me in. Not wishing
to be unmannerly, I waited a long time, and watched
the sea, from which the wind was blowing; and whose

many lips of waves—though the tide was half-way out
—spoke to and refreshed me. After a while I knocked
again, for my horse was becoming hungry; and a good
while after that again, a voice came through the key-
hole :

"Who is that wishes to enter?"

"The boy who was at the pump," said I, "when the
carriage broke down at Dulverton. The boy that lives
at oh—ah; and some day you would come seek for
him."

"Oh yes, I remember certainly. My leetle boy,
with the fair white skin. I have desired to see him,
oh many, yes many times."

She was opening the door, while saying this, and
then she started back in affright that the little boy
should have grown so.

"You cannot be that leetle boy. It is quite impos-
seeble. Why do you impose on me?"

"Not only am I that little boy, who made the water
to flow for you, till the nebule came upon the glass; but
also I am come to tell you all about your little girl."

"Come in, you very great leetle boy;" she answered,
with her dark eyes brightened. And I went in, and
looked at her. She was altered by time, as much as I
was. The slight and graceful shape was gone; not that
I remembered anything of her figure, if you please;
for boys of twelve are not yet prone to note the shapes
of women; but that her lithe straight gait had struck
me, as being so unlike our people. Now her time for
walking so was past, and transmitted to her children.

Yet her face was comely still, and full of strong intelligence. I gazed at her, and she at me: and we were sure of one another.

"Now what will ye please to eat?" she asked, with a lively glance at the size of my mouth: "that is always the first thing you people ask, in these barbarous places."

"I will tell you, by-and-by," I answered, misliking this satire upon us: "but I might begin with a quart of ale, to enable me to speak, madam."

"Very well. One quevart of be-or:" she called out to a little maid, who was her eldest child, no doubt. "It is to be expected, sir. Be-or, be-or, be-or, all day long, with you Englishmen!"

"Nay," I replied; "not all day long, if madam will excuse me. Only a pint at breakfast-time, and a pint and a-half at eleven o'clock; and a quart or so at dinner. And then no more till the afternoon; and half a gallon at supper time. No one can object to that."

"Well, I suppose it is right," she said, with an air of resignation: "God knows. But I do not understand it. It is 'good for business;' as you say, to preclude everything."

"And it is good for us, madam," I answered with indignation, for beer is my favourite beverage: "and I am a credit to beer, madam; and so are all who trust to it."

"At any rate you are, young man. If beer has made you grow so large, I will put my children upon it; it is too late for me to begin. The smell to me is hateful."

Now I only set down that, to show how perverse those foreign people are. They will drink their wretched heartless stuff, such as they call claret, or wine of Medoc, or Bordeaux, or what not; with no more meaning than sour rennet, stirred with the pulp from the cider press, and strained through the cap of our Betty. This is very well for them; and as good as they deserve, no doubt; and meant perhaps by the will of God for those unhappy natives. But to bring it over to England, and set it against our home-brewed ale (not to speak of wines from Portugal) and sell it at ten times the price, as a cure for British bile, and a great enlightenment; this I say is the vilest feature of the age we live in.

Madam Benita Odam—for the name of the man who turned the wheel proved to be John Odam— showed me into a little room containing two chairs and a fir-wood table, and sate down in a three-legged seat, and studied me very steadfastly. This she had a right to do; and I, having all my clothes on now, was not disconcerted. It would not become me to repeat her judgment upon my appearance; which she delivered as calmly as if I were a pig at market, and as proudly as if her own pig. And she asked me whether I had ever got rid of the black marks on my breast.

Not wanting to talk about myself (though very fond of doing so, when time and season favour) I led her

back to that fearful night of the day when first I had
seen her. She was not desirous to speak of it, because of
her own little children: however, I drew her gradually
to recollection of Lorna, and then of the little boy who
died, and the poor mother buried with him. And her
strong hot nature kindled, as she dwelled upon these
things; and my wrath waxed within me; and we for-
got reserve and prudence under the sense of so vile a
wrong. She told me (as nearly as might be) the very
same story which she had told to Master Jeremy
Stickles; only she dwelled upon it more, because of
my knowing the outset. And being a woman, with an
inkling of my situation, she enlarged upon the little
maid, more than to dry Jeremy.

"Would you know her again?" I asked, being
stirred by these accounts of Lorna, when she was five
years old: "would you know her as a full-grown
maiden?"

"I think I should," she answered; "it is not possible to say until one sees the person: but from the
eyes of the little girl, I think that I must know her.
Oh, the poor young creature! Is it to be believed that
the cannibals devoured her? What a people you are
in this country! Meat, meat, meat!"

As she raised her hands and eyes in horror at our
carnivorous propensities, to which she clearly attributed
the disappearance of Lorna, I could scarce help laughing, even after that sad story. For though it is said
at the present day, and will doubtless be said hereafter,
that the Doones had devoured a baby once, as they

came up Porlock hill, after fighting hard in the
market-place, I knew that the tale was utterly false:
for cruel and brutal as they were, their taste was very
correct and choice, and indeed one might say fastidious. Nevertheless, I could not stop to argue that
matter with her.

"The little maid has not been devoured," I said to
Mistress Odam: "and now she is a tall young lady,
and as beautiful as can be. If I sleep in your good
hostel to-night, after going to Watchett town, will
you come with me to Oare to-morrow, and see your
little maiden?"

"I would like—and yet I fear. This country is so
barbarous. And I am good to eat—my God, there is
much picking on my bones!"

She surveyed herself with a glance so mingled of
pity and admiration; and the truth of her words was
so apparent (only that it would have taken a week to
get at the bones, before picking) that I nearly lost
good manners; for she really seemed to suspect even
me of cannibal inclinations. However, at last I made
her promise to come with me on the morrow, pre-
suming that Master Odam could by any means be
persuaded to keep her company in the cart, as pro-
priety demanded. Having little doubt that Master
Odam was entirely at his wife's command, I looked
upon that matter as settled, and set off for Watchett,
to see the grave of Lorna's poor mother, and to hire a
cart for the morrow.

And here (as so often happens with men) I succeeded without any trouble or hindrance, where I had looked for both of them, namely in finding a suitable cart; whereas the other matter, in which I could have expected no difficulty, came very near to defeat me. For when I heard that Lorna's father was the Earl of Dugal—as Benita impressed upon me with a strong enforcement, as much as to say, "Who are you, young man, to come even asking about her?"—then I never thought but that everybody in Watchett town must know all about the tombstone of the Countess of Dugal.

This however proved otherwise. For Lord Dugal had never lived at Watchett Grange, as their place was called; neither had his name become familiar as its owner. Because the Grange had only devolved to him by will, at the end of a long entail, when the last of the Fitz-Paines died out; and though he liked the idea of it, he had gone abroad, without taking seisin. And upon news of his death, John Jones, a rich gentleman from Llandaff, had taken possession, as next of right, and hushed up all the story. And though, even at the worst of times, a lady of high rank and wealth could not be robbed, and as bad as murdered, and then buried in a little place, without moving some excitement; yet it had been given out, on purpose and with diligence, that this was only a foreign lady, travelling for her health and pleasure, along the sea-coast of England. And as the poor thing never spoke; and several of her servants, and her baggage looked so foreign, and she herself died in

a collar of lace unlike any made in England, all
Watchett, without hesitation, pronounced her to be a
foreigner. And the English serving-man and maid,
who might have cleared up everything, either were
bribed by Master Jones, or else decamped of their
own accord with the relics of the baggage. So the
poor Countess of Dugal, almost in sight of her own
grand house, was buried in an unknown grave, with
her pair of infants; without a plate, without a tombstone, (worse than all) without a tear, except from
the hired Italian woman. Surely my poor Lorna came
of an ill-starred family.

Now, in spite of all this, if I had only taken Benita
with me, or even told her what I wished, and craved
her directions, there could have been no trouble. But
I do assure you that among the stupid people at
Watchett (compared with whom our folk of Oare,
exceeding dense though being, are as Hamlet against
Dogberry), what with one of them and another, and
the firm conviction of all the town that I could be
come only to wrestle; I do assure you (as I said
before) that my wits almost went out of me. And
what vexed me yet more about it, was that I saw
my own mistake, in coming myself to seek out the
matter, instead of sending some unknown person. For
my face and form were known at that time (and still
are so) to nine people out of every ten living in forty
miles of me. Not through any excellence, or anything
of good desert, in either the one or the other; but
simply because folks will be fools on the rivalry of

wrestling. The art is a fine one in itself, and demands a little wit of brain, as well as strength of
body: it binds the man who studies it to temperance,
and chastity, to self-respect, and most of all to an
even and sweet temper; for I have thrown stronger
men than myself (when I was a mere saplin, and
before my strength grew hard on me) through their
loss of temper. But though the art is an honest one,
surely they who excel therein have a right (like all
the rest of mankind) to their own private life.

Be that either way — and I will not speak too
strongly, for fear of indulging my own annoyance—
anyhow all Watchett town cared ten times as much to
see John Ridd, as to show him what he wanted. I was
led to every public-house, instead of to the churchyard;
and twenty tables were ready for me, in lieu of a single
gravestone. "Zummerzett thou bee'st, Jan Ridd, and
Zummerzett thou shalt be. Thee carl theezell a
Davonsheer man! Whoy, thee lives in Zummerzett;
and in Zummerzett thee wast barn, lad." And so it
went on, till I was weary; though very much obliged
to them.

Dull and solid as I am, and with a wild duck waiting
for me at good Mistress Odam's, I saw that there was
nothing for it but to yield to these good people, and
prove me a man of Somerset by eating a dinner at
their expense. As for the churchyard, none would
hear of it; and I grieved for broaching the matter.

But how was I to meet Lorna again, without having
done the thing of all things which I had promised to

see to? It would never do to tell her that so great
was my popularity, and so strong the desire to feed me,
that I could not attend to her mother. Least of all
could I say that every one in Watchett knew John
Ridd; while none had heard of the Countess of Dugal.
And yet that was about the truth: as I hinted very
delicately to Mistress Odam that evening. But she
(being vexed about her wild duck, and not having
English ideas on the matter of sports, and so on) made
a poor unwitting face at me. Nevertheless, Master
Odam restored me to my self-respect; for he stared
at me till I went to bed; and he broke his hose with
excitement. For being in the leg-line myself, I wanted
to know what the muscles were of a man who turned a
wheel all day. I had never seen a tread-mill (though
they have one now at Exeter) and it touched me much
to learn whether it were good exercise. And herein,
from what I saw of Odam, I incline to think that it
does great harm; as moving the muscles too much in
a line, and without variety.

## CHAPTER V.

HAVING obtained from Benita Odam a very close and full description of the place where her poor mistress lay, and the marks whereby to know it, I hastened to Watchett the following morning, before the sun was up, or any people were about. And so, without interruption, I was in the churchyard at sunrise.

In the furthest and darkest nook, overgrown with grass, and overhung by a weeping tree, a little bank of earth betokened the rounding off of a hapless life. There was nothing to tell of rank, or wealth, of love, or even pity: nameless as a peasant lay the last (as supposed) of a mighty race. Only some unskilful hand, probably Master Odam's, under his wife's teaching, had carved a rude L., and a ruder D., upon a large pebble from the beach, and set it up as a headstone.

I gathered a little grass for Lorna, and a sprig of the weeping tree; and then returned to the "Forest-cat," as Benita's lonely inn was called. For the way is long from Watchett to Oare; and though you may

ride it rapidly, as the Doones had done on that fatal
night; to travel on wheels, with one horse only, is a
matter of time, and of prudence. Therefore we set
out pretty early, three of us, and a baby, who could
not well be left behind. The wife of the man who
owned the cart had undertaken to mind the business,
and the other babies; upon condition of having the
keys of all the taps left with her.

As the manner of journeying over the moor has
been described oft enough already, I will say no more,
except that we all arrived, before dusk of the summer's
day, safe at Plover's Barrows. Mistress Benita was
delighted with the change from her dull hard life;
and she made many excellent observations, such as
seem natural to a foreigner looking at our country.

As luck would have it, the first who came to meet
us at the gate was Lorna, with nothing whatever upon
her head (the weather being summerly), but her beautiful hair shed round her; and wearing a sweet white
frock tucked in, and showing her figure perfectly.
In her joy she ran straight up to the cart; and then
stopped and gazed at Benita. At one glance her old
nurse knew her: "Oh the eyes, the eyes!" she cried,
and was over the rail of the cart in a moment, in spite
of all her substance. Lorna, on the other hand, looked
at her, with some doubt and wonder; as though having
right to know much about her, and yet unable to do so.
But when the foreign woman said something in Roman
language, and flung new hay from the cart upon her,
as if in a romp of childhood, the young maid cried,

"Oh, Nita, Nita!" and fell upon her breast, and wept; and after that looked round at us.

This being so, there could be no doubt as to the power of proving Lady Lorna's birth, and rights, both by evidence and token. For though we had not the necklace now—thanks to Annie's wisdom—we had the ring of heavy gold, a very ancient relic, with which my maid (in her simple way) had pledged herself to me. And Benita knew this ring as well as she knew her own fingers, having heard a long history about it; and the effigy on it of the wild cat was the bearing of the house of Lorne.

For though Lorna's father was a nobleman of high and goodly lineage, her mother was of yet more ancient and renowned descent, being the last in line direct from the great and kingly chiefs of Lorne. A wild and headstrong race they were, and must have everything their own way. Hot blood was ever among them, even of one household; and their sovereignty (which more than once had defied the King of Scotland) waned and fell among themselves, by continual quarrelling. And it was of a piece with this, that the Doones (who were an offset, by the mother's side, holding in co-partnership some large property, which had come by the spindle, as we say) should fall out with the Earl of Lorne, the last but one of that title.

The daughter of this nobleman had married Sir Ensor Doone; but this, instead of healing matters, led to fiercer conflict. I never could quite understand all the ins and outs of it; which none but a lawyer may

go through, and keep his head at the end of it. The
motives of mankind are plainer than the motions they
produce. Especially when charity (such as found
among us) sits to judge the former, and is never weary
of it: while reason does not care to trace the latter
complications, except for fee or title.

Therefore it is enough to say, that knowing Lorna
to be direct in heirship to vast property, and bearing
especial spite against the house of which she was the
last, the Doones had brought her up with full intention
of lawful marriage; and had carefully secluded her
from the wildest of their young gallants. Of course,
if they had been next in succession, the child would
have gone down the waterfall, to save any further
trouble; but there was an intercepting branch of some
honest family; and they being outlaws, would have a
poor chance (though the law loves outlaws) against
them. Only Lorna was of the stock; and Lorna they
must marry. And what a triumph against the old
Earl, for a cursed Doone to succeed him!

As for their outlawry, great robberies, and grand
murders, the veriest child, now-a-days, must know that
money heals the whole of that. Even if they had
murdered people of a good position, it would only
cost about twice as much, to prove their motives loyal.
But they had never slain any man above the rank of
yeoman; and folk even said that my father was the
highest of their victims; for the death of Lorna's
mother and brother was never set to their account.

Pure pleasure it is to any man, to reflect upon all

these things. How truly we discern clear justice, and how well we deal it. If any poor man steals a sheep, having ten children starving, and regarding it as mountain game (as a rich man does a hare), to the gallows with him. If a man of rank beats down a door, smites the owner upon the head, and honours the wife with attention; it is a thing to be grateful for, and to slouch smitten head the lower.

While we were full of all these things, and wondering what would happen next, or what we ought ourselves to do, another very important matter called for our attention. This was no less than Annie's marriage to the Squire Faggus. We had tried to put it off again; for in spite of all advantages, neither my mother nor myself had any real heart for it. Not that we dwelled upon Tom's short-comings, or rather perhaps his going too far, at the time when he worked the road so. All that was covered by the King's pardon, and universal respect of the neighbourhood. But our scruple was this—and the more we talked the more it grew upon us—that we both had great misgivings as to his future steadiness.

For it would be a thousand pities we said, for a fine, well-grown, and pretty maiden (such as our Annie was) useful too in so many ways, and lively, and warmhearted, and mistress of £500, to throw herself away on a man with a kind of a turn for drinking. If that last were even hinted, Annie would be most indignant, and ask, with cheeks as red as roses, who had ever seen Master Faggus any the worse for liquor indeed? Her

own opinion was, in truth, that he took a great deal
too little; after all his hard work, and hard riding, and
coming over the hills to be insulted! And if ever it
lay in her power, and with no one to grudge him his
trumpery glass, she would see that poor Tom had the
nourishment which his cough and his lungs required.

His lungs being quite as sound as mine, this matter
was out of all argument; so mother and I looked at
one another, as much as to say, "let her go upstairs:
she will cry, and come down more reasonable." And
while she was gone, we used to say the same thing
over and over again; but without perceiving a cure
for it. And we almost always finished up with the
following reflection, which sometimes came from
mother's lips, and sometimes from my own: "Well,
well, there is no telling. None can say how a man may
alter, when he takes to matrimony. But if we could
only make Annie promise to be a little firm with him!"

I fear that all this talk on our part only hurried
matters forward, Annie being more determined every
time we pitied her. And at last Tom Faggus came,
and spoke as if he were on the King's road, with a
pistol at my head, and one at mother's. "No more
fast and loose," he cried: "either one thing, or the
other. I love the maid, and she loves me: and we
will have one another, either with your leave, or without it. How many more times am I to dance over
these vile hills, and leave my business, and get nothing
more than a sigh or a kiss, and 'Tom, I must wait for
mother?' You are famous for being straightforward,

you Ridds. Just treat me as I would treat you, now."

I looked at my mother; for a glance from her would have sent Tom out of the window; but she checked me with her hand, and said, " You have some ground of complaint, sir : I will not deny it. Now I will be as straightforward with you, as even a Ridd is supposed to be. My son and myself have all along disliked your marriage with Annie. Not for what you have been so much, as for what we fear you will be. Have patience, one moment, if you please. We do not fear your taking to the highway life again; for that you are too clever, no doubt, now that you have property. But we fear that you will take to drinking, and to squandering money. There are many examples of this around us : and we know what the fate of the wife is. It has been hard to tell you this, under our own roof, and with our own "—— Here mother hesitated.

"Spirits, and cider, and beer," I broke in; "out with it, like a Ridd, mother; as he will have all of it."

"Spirits, and cider, and beer," said mother very firmly after me; and then she gave way and said, " You know, Tom, you are welcome to every drop and more of it."

Now Tom must have had a far sweeter temper than ever I could claim; for I should have thrust my glass away, and never taken another drop in the house where such a check had met me. But instead of that, Master Faggus replied, with a pleasant smile :

"I know that I am welcome, good mother; and to prove it, I will have some more."

And thereupon he mixed himself another glass of hollands with lemon, and hot water; yet pouring it very delicately.

"Oh, I have been so miserable—take a little more, Tom," said mother, handing the bottle.

"Yes, take a little more," I said; "you have mixed it over weak, Tom."

"If ever there was a sober man," cried Tom, complying with our request; "if ever there was in Christendom a man of perfect sobriety, that man is now before you. Shall we say to-morrow week, mother? It will suit your washing-day."

"How very thoughtful you are, Tom! Now John would never have thought of that, in spite of all his steadiness."

"Certainly not," I answered proudly; "when my time comes for Lorna, I shall not study Betty Muxworthy."

In this way the Squire got over us; and Farmer Nicholas Snowe was sent for, to counsel with mother about the matter, and to set his two daughters sewing.

When the time for the wedding came, there was such a stir and commotion as had never been known in the parish of Oare, since my father's marriage. For Annie's beauty and kindliness had made her the pride of the neighbourhood; and the presents sent her, from all around, were enough to stock a shop with. Master Stickles, who now could walk, and who certainly owed his recovery, with the blessing of God, to Annie, presented her with a mighty Bible, silver-clasped, and very handsome, beating the parson's out and out, and for which he had sent to Taunton. Even the common troopers, having tasted her cookery many times (to help out their poor rations), clubbed together, and must have given at least a week's pay apiece, to have turned out what they did for her. This was no less than a silver pot, well-designed, but suited surely rather to the bridegroom's taste, than bride's. In a word, everybody gave her things.

And now my Lorna came to me, with a spring of tears in appealing eyes—for she was still somewhat childish; or rather, I should say, more childish now than when she lived in misery,—and she placed her little hand in mine, and she was half afraid to speak, and dropped her eyes for me to ask.

"What is it, little darling?" I asked, as I saw her breath come fast; for the smallest emotion moved her form.

"You don't think, John, you don't think, dear, that you could lend me any money?"

"All I have got," I answered: "how much do you want, dear heart?"

"I have been calculating; and I fear that I cannot do any good with less than ten pounds, John."

Here she looked up at me, with horror at the grandeur of the sum, and not knowing what I could think of it. But I kept my eyes from hers. "Ten pounds!" I said, in my deepest voice, on purpose to

have it out in comfort, when she should be frightened :
"what can you want with ten pounds, child ? "

"That is my concern," said Lorna, plucking up her
spirit at this : "when a lady asks for a loan, no gentleman pries into the cause of her asking it."

"That may be, as may be," I answered in a judicial
manner : "ten pounds, or twenty, you shall have. But
I must know the purport."

"Then that you never shall know, John. I am
very sorry for asking you. It is not of the smallest
consequence. Oh dear, no." Herewith she was running away.

"Oh dear, yes," I replied ; "it is of very great
consequence ; and I understand the whole of it. You
want to give that stupid Annie, who has lost you a
hundred thousand pounds, and who is going to be
married before us, dear — God only can tell why,
being my younger sister—you want to give her a
wedding-present. And you shall do it, darling ; because it is so good of you. Don't you know your title,
love ? How humble you are with us humble folk.
You are Lady Lorna something, so far as I can make
out yet : and you ought not even to speak to us. You
will go away, and disdain us."

"If you please, talk not like that, John. I will
have nothing to do with it ; if it comes between you
and me, John."

"You cannot help yourself," said I. And then she
vowed that she could and would. And rank and birth
were banished from between our lips, in no time.

"What can I get her good enough? I am sure I
do not know," she asked: "she has been so kind and
good to me, and she is such a darling. How I shall
miss her, to be sure! By-the-by, you seem to think,
John, that I shall be rich some day?"

"Of course you will. As rich as the French king
who keeps ours. Would the Lord Chancellor trouble
himself about you, if you were poor?"

"Then if I am rich, perhaps you would lend me
twenty pounds, dear John. Ten pounds would be
very mean for a wealthy person to give her."

To this I agreed, upon condition that I should make
the purchase myself, whatever it might be. For nothing could be easier than to cheat Lorna about the
cost, until time should come for her paying me.. And
this was better than to cheat her for the benefit of our
family. For this end, and for many others, I set off to
Dulverton, bearing more commissions, more messages,
and more questions, than a man of thrice my memory
might carry so far as the corner where the saw-pit is.
And to make things worse, one girl or other would
keep on running up to me, or even after me (when
started), with something or other she had just thought
of, which she could not possibly do without, and which
I must be sure to remember, as the most important of
the whole.

To my dear mother, who had partly outlived the
exceeding value of trifles, the most important matter
seemed to ensure Uncle Reuben's countenance and
presence at the marriage. And if I succeeded in this,

I might well forget all the maidens' trumpery. This she would have been wiser to tell me when they were out of hearing; for I left her to fight her own battle with them; and laughing at her predicament, promised to do the best I could for all, so far as my wits would go.

Uncle Reuben was not at home; but Ruth, who received me very kindly, although without any expressions of joy, was sure of his return in the afternoon, and persuaded me to wait for him. And by the time that I had finished all I could recollect of my orders, even with paper to help me, the old gentleman rode into the yard, and was more surprised than pleased to see me. But if he was surprised, I was more than that,—I was utterly astonished at the change in his appearance since the last time I had seen him. From a hale, and rather heavy man, grey-haired, but plump, and ruddy, he was altered to a shrunken, wizened, trembling, and almost decrepit figure. Instead of curly and comely locks, grizzled indeed, but plentiful, he had only a few lank white hairs scattered and flattened upon his forehead. But the greatest change of all was in the expression of his eyes, which had been so keen, and restless, and bright, and a little sarcastic. Bright indeed they still were, but with a slow unhealthy lustre; their keenness was turned to perpetual outlook, their restlessness to a haggard want. As for the humour which once gleamed there (which people who fear it call sarcasm), it had been succeeded by stares of terror, and then mistrust, and shrinking.

There was none of the interest in mankind, which is needful even for satire.

"Now what can this be?" thought I to myself: "has the old man lost all his property, or taken too much to strong waters?"

"Come inside, John Ridd," he said: "I will have a talk with you. It is cold out here; and it is too light. Come inside, John Ridd, boy."

I followed him into a little dark room, quite different from Ruth Huckaback's. It was closed from the shop by an old division of boarding, hung with tanned canvass; and the smell was very close and faint. Here there was a ledger-desk, and a couple of chairs, and a long-legged stool.

"Take the stool," said Uncle Reuben, showing me in very quietly; "it is fitter for your height, John. Wait a moment; there is no hurry."

Then he slipped out by another door, and closing it quickly after him, told the foreman, and waiting-men, that the business of the day was done. They had better all go home at once; and he would see to the fastenings. Of course, they were only too glad to go; but I wondered at his sending them, with at least two hours of daylight left.

However, that was no business of mine; and I waited, and pondered whether fair Ruth ever came into this dirty room; and if so, how she kept her hands from it. For Annie would have had it upside down, in about two minutes, and scrubbed, and brushed, and dusted, until it looked quite another place; and

yet all this done without scolding and crossness; which
are the curse of clean women, and ten times worse
than the dustiest dust.

Uncle Ben came reeling in, not from any power
of liquor, but because he was stiff from horse-back,
and weak from work and worry.

"Let me be, John, let me be," he said, as I went
to help him: "this is an unkid dreary place; but many
a hundred of good gold Carolus has been turned in
this place, John."

"Not a doubt about it, sir," I answered, in my loud
and cheerful manner; "and many another hundred,
sir; and may you long enjoy them!"

"My boy, do you wish me to die?" he asked,
coming up close to my stool, and regarding me with
a shrewd, though blear-eyed gaze: "many do. Do
you, John?"

"Come," said I: "don't ask such nonsense. You
know better than that, Uncle Ben. Or else, I am
sorry for you. I want you to live as long as possible,
for the sake of"—— Here I stopped.

"For the sake of what, John? I know it is not for
my own sake. For the sake of what, my boy?"

"For the sake of Ruth," I answered; "if you must
have all the truth. Who is to mind her when you are
gone?"

"But if you knew that I had gold, or a manner of
getting gold, far more than ever the sailors got out of
the Spanish galleons, far more than ever was heard of;
and the secret was to be yours, John; yours after me,

and no other soul's—then you would wish me dead,
John." Here he eyed me as if a speck of dust in my
eyes should not escape him.

"You are wrong, Uncle Ben; altogether wrong.
For all the gold ever heard, or dreamed of, not a
wish would cross my heart to rob you of one day of
life."

At last he moved his eyes from mine; but without
any word, or sign, to show whether he believed or disbelieved. Then he went to a chair, and sate with his
chin upon the ledger-desk; as if the effort of probing
me had been too much for his weary brain. "Dreamed
of! All the gold ever dreamed of! As if it were but
a dream!" he muttered: and then he closed his eyes,
to think.

"Good Uncle Reuben," I said to him, "you have
been a long way to-day, sir. Let me go and get you
a glass of good wine. Cousin Ruth knows where to
find it."

"How do you know how far I have been?" he
asked, with a vicious look at me. "And Cousin Ruth!
You are very pat with my grand-daughter's name,
young man!"

"It would be hard upon me, sir, not to know my
own cousin's name."

"Very well. Let that go by. You have behaved
very badly to Ruth. She loves you; and you love her
not."

At this I was so wholly amazed—not at the thing
itself I mean, but at his knowledge of it—that I could

G 2

not say a single word: but looked, no doubt, very foolish.

"You may well be ashamed, young man," he cried, with some triumph over me: "you are the biggest of all fools, as well as a conceited coxcomb. What can you want more than Ruth? She is a little damsel truly: but finer men than you, John Ridd, with all your boasted strength and wrestling, have wedded smaller maidens. And as for quality, and value,— bots! one inch of Ruth is worth all your seven feet put together."

Now I am not seven feet high; nor ever was six feet eight inches, in my very prime of life; and nothing vexes me so much as to make me out a giant, and above human sympathy, and human scale of weakness. It cost me hard to hold my tongue; which luckily is not in proportion to my stature. And only for Ruth's sake I held it. But Uncle Ben (being old and worn) was vexed by not having any answer, almost as much as a woman is.

"You want me to go on," he continued, with a look of spite at me; "about my poor Ruth's love for you, to feed your cursed vanity. Because a set of asses call you the finest man in England; there is no maid (I suppose) who is not in love with you. I believe you are as deep as you are long, John Ridd. Shall I ever get to the bottom of your character?"

This was a little too much for me. Any insult I could take (with good will) from a white-haired man, and one who was my relative; unless it touched my

love for Lorna, or my conscious modesty. Now both
of these were touched to the quick, by the sentences of
the old gentleman. Therefore, without a word, I
went; only making a bow to him.

But women, who are (beyond all doubt) the mothers
of all mischief, also nurse that babe to sleep, when he
is too noisy. And there was Ruth, as I took my horse
(with a trunk of frippery on him), poor little Ruth was
at the bridle, and rusting all the knops of our town-
going harness with tears.

"Good-bye, dear," I said, as she bent her head away
from me; "shall I put you up on the saddle, dear?"

"Cousin Ridd, you may take it lightly," said Ruth,
turning full upon me: "and very likely you are right,
according to your nature"—this was the only cutting
thing the little soul ever said to me—"but oh, Cousin
Ridd, you have no idea of the pain you will leave
behind you."

"How can that be so, Ruth, when I am as good as
ordered to be off the premises?"

"In the first place, Cousin Ridd, grandfather will be
angry with himself, for having so ill-used you. And
now he is so weak and poorly, that he is always
repenting. In the next place, I shall scold him first,
until he admits his sorrow; and when he has admitted
it, I shall scold myself for scolding him. And then he
will come round again, and think that I was hard on
him; and end perhaps by hating you—for he is like a
woman now, John."

That last little touch of self-knowledge in Ruth,

which she delivered with a gleam of some secret pleasantry, made me stop and look closely at her: but she pretended not to know it. "There is something in this child," I thought, "very different from other girls. What it is, I cannot tell; for one very seldom gets at it."

At any rate, the upshot was that the good horse went back to stable, and had another feed of corn; while my wrath sank within me. There are two things, according to my experience (which may not hold with another man) fitted beyond any others to take hot tempers out of us. The first is to see our favourite creatures feeding, and licking up their food, and happily snuffling over it, yet sparing time to be grateful, and showing taste and perception; the other is to go gardening boldly, in the spring of the year, without any misgiving about it, and hoping the utmost of everything. If there be a third anodyne, approaching these two in power, it is to smoke good tobacco well, and watch the setting of the moon; and if this should only be over the sea, the result is irresistible.

Master Huckaback showed no especial signs of joy at my return; but received me with a little grunt, which appeared to me to mean: "Ah, I thought he would hardly be fool enough to go." I told him how sorry I was for having in some way offended him; and he answered that I did well to grieve for one at least of my offences. To this I made no reply, as behoves a man dealing with cross and fractious people: and presently he became better tempered, and sent little Ruth

for a bottle of wine. She gave me a beautiful smile of
thanks for my forbearance, as she passed; and I knew
by her manner that she would bring the best bottle in
all the cellar.

As I had but little time to spare (although the days
were long and light) we were forced to take our wine
with promptitude and rapidity; and whether this
loosened my uncle's tongue, or whether he meant
beforehand to speak, is now almost uncertain. But
true it is that he brought his chair very near to mine,
after three or four glasses, and sent Ruth away upon
some errand which seemed of small importance. At
this I was vexed; for the room always looked so different without her.

"Come, Jack," he said; "here's your health, young
fellow, and a good and obedient wife to you. Not that
your wife will ever obey you though; you are much
too easy tempered. Even a bitter and stormy woman
might live in peace with you, Jack. But never you
give her the chance to try. Marry some sweet little
thing, if you can. If not, don't marry any. Ah, we
have the maid to suit you, my lad, in this old town of
Dulverton."

"Have you so, sir? But perhaps the maid might
have no desire to suit me."

"That you may take my word she has. The colour
of this wine will prove it. The sly little hussy has
been to the cobwebbed arch of the cellar, where she
has no right to go, for any one under a magistrate.
However, I am glad to see it; and we will not spare

it, John.   After my time, somebody, whoever marries
little Ruth, will find some rare wine there, I trow, and
perhaps not know the difference."

Thinking of this the old man sighed, and expected
me to sigh after him.   But a sigh is not (like a yawn)
infectious; and we are all more prone to be sent to
sleep than to sorrow by one another.   Not but what a
sigh sometimes may make us think of sighing.

"Well, sir," cried I, in my sprightliest manner,
which rouses up most people; "here's to your health,
and dear little Ruth's; and may you live to knock off
the cobwebs from every bottle in under the arch.
Uncle Reuben, your life, and health, sir!"

With that I took my glass thoughtfully, for it was
wondrous good; and Uncle Ben was pleased to see me
dwelling pleasantly on the subject, with parenthesis,
and self-commune, and oral judgment unpronounced,
though smacking of fine decision.   "Curia vult advi-
sari," as the lawyers say; which means, "Let us have
another glass, and then we can think about it."

"Come now, John," said Uncle Ben, laying his
wrinkled hand on my knee, when he saw that none
could heed us: "I know that you have a sneaking
fondness for my grandchild Ruth.   Don't interrupt me
now; you have; and to deny it will only provoke me."

"I do like Ruth, sir," I said boldly, for fear of misunderstanding; "but I do not love her."

"Very well; that makes no difference.   Liking may
very soon be loving (as some people call it) when the
maid has money to help her."

"But if there be, as there is in my case "——

, "Once for all, John, not a word. I do not attempt
to lead you into any engagement with little Ruth;
neither will I blame you (though I may be disappointed) if. no such engagement should ever be. But
whether you will have my grandchild, or whether you
will not—and such a chance is rarely offered to a
fellow of your standing"—Uncle Ben despised all
farmers—"in any case I have at last resolved to let
you know my secret; and for two good reasons. The
first is that it wears me out to dwell upon it, all alone:
and the second is that I can trust you to fulfil a promise. Moreover you are my next of kin, except among
the womankind; and you are just the man I want, to
help me in my enterprise."

"And I will help you, sir," I answered, fearing
some conspiracy, "in anything that is true, and loyal,
and according to the laws of the realm."

"Ha, ha!" cried the old man, laughing until his
eyes ran over, and spreading out his skinny hands upon
his shining breeches; "thou hast gone the same fools'
track as the rest; even as spy Stickles went, and all
his precious troopers. Landing of arms at Glenthorne,
and Lynmouth, waggons escorted across the moor,
sounds of metal, and booming noises! Ah but we
managed it cleverly, to cheat even those so near to us.
Disaffection at Taunton, signs of insurrection at Dulverton, revolutionary tanner at Dunster! We set it
all abroad, right well. And not even you to suspect
our work; though we thought at one time that you

watched us. Now who, do you suppose, is at the bottom of all this Exmoor insurgency, all this western rebellion—not that I say there is none, mind—but who is at the bottom of it?"

"Either Mother Melldrum," said I, being now a little angry; "or else old Nick himself."

"Nay, old Uncle Reuben!" Saying this, Master Huckaback cast back his coat, and stood up, and made the most of himself.

"Well!" cried I, being now quite come to the limits of my intellect: "then after all Captain Stickles was right in calling you a rebel, sir!"

"Of course he was: could so keen a man be wrong about an old fool like me? But come, and see our rebellion, John. I will trust you now with everything. I will take no oath from you; only your word to keep silence; and most of all from your mother."

"I will give you my word," I said, although liking not such pledges; which make a man think, before he speaks in ordinary company, against his usual practice. However I was now so curious, that I thought of nothing else; and scarcely could believe at all that Uncle Ben was quite right in his head.

"Take another glass of wine, my son," he cried, with a cheerful countenance, which made him look more than ten years younger; "you shall come into partnership with me: your strength will save us two horses, and we always fear the horse work. Come and see our rebellion, my boy; you are a made man from to-night."

"But where am I to come and see it? Where am I to find it, sir?"

"Meet me," he answered, yet closing his hands, and wrinkling with doubt his forehead; "come alone, of course; and meet me at the Wizard's Slough, at ten to-morrow morning."

## CHAPTER VI.

KNOWING Master Huckaback to be a man of his word, as well as one who would have others so, I was careful to be in good time the next morning, by the side of the Wizard's Slough. I am free to admit that the name of the place bore a feeling of uneasiness, and a love of distance, in some measure, to my heart. But I did my best not to think of this: only I thought it a wise precaution, and due for the sake of my mother and Lorna, to load my gun with a dozen slugs made from the lead of the old church-porch, laid by, long since, against witchcraft.

I am well aware that some people now begin to doubt about witchcraft; or at any rate feign to do so, being desirous to disbelieve whatever they are afraid of. This spirit is growing too common among us, and will end (unless we put stop to it) in the destruction of all religion. And as regards witchcraft, a man is bound either to believe in it, or to disbelieve the Bible. For even in the New Testament; discarding many things of the Old, such as sacrifices, and sabbath, and fasting, and other miseries; witchcraft is clearly spoken of as a thing that must continue; that the Evil One be not utterly robbed of his vested interests. Hence let no one tell me, that witchcraft is done away with: for I will meet him with St. Paul, than whom no better man, and few less superstitious, can be found in all the Bible.

Feeling these things more in those days, than I feel them now, I fetched a goodish compass round, by the way of the Cloven rocks, rather than cross Black Barrow Down, in a reckless and unholy manner. There were several spots, upon that Down, cursed, and smitten, and blasted, as if thunderbolts had fallen there, and Satan sate to keep them warm. At any rate it was good (as every one acknowledged) not to wander there too much; even with a doctor of divinity upon one arm, and of medicine upon the other.

Therefore I, being all alone, and on foot (as seemed the wisest) preferred a course of roundabout; and starting about eight o'clock, without mentioning my business, arrived at the mouth of the deep descent, such as John Fry described it. Now this (though I have not spoken of it) was not my first time of being there. For, although I could not bring myself to spy upon Uncle Reuben, as John Fry had done, yet I thought it no ill manners, after he had left our house, to have a look at the famous place, where the malefactor came to life, at least in John's opinion. At that time, however, I saw nothing, except the great ugly black morass, with the grisly reeds around it: and I

did not care to go very near it, much less to pry on
the further side.

Now, on the other hand, I was bent to get at the
very bottom of this mystery (if there were any), having
less fear of witch or wizard, with a man of Uncle
Reuben's wealth to take my part, and see me through.
So I rattled the ramrod down my gun, just to know if
the charge were right, after so much walking; and
finding it full six inches deep, as I like to have it, went
boldly down the steep gorge of rock, with a firm resolve
to shoot any witch, unless it were good Mother Melldrum. Nevertheless, to my surprise, all was quiet,
and fair to look at, in the decline of the narrow way;
with great stalked ferns coming forth like trees, yet
hanging like cobwebs over one. And along one side,
a little spring was getting rid of its waters. Any man
might stop and think; or he might go on and think;
and in either case, there was none to say that he was
making a fool of himself.

When I came to the foot of this ravine, and ove
against the great black slough, there was no sign o
Master Huckaback, nor of any other living man,
except myself, in the silence. Therefore I sate in a
niche of rock, gazing at the slough, and pondering the
old tradition about it.

They say that, in the ancient times, a mighty necromancer lived in the wilderness of Exmoor. Here, by
spell and incantation, he built himself a strong high
palace, eight-sided like a spider's web, an d standing on
a central steep; so that neither man nor beast could

cross the moor without his knowledge. If he wished to rob and slay a traveller, or to have wild ox, or stag for food, he had nothing more to do than sit at one of his eight windows, and point his unholy book at him. Any moving creature, at which that book was pointed, must obey the call, and come from whatever distance; if sighted once by the wizard.

This was a bad condition of things, and all the country groaned under it; and Exmoor (although the most honest place that a man could wish to live in) was beginning to get a bad reputation, and all through that vile wizard. No man durst even go to steal a sheep, or a pony, or so much as a deer for dinner, lest he should be brought to book by a far bigger rogue than he was. And this went on for many years; though they prayed to God to abate it. But at last, when the wizard was getting fat and haughty upon his high stomach, a mighty deliverance came to Exmoor, and a warning, and a memory. For one day the sorcerer gazed from his window facing the south-east of the compass; and he yawned, having killed so many men, that now he was weary of it.

"'Ifackins," he cried, or some such oath, both profane and uncomely; "I see a man on the verge of the sky-line, going along laboriously. A pilgrim, I trow, or some such fool, with the nails of his boots inside them. Too thin to be worth eating: but I will have him for the fun of the thing: and most of those saints have got money."

With these words, he stretched forth his legs on a

stool, and pointed the book of heathenish spells, back upwards, at the pilgrim. Now this good pilgrim was plodding along, soberly and religiously; with a pound of flints in either boot, and not an ounce of meat inside him. He felt the spell of the wicked book, but only as a horse might feel a "gee-wug!" addressed to him. It was in the power of this good man, either to go on, or turn aside, and see out the wizard's meaning. And for a moment he halted and stood, like one in two minds about a thing. Then the wizard clapped one cover to, in a jocular and insulting manner; and the sound of it came to the pilgrim's ear, about five miles in the distance: like a great gun fired at him.

"By our Lady," he cried; "I must see to this; although my poor feet have no skin below them. I will teach this heathen miscreant how to scoff at Glastonbury."

Thereupon he turned his course, and ploughed along through the moors and bogs, towards the eight-sided palace. The wizard sate on his chair of comfort; and with the rankest contempt observed the holy man ploughing toward him. "He has something good in his wallet, I trow," said the black thief to himself; "these fellows get always the pick of the wine, and the best of a woman's money." Then he cried, "Come in, come in, good sir;" as he always did to every one.

"Bad sir, I will not come in," said the pilgrim; "neither shall you come out again. Here are the bones of all you have slain; and here shall your own bones be."

"Hurry me not," cried the sorcerer; "that is a thing to think about. How many miles hast thou travelled this day?"

But the pilgrim was too wide awake; for if he had spoken of any number, bearing no cross upon it, the necromancer would have had him, like a ball at bando-play. Therefore he answered, as truly as need be, "By the grace of our Lady, nine."

Now nine is the crossest of all cross numbers, and full to the lip of all crotchets. So the wizard staggered back, and thought, and inquired again with bravery: "Where can you find a man and wife, one going up-hill, and one going down, and not a word spoken between them?"

"In a cucumber plant," said the modest saint; blushing even to think of it: and the wizard knew he was done for.

"You have tried me with ungodly questions," continued the honest pilgrim; with one hand still over his eyes, as he thought of the feminine cucumber; "and now I will ask you a pure one. To whom of mankind have you ever done good, since God saw fit to make you?"

The wizard thought, but could quote no one: and he looked at the saint, and the saint at him, and both their hearts were trembling. "Can you mention only one?" asked the saint, pointing a piece of the true cross at him, hoping he might cling to it: "even a little child will do: try to think of some one."

The earth was rocking beneath their feet, and the

VOL. III. H

palace windows darkened on them, with a tint of blood :
for now the saint was come inside, hoping to save the
wizard.

"If I must tell the pure truth," said the wizard,
looking up at the arches of his windows; "I can tell of
only one to whom I ever have done good."  .

" One will do: one is quite enough: be quick
before the ground opens.　The name of one — and
this cross will save you.　Lay your thumb on the end
of it."

" Nay, that I cannot do, great saint.　The devil
have mercy upon me !"

All this while the palace was sinking, and blackness
coming over them.

" Thou hast all but done for thyself," said the saint,
with a glory burning round his head; " by that last
invocation.　Yet give us the name of the one, my
friend, if one there be, it will save thee, with the cross
upon thy breast.　All is crashing round us ; dear
brother, who is that one ? "

" My own self," cried the wretched wizard.

" Then there is no help for thee."　And with that
the honest saint went upward, and the wizard, and all
his palace, and even the crag that bore it sank to the
bowels of the earth; and over them was nothing left
except a black bog fringed with reed, of the tint of the
wizard's whiskers.　The saint however was all right,
after sleeping off the excitement; and he founded a
chapel, some three miles westward; and there he lies
with his holy relic; and thither in after ages came (as

we all come home at last) both my Lorna's Aunt
Sabina, and her guardian Ensor Doone.

While yet I dwelled upon this strange story, wondering if it all were true, and why such things do not
happen now, a man on horseback appeared as suddenly
as if he had risen out of the earth, on the other side of
the great black slough. At first I was a little scared, my
mind being in the tune for wonders; but presently the
white hair, whiter from the blackness of the bog between
us, showed me that it was Uncle Reuben come to look
for me, that way. Then I left my chair of rock, and
waved my hat and shouted to him, and the sound of
my voice among the crags and lonely corners frightened me.

Old Master Huckaback made no answer; but (so
far as I could guess) beckoned me to come to him.
There was just room between the fringe of reed and
the belt of rock around it, for a man going very carefully to escape that horrible pit-hole. And so I went
round to the other side, and there found open space
enough, with stunted bushes, and starveling trees, and
straggling tufts of rushes.

"You fool, you are frightened," said Uncle Ben,
as he looked at my face after shaking hands: "I
want a young man of steadfast courage, as well as of
strength and silence. And after what I heard of the
battle at Glen Doone, I thought I might trust you for
courage."

"So you may," said I, "wherever I see mine enemy;
but not where witch and wizard be."

"Tush, great fool!" cried Master Huckaback:
"the only witch or wizard here is the one that bewitcheth all men. Now fasten up my horse, John Ridd,
and not too near the slough, lad. Ah, we have chosen
our entrance wisely. Two good horsemen, and their
horses, coming hither to spy us out, are gone mining
on their own account (and their last account it is)
down this good wizard's bog-hole."

With these words, Uncle Reuben clutched the mane
of his horse and came down, as a man does when his
legs are old; and as I myself begin to do, at this time
of writing. I offered a hand, but he was vexed, and
would have nought to do with it.

"Now follow me, step for step," he said, when I
had tethered his horse to a tree; "the ground is not
death (like the wizard's hole), but many parts are
treacherous. I know it well by this time."

Without any more ado, he led me in and out the
marshy places, to a great round hole or shaft, bratticed
up with timber. I never had seen the like before,
and wondered how they could want a well, with so
much water on every side. Around the mouth were a
few little heaps of stuff unused to the daylight; and I
thought at once of the tales I had heard concerning
mines in Cornwall, and the silver cup at Combe-Martin,
sent to the Queen Elizabeth.

"We had a tree across it, John," said Uncle
Reuben, smiling grimly at my sudden shrink from
it: "but some rogue came spying here, just as one
of our men went up. He was frightened half out of

his life, I believe, and never ventured to come again.
But we put the blame of that upon you. And I see
that we were wrong, John." Here he looked at me
with keen eyes, though weak.

"You were altogether wrong," I answered. "Am
I mean enough to spy upon any one dwelling with us?
And more than that, Uncle Reuben, it was mean of
you to suppose it."

"All ideas are different," replied the old man to
my heat, like a little worn-out rill running down a
smithy; "you with your strength, and youth, and all
that, are inclined to be romantic. I take things as I
have known them, going on for seventy years. Now
will you come and meet the wizard, or does your
courage fail you?"

"My courage must be none," said I, "if I would
not go where you go, sir."

He said no more, but signed to me to lift a heavy
wooden corb with an iron loop across it, and sunk in a
little pit of earth, a yard or so from the mouth of the
shaft. I raised it, and by his direction dropped it into
the throat of the shaft, where it hung and shook from
a great cross-beam laid at the level of the earth. A
very stout thick rope was fastened to the handle of the
corb, and ran across a pulley hanging from the centre of
the beam, and thence out of sight in the nether places.

"I will first descend," he said; "your weight is too
great for safety. When the bucket comes up again,
follow me, if your heart is good."

Then he whistled down, with a quick sharp noise,

and a whistle from below replied: and he clomb into the vehicle, and the rope ran through the pulley, and Uncle Ben went merrily down, and was out of sight, before I had time to think of him.

Now being left on the bank like that, and in full sight of the goodly heaven, I wrestled hard with my flesh and blood, about going down into the pit-hole. And but for the pale shame of the thing, that a white-headed man should adventure so, and green youth doubt about it, never could I have made up my mind; for I do love air and heaven. However, at last up came the bucket; and with a short sad prayer I went into whatever might happen.

My teeth would chatter, do all I could; but the strength of my arms was with me; and by them I held on the grimy rope, and so eased the foot of the corb, which threatend to go away fathoms under me. Of course I should still have been safe enough, being like an egg in an egg-cup, too big to care for the bottom; still I wished that all should be done, in good order, without excitement.

The scoopings of the side grew black, and the patch of sky above more blue, as with many thoughts of Lorna, a long way underground I sank. Then I was fetched up at the bottom with a jerk and rattle; and but for holding by the rope so, must have tumbled over. Two great torches of bale-resin showed me all the darkness, one being held by Uncle Ben and the other by a short square man with a face which seemed well known to me.

"Hail to the world of gold, John Ridd," said Master Huckaback, smiling in the old dry manner: "bigger coward never came down the shaft, now did he, Carfax?"

"They be all alike," said the short square man, "fust time as they doos it."

"May I go to heaven," I cried; "which is a thing quite out of sight"—for I always have a vein of humour, too small to be followed by any one—"if ever again of my own accord I go so far away from it!" Uncle Ben grinned less at this than at the way I knocked my shin in getting out of the bucket; and as for Master Carfax, he would not even deign to smile. And he seemed to look upon my entrance as an interloping.

For my part, I had nought to do, after rubbing my bruised leg, except to look about me, so far as the dulness of light would help. And herein I seemed, like a mouse in a trap, able no more than to run to and fro, and knock himself, and stare at things. For here was a little channel grooved with posts on either side of it, and ending with a heap of darkness, whence the sight came back again; and there was a scooped place, like a funnel, but pouring only to darkness. So I waited for somebody to speak first, not seeing my way to anything.

"You seem to be disappointed, John," said Uncle Reuben, looking blue by the light of the flambeaux; "did you expect to see the roof of gold, and the sides of gold, and the floor of gold, John Ridd?"

"Ha, ha!" cried Master Carfax: "I reckon her did; no doubt her did."

"You are wrong," I replied: "but I did expect to see something better than dirt and darkness."

"Come on then, my lad; and we will show you something better. We want your great arm on here, for a job that has beaten the whole of us."

With these words Uncle Ben led the way along a narrow passage, roofed with rock and floored with slate-coloured shale and shingle, and winding in and out, until we stopped at a great stone block or boulder, lying across the floor, and as large as my mother's best oaken wardrobe. Beside it were several sledge-hammers, battered, and some with broken helves.

"Thou great villain!" cried Uncle Ben, giving the boulder a little kick; "I believe thy time is come at last. Now, John, give us a sample of the things they tell of thee. Take the biggest of them sledge-hammers and crack this rogue in two for us. We have tried at him for a fortnight, and he is a nut worth cracking. But we have no man who can swing that hammer, though all in the mine have handled it."

"I will do my very best," said I, pulling off my coat and waistcoat, as if I were going to wrestle: "but I fear he will prove too tough for me."

"Ay, that her wull," grunted Master Carfax; "lack'th a Carnishman, and a beg one too, not a little charp such as I be. There be no man outside Carnwall, as can crack that boolder."

"Bless my heart," I answered; "but I know something of you, my friend, or at any rate of your family. Well, I have beaten most of your Cornish men, though not my place to talk of it. But mind, if I crack this rock for you, I must have some of the gold inside it."

"Dost think to see the gold come tumbling out like the kernel of a nut, thou zany?" asked Uncle Reuben pettishly: "now wilt thou crack it, or wilt thou not? For I believe thou can'st do it, though only a lad of Somerset."

Uncle Reuben showed by saying this, and by his glance at Carfax, that he was proud of his county, and would be disappointed for it, if I failed to crack the boulder. So I begged him to stoop his torch a little, that I might examine my subject. To me there appeared to be nothing at all remarkable about it, except that it sparkled here and there, when the flash of the flame fell upon it. A great, obstinate, oblong, sullen stone: how could it be worth the breaking, except for making roads with?

Nevertheless, I took up the hammer, and swinging it far behind my head, fetched it down, with all my power, upon the middle of the rock. The roof above rang mightily, and the echo went down delven galleries, so that all the miners flocked to know what might be doing. But Master Carfax only smiled, although the blow shook him where he stood, for behold the stone was still unbroken, and as firm as ever. Then I smote it again, with no better fortune, and Uncle Ben looked vexed and angry, but all the miners grinned with triumph.

"This little tool is too light," I cried; "one of you give me a piece of strong cord."

Then I took two more of the weightiest hammers, and lashed them fast to the back of mine, not so as to strike, but to burden the fall. Having made this firm, and with room to grasp the handle of the largest one only—for the helves of the others were shorter—I smiled at Uncle Ben, and whirled the mighty implement round my head, just to try whether I could manage it. Upon that the miners gave a cheer, being honest men, and desirous of seeing fair play between this "shameless stone" (as Dan Homer calls it) and me with my hammer hammering.

Then I swung me on high to the swing of the sledge, as a thresher bends back to the rise of his flail, and with all my power descending delivered the ponderous onset. Crashing and crushed the great stone fell over, and threads of sparkling gold appeared in the jagged sides of the breakage.

"How now, Simon Carfax?" cried Uncle Ben triumphantly; "wilt thou find a man in Cornwall can do the like of that?"

"Ay and more," he answered: "however, it be pretty fair for a lad of these outlandish parts. Get your rollers, my lads, and lead it to the crushing engine."

I was glad to have been of some service to them: for it seems that this great boulder had been too large to be drawn along the gallery and too hard to crack. But now they moved it very easily, taking piece by piece, and carefully picking up the fragments.

"Thou hast done us a good turn, my lad," said Uncle Reuben, as the others passed out of sight at the corner; "and now I will show thee the bottom of a very wondrous mystery. But we must not do it more than once, for the time of day is the wrong one."

The whole affair being a mystery to me, and far beyond my understanding, I followed him softly, without a word, yet thinking very heavily, and longing to be above ground again. He led me, through small passages, to a hollow place near the descending-shaft, where I saw a most extraordinary monster fitted up. In form it was like a great coffee-mill, such as I had seen in London, only a thousand times larger, and with a heavy windlass to work it.

"Put in a barrow-load of the smoulder," said Uncle Ben to Carfax; "and let them work the crank, for John to understand a thing or two."

"At this time of day!" cried Simon Carfax; "and the watching as has been o' late!"

However, he did it without more remonstrance; pouring into the scuttle at the top of the machine about a basketful of broken rock; and then a dozen men went to the wheel, and forced it round, as sailors do. Upon that such a hideous noise arose, as I never should have believed any creature capable of making: and I ran to the well of the mine for air, and to ease my ears, if possible.

"Enough, enough!" shouted Uncle Ben, by the time I was nearly deafened; "we will digest our goodly boulder, after the devil is come abroad for his evening work. Now, John, not a word about what you have learned: but henceforth you will not be frightened by the noise we make at dusk."

I could not deny but what this was very clever management. If they could not keep the echoes of the upper air from moving, the wisest plan was to open their valves during the discouragement of the falling evening; when folk would rather be driven away, than drawn into the wilds and quagmires, by a sound so deep and awful, coming through the darkness.

## CHAPTER VII.

ALTHOUGH there are very ancient tales of gold being
found upon Exmoor, in lumps and solid hummocks,
and of men who slew one another for it; this deep
digging and great labour seemed to me a dangerous
and unholy enterprise. And Master Huckaback confessed that up to the present time, his two partners
and himself (for they proved to be three adventurers)
had put into the earth more gold than they had taken
out of it. Nevertheless he felt quite sure that it must
in a very short time succeed, and pay them back an
hundredfold; and he pressed me with great earnestness to join them, and work there as much as I could,
without moving my mother's suspicions. I asked him
how they had managed so long to carry on, without
discovery; and he said that this was partly through
the wildness of the neighbourhood, and the legends
that frightened people of a superstitious turn; partly
through their own great caution, and manner of fetch-
ing both supplies and implements by night; but most
of all, they had to thank the troubles of the period,

the suspicions of rebellion, and the terror of the
Doones, which (like the wizard I was speaking of)
kept folk from being too inquisitive, where they had
no business. The slough, moreover, had helped them
well, both by making their access dark, and yet more
by swallowing up and concealing all that was cast
from the mouth of the pit. Once, before the attack
on Glen Doone, they had a narrow escape from the
King's Commissioner: for Captain Stickles, having
heard no doubt the story of John Fry, went with
half-a-dozen troopers, on purpose to search the neighbourhood. Now if he had ridden alone, most likely
he would have discovered everything; but he feared
to venture so, having suspicion of a trap. Coming as
they did in a company, all mounted and conspicuous,
the watchman (who was posted now on the top of the
hill, almost every day, since John Fry's appearance)
could not help espying them, miles distant, over the
moorland. He watched them under the shade of his
hand, and presently ran down the hill, and raised a
great commotion. Then Simon Carfax and all his
men came up, and made things natural, removing
every sign of work; and finally, sinking underground,
drew across the mouth of the pit a hurdle thatched
with sedge and heather. Only Simon himself was left
behind, ensconced in a hole of the crags, to observe the
doings of the enemy.

Captain Stickles rode very bravely, with all his men
clattering after him, down the rocky pass, and even to
the margin of the slough. And there they stopped,

and held council; for it was a perilous thing to risk
the passage upon horseback, between the treacherous
brink and the cliff, unless one knew it thoroughly.
Stickles, however, and one follower, carefully felt the
way along, having their horses well in hand, and
bearing a rope ·to draw them out, in case of being
foundered. Then they spurred across the rough boggy
land, further away than the shaft was.   Here the
ground lay jagged and shaggy, wrought up with high
tufts of reed, or scragged with stunted brushwood.
And between the ups and downs (which met anybody
anyhow) green covered places tempted the foot, and
black bog-holes discouraged it.   It is not to be
marvelled at that amid such place as this, for the
first time visited, the horses were a little skeary; and
their riders partook of the feeling, as all good riders
do.   In and out the tufts they went, with their eyes
dilating; wishing to be out of harm, if conscience
were but satisfied.   And of this tufty flaggy ground,
pocked with bogs and boglets, one especial nature is
that it will not hold impressions.

Seeing thus no track of men, nor anything but
marshwork, and stormwork, and of the seasons, these
two honest men rode back, and were glad to do
so.   For above them hung the mountains, cowled with
fog, and seamed with storm; and around them desolation; and below their feet the grave. Hence they
went, with all good will; and vowed for ever afterwards that fear of a simple place like that was only
too ridiculous. So they all rode home with mutual

praises, and their courage well-approved; and the only result of the expedition was to confirm John Fry's repute, as a bigger liar than ever.

Now I had enough of that underground work, as before related, to last me for a year to come; neither would I, for sake of gold, have ever stepped into that bucket, of my own good will again.   But when I told Lorna—whom I could trust in any matter of secresy, as if she had never been a woman—all about my great descent, and the honeycombing of the earth, and the mournful noise at eventide, when the gold was under the crusher and bewailing the mischief it must do; then Lorna's chief desire was to know more about Simon Carfax.

"It must be our Gwenny's father," she cried; "the man who disappeared underground, and whom she has ever been seeking.   How grieved the poor little thing will be, if it should turn out, after all, that he left his child on purpose!   I can hardly believe it; can you, John?"

"Well," I replied; "all men are wicked, more or less, to some extent: and no man may say otherwise."

For I did not wish to commit myself to an opinion about Simon, lest I might be wrong, and Lorna think less of my judgment.

But being resolved to see this out, and do a good turn, if I could, to Gwenny, who had done me many a good one, I begged my Lorna to say not a word of this matter to the handmaiden, until I had further searched it out.   And to carry out this resolve, I went again to the place of business where they were grinding gold as freely as an apothecary at his pills.

Having now true right of entrance, and being known to the watchman, and regarded (since I cracked the boulder) as one who could pay his footing, and perhaps would be the master, when Uncle Ben should be choked with money; I found the corb sent up for me, rather sooner than I wished it. For the smell of the places underground, and the way men's eyes come out of them, with links, and brands, and flambeaux, instead of God's light to look at, were to me a point of caution, rather than of pleasure.

No doubt but what some men enjoy it, being born, like worms, to dig, and to live in their own scoopings. Yet even the worms come up sometimes, after a good soft shower of rain, and hold discourse with one another; whereas these men, and the horses let down, come above ground never.

And the changing of the sky is half the change our nature calls for. Earth we have, and all its produce (moving from the first appearance, and the hope with infant's eyes, through the bloom of beauty's promise, to the rich and ripe fulfilment, and the falling back to rest); sea we have (with all its wonder shed on eyes, and ears, and heart; and the thought of something more)—but without the sky to look at, what would earth, and sea, and even our ownselves, be to us?

Do we look at earth with hope? Yes, for victuals only. Do we look at sea with hope? Yes, that we may escape it. At the sky alone (though questioned with the doubts of sunshine, or scattered with uncertain stars), at the sky alone we look, with pure hope and with memory.

Hence it always hurt my feelings when I got into that bucket, with my small-clothes turned up over, and a kerchief round my hat. But knowing that my purpose was sound, and my motives pure, I let the sky grow to a little blue hole, and then to nothing over me. At the bottom, Master Carfax met me, being Captain of the mine, and desirous to know my business. He wore a loose sack round his shoulders, and his beard was two feet long.

"My business is to speak with you," I answered rather sternly; for this man, who was nothing more than Uncle Reuben's servant, had carried things too far with me, showing no respect whatever; and though I do not care for much, I liked to receive a little, even in my early days.

"Coom into the muck-hole then," was his gracious answer; and he led me into a filthy cell, where the miners changed their jackets.

"Simon Carfax," I began, with a manner to discourage him: "I fear you are a shallow fellow, and not worth my trouble."

"Then don't take it," he replied; "I want no man's trouble."

"For your sake I would not," I answered; "but for your daughter's sake I will: the daughter whom you left to starve so pitifully in the wilderness."

The man stared at me with his pale grey eyes,

whose colour was lost from candle-light; and his voice as well as his body shook, while he cried—

"It is a lie, man. No daughter, and no son have I. Nor was ever child of mine left to starve in the wilderness. You are too big for me to tackle, and that makes you a coward for saying it." His hands were playing with a pickaxe-helve, as if he longed to have me under it.

"Perhaps I have wronged you, Simon," I answered very softly; for the sweat upon his forehead shone in the smoky torchlight: "if I have, I crave your pardon. But did you not bring up from Cornwall, a little maid named 'Gwenny,' and supposed to be your daughter?"

"Ay, and she was my daughter, my last and only child of five: and for her I would give this mine, and all the gold will ever come from it."

"You shall have her, without either mine or gold: if you only prove to me that you did not abandon her."

"Abandon her! I abandon Gwenny!" He cried with such a rage of scorn, that I at once believed him. "They told me she was dead, and crushed, and buried in the drift here; and half my heart died with her. The Almighty blast their mining-work, if the scoundrels lied to me!"

"The scoundrels must have lied to you," I answered, with a spirit fired by his heat of fury: "the maid is living, and with us. Come up; and you shall see her."

I 2

"Rig the bucket," he shouted out along the echoing gallery; and then he fell against the wall, and through the grimy sack I saw the heaving of his breast, as I have seen my opponent's chest, in a long hard bout of wrestling. For my part, I could do no more than hold my tongue, and look at him.

Without another word we rose to the level of the moors and mires; neither would Master Carfax speak, as I led him across the barrows. In this he was welcome to his own way, for I do love silence; so little harm can come of it. And though Gwenny was no beauty, her father might be fond of her.

So I put him in the cow-house (not to frighten the little maid) and the folding shutters over him, such as we used at the beestings; and he listened to my voice outside, and held on, and preserved himself. For now he would have scooped the earth, as cattle do at yearning-time, and as meekly and as patiently, to have his child restored to him. Not to make long tale of it—for this thing is beyond me, through want of true experience — I went and fetched his Gwenny forth from the back kitchen, where she was fighting, as usual, with our Betty.

"Come along, you little Vick," I said, for so we called her; "I have a message to you, Gwenny, from the Lord in heaven."

"Dont'ee talk about He," she answered; "Her have long forgatten me."

"That He has never done, you stupid. Come, and see who is in the cow-house."

Gwenny knew; she knew in a moment. Looking into my eyes, she knew; and hanging back from me to sigh, she knew it even better.

She had not much elegance of emotion, being flat and square all over; but none the less for that her heart came quick, and her words came slowly.

"Oh, Jan, you are too good to cheat me. Is it joke you are putting upon me?"

I answered her with a gaze alone; and she tucked up her clothes and followed me, because the road was dirty. Then I opened the door just wide enough for the child to go to her father; and left those two to have it out, as might be most natural. And they took a long time about it.

Meanwhile I needs must go and tell my Lorna all the matter; and her joy was almost as great as if she herself had found a father. And the wonder of the whole was this, that I got all the credit; of which not a thousandth part belonged by right and reason to me. Yet so it almost always is. If I work for good desert, and slave, and lie awake at night, and spend my unborn life in dreams; not a blink, nor wink, nor inkling of my labour ever tells. It would have been better to leave unburned, and to keep undevoured, the fuel and the food of life. But if I have laboured not, only acted by some impulse, whim, caprice, or anything; or even acting not at all, only letting things float by; piled upon me commendations, bravohs, and applauses, almost work me up to tempt, once again (though sick of it) the ill-luck of deserving.

Without intending any harm, and meaning only
good indeed, I had now done serious wrong to Uncle
Reuben's prospects.   For Captain Carfax was full as
angry at the trick played on him, as he was happy
in discovering the falsehood and the fraud of it.   Nor
could I help agreeing with him, when he told me all of
it, as with tears in his eyes he did, and ready to be my
slave thenceforth; I could not forbear from owning
that it was a low and heartless trick, unworthy of men
who had families; and the recoil whereof was well
deserved whatever it might end in.

For when this poor man left his daughter, asleep
as he supposed, and having his food, and change of
clothes, and Sunday hat to see to, he meant to return
in an hour or so, and settle about her sustenance in
some house of the neighbourhood.   But this was the
very thing of all things which the leaders of the enterprise, who had brought him up from Cornwall, for his
noted skill in metals, were determined, whether by
fair means or foul, to stop at the very outset.   Secresy
being their main object, what chance could there be
of it, if the miners were allowed to keep their children
in the neighbourhood ?   Hence, on the plea of feasting
Simon, they kept him drunk for three days and three
nights, assuring him (whenever he had gleams enough
to ask for her) that his daughter was as well as could
be, and enjoying herself with the children.   Not wishing the maid to see him tipsy, he pressed the matter
no further; but applied himself to the bottle again,
and drank her health with pleasure.

However, after three days of this, his constitution
rose against it; and he became quite sober; with a
certain lownesss of heart moreover, and a sense of
error. And his first desire to right himself, and easiest
way to do it, was by exerting parental authority upon
Gwenny. Possessed with this intention (for he was not
a sweet-tempered man, and his head was aching sadly),
he sought for Gwenny high and low; first with threats,
and then with fears, and then with tears and wailing.
And so he became to the other men a warning and
great annoyance. Therefore they combined to swear
what seemed a very likely thing, and might be true for
all they knew; to wit, that Gwenny had come to seek
for her father down the shaft-hole, and peering too
eagerly into the dark, had toppled forward, and gone
down, and lain at the bottom as dead as a stone.

" And thou being so happy with drink," the villains
finished up to him, " and getting drunker every day,
we thought it shame to trouble thee; and we buried
the wench in the lower drift; and no use to think more
of her; but come and have a glass, Sim."

But Simon Carfax swore that drink had lost him his
wife, and now had lost him the last of his five children,
and would lose him his own soul, if further he went
on with it; and from that day to his death he never
touched strong drink again. Nor only this; but being
soon appointed captain of the mine, he allowed no man
on any pretext to bring cordials thither; and to this
and his stern hard rule, and stealthy secret management (as much as to good luck and place) might it

be attributed that scarcely any but themselves had dreamed about this Exmoor mine.

As for me, I had no ambition to become a miner; and the state to which gold-seeking had brought poor Uncle Ben was not at all encouraging. My business was to till the ground, and tend the growth that came of it, and store the fruit in heaven's good time, rather than to scoop and burrow like a weasel or a rat for the yellow root of evil. Moreover, I was led from home, between the hay and corn harvests (when we often have a week to spare) by a call there was no resisting; unless I gave up all regard for wrestling, and for my county.

. Now here many persons may take me amiss, and there always has been some confusion; which people who ought to have known better have wrought into subject of quarrelling. By birth it is true, and cannot be denied, that I am a man of Somerset; nevertheless by breed I am, as well as by education, a son of Devon also. And just as both of our two counties vowed that Glen Doone was none of theirs, but belonged to the other one; so now, each with hot claim and jangling (leading even to blows sometimes) asserted and would swear to it (as I became more famous) that John Ridd was of its own producing, bred of its own true blood, and basely stolen by the other.

Now I have not judged it in any way needful, or even becoming and delicate, to enter into my wrestling adventures, or describe my progress. The whole thing is so different from Lorna, and her gentle manners, and her style of walking; moreover I must seem (even to kind people) to magnify myself so much, or at least attempt to do it, that I have scratched out written pages, through my better taste and sense.

Neither will I, upon this head, make any difference even now; being simply betrayed into mentioning the matter, because bare truth requires it, in the tale of Lorna's fortunes.

For a mighty giant had arisen in a part of Cornwall; and his calf was twenty-five inches round, and the breadth of his shoulders two feet and a quarter; and his stature seven feet and three quarters. Round the chest he was seventy inches, and his hand a foot across, and there were no scales strong enough to judge of his weight in the market-place. Now this man—or I should say, his backers and his boasters, for the giant himself was modest—sent me a brave and haughty challenge, to meet him in the ring at Bodmin-town, on the first day of August; or else to return my champion's belt to them by the messenger.

It is no use to deny, but that I was greatly dashed and scared at first. For my part, I was only, when measured without clothes on, sixty inches round the breast, and round the calf scarce twenty-one, only two feet across the shoulders, and in height not six and three quarters. However, my mother would never believe that this man could beat me; and Lorna being of the same mind, I resolved to go and try him, as they would pay all expenses, and a hundred pounds, if I conquered him; so confident were those Cornishmen.

Now this story is too well-known for me to go

through it again and again. Every child in Devonshire knows, and his grandson will know, the song which some clever man made of it; after I had treated him to water, and to lemon, and a little sugar, and a drop of eau-de-vie. Enough that I had found the giant quite as big as they had described him, and enough to terrify any one. But trusting in my practice and study of the art, I resolved to try a back with him; and when my arms were round him once, the giant was but a farthingale put into the vice of a blacksmith. The man had no bones; his frame sank in, and I was afraid of crushing him. He lay on his back, and smiled at me; and I begged his pardon.

Now this affair made a noise at the time, and redounded so much to my credit, that I was deeply grieved at it, because deserving none. For I do'like a good strife and struggle; and the doubt makes the joy of victory; whereas in this case I might as well have been sent for a match with a hay-mow. However, I got my hundred pounds, and made up my mind to spend every farthing in presents for mother and Lorna.

For Annie was married by this time, and long before I went away; as need scarcely be said perhaps, if any one follows the weeks and the months. The wedding was quiet enough, except for everybody's good wishes; and I desire not to dwell upon it, because it grieved me in many ways.

But now that I had tried to hope the very best for dear Annie, a deeper blow than could have come, even through her, awaited me. For after that visit to Cornwall, and with my prize-money about me, I came on foot from Okehampton to Oare, so as to save a little sum towards my time of marrying. For Lorna's fortune I would not have; small or great I would not have it; only if there were no denying, we would devote the whole of it to charitable uses, as Master Peter Blundell had done; and perhaps the future ages would endeavour to be grateful. Lorna and I had settled this question, at least twice a day, on the average; and each time with more satisfaction.

Now coming into the kitchen with all my cash in my breeches pocket (golden guineas, with an elephant on them, for the stamp of the Guinea Company), I found dear mother most heartily glad to see me safe and sound again—for she had dreaded that giant, and dreamed of him—and she never asked me about the money. Lizzie also was softer, and more gracious than usual; especially when she saw me pour guineas, like pepper-corns, into the pudding-basin. But by the way they hung about, I knew that something was gone wrong.

"Where is Lorna?" I asked at length, after trying not to ask it: "I want her to come, and see my money. She never saw so much before."

"Alas!" said mother, with a heavy sigh; "she will see a great deal more, I fear; and a deal more than is good for her. Whether you ever see her again will depend upon her nature, John."

"What do you mean, mother? Have you quarrelled?

Why does not Lorna come to me? Am I never
to know?"

"Now, John, be not so impatient," my mother
replied, quite calmly, for in truth she was jealous
of Lorna: "you could wait now very well, John, if it
were till this day week, for the coming of your mother,
John. And yet your mother is your best friend.
Who can ever fill her place?"

Thinking of her future absence, mother turned
away and cried; and the box-iron singed the blanket.

"Now," said I, being wild by this time; "Lizzie,
you have a little sense; will you tell me where is
Lorna?"

"The Lady Lorna Dugal," said Lizzie, screwing up
her lips, as if the title were too grand; "is gone
to London, brother John; and not likely to come back
again. We must try to get on without her."

"You little"—[something] I cried, which I dare not
write down here, as all you are too good for such
language; but Lizzie's lip provoked me so—"my
Lorna gone, my Lorna gone! And without good-
bye to me even! It is your spite has sickened
her."

"You are quite mistaken there," she replied; "how
can folk of low degree have either spite or liking
towards the people so far above them? The Lady
Lorna Dugal is gone, because she could not help
herself; and she wept enough to break ten hearts—if
hearts are ever broken, John."

"Darling Lizzie, how good you are!" I cried,

without noticing her sneer: " tell me all about it, dear; tell me every word she said."

"That will not take long," said Lizzie, quite as unmoved by soft coaxing as by urgent cursing: " the lady spoke very little to any one, except indeed to mother, and to Gwenny Carfax: and Gwenny is gone with her, so that the benefit of that is lost. But she left a letter for ' poor John,' as in charity she called him. How grand she looked, to be sure, with the fine clothes on that were come for her ! "

" Where is the letter, you utter vixen? Oh, may you have a husband ! "

" Who will thresh it out of you, and starve it, and swear it out of you!" was the meaning of my imprecation; but Lizzie, not dreaming as yet of such things, could not understand me, and was rather thankful; therefore she answered quietly,

" The letter is in the little cupboard, near the head of Lady Lorna's bed, where she used to keep the diamond necklace, which we contrived to get stolen."

Without another word, I rushed (so that every board in the house shook) up to my lost Lorna's room, and tore the little wall-niche open, and espied my treasure. It was as simple, and as homely, and loving, as even I could wish. Part of it ran as follows—the other parts it behoves me not to open out to strangers: " My own love, and sometime lord,—Take it not amiss of me, that even without farewell, I go; for I cannot persuade the men to wait, your return being doubtful. My great uncle, some grand lord, is awaiting me at

Dunster, having fear of venturing too near this Exmoor country. I, who have been so lawless always, and the child of outlaws, am now to atone for this, it seems, by living in a court of law, and under special surveillance (as they call it, I believe) of His Majesty's Court of Chancery. My uncle is appointed my guardian and master; and I must live beneath his care, until I am twenty-one years old. To me this appears a dreadful thing, and very unjust, and cruel; for why should I lose my freedom, through heritage of land and gold? I offered to abandon all if they would only let me go: I went down on my knees to them, and said I wanted titles not, neither land, nor money; only to stay where I was, where first I had known happiness. But they only laughed, and called me 'child,' and said that I must talk of that to the King's High Chancellor. Their orders they had, and must obey them; and Master Stickles was ordered too to help, as the King's Commissioner. And then, although it pierced my heart not to say one 'good bye, John,' I was glad upon the whole that you were not here to dispute it. For I am almost certain that you would not, without force to yourself, have let your Lorna go to people who never, never can care for her."

Here my darling had wept again, by the tokens on the paper; and then there followed some sweet words, too sweet for me to chatter them. But she finished with these noble lines, which (being common to all humanity, in a case of steadfast love) I do no harm, but rather help all true love, by repeating. "Of one thing rest you well assured—and I do hope that it may prove of service to your rest, love; else would my own be broken—no difference of rank, or fortune, or of life itself, shall ever make me swerve from truth to you. We have passed through many troubles, dangers, and dispartments; but never yet was doubt between us; neither ever shall be. Each has trusted well the other; and still each must do so. Though they tell you I am false, though your own mind harbours it, from the sense of things around, and your own under-valuing; yet take counsel of your heart, and cast such thoughts away from you; being unworthy of itself, they must be unworthy also of the one who dwells there: and that one is, and ever shall be, your own Lorna Dugal."

Some people cannot understand that tears should come from pleasure; but whether from pleasure or from sorrow (mixed as they are in the twisted strings of a man's heart, or a woman's), great tears fell from my stupid eyes, even on the blots of Lorna's.

"No doubt, it is all over:" my mind said to me bitterly: "trust me, all shall yet be right:" my heart replied very sweetly.

## CHAPTER VIII.

SOME people may look down upon us for our slavish ways (as they may choose to call them), but in our part of the country, we do love to mention title, and to roll it on our tongues, with a conscience and a comfort. Even if a man knows not, through fault of education, who the Duke of this is, or the Earl of that, it will never do for him to say so, lest the room look down on him. Therefore he must nod his head, and say, " Ah, to be sure ! I know him as well as ever I know my own good woman's brother. He married Lord Flipflap's second daughter, and a precious life she led him." Whereupon the room looks up at him. But I, being quite unable to carry all this in my head, as I ought, was speedily put down by people of a noble tendency, apt at Lords, and pat with Dukes, and knowing more about the King than His Majesty would have requested. Therefore, I fell back in thought, not daring in words to do so, upon the titles of our horses. And all these horses deserved their names, not having merely inherited, but by their own doing

earned them. Smiler, for instance, had been so called,
not so much from a habit of smiling, as from his general
geniality, white nose, and white ankle. This worthy
horse was now in years, but hale and gay as ever;
and when you let him out of stable, he could neigh
and whinny, and make men and horses know it. On
the other hand, Kickums was a horse of morose and
surly order; harbouring up revenge, and leading a
rider to false confidence. Very smoothly he would go,
and as gentle as a turtle-dove; until his rider fully
believed that a pack-thread was enough for him, and a
pat of approval upon his neck the aim and crown of his
worthy life. Then suddenly up went his hind feet to
heaven, and the rider for the most part flew over his
nose: whereupon good Kickums would take advantage
of his favourable position to come and bite a piece out
of his back. Now in my present state of mind, being
understood of nobody, having none to bear me company, neither wishing to have any, an indefinite kind
of attraction drew me into Kickums' society. A bond
of mutual sympathy was soon established between us:
I would ride no other horse, neither Kickums be ridden
by any other man. And this good horse became as
jealous about me, as a dog might be; and would lash
out, or run teeth foremost, at any one who came near
him when I was on his back.

Now the reaping of the corn, which had been, but a
year ago, so pleasant and so lightsome, was become a
heavy labour, and a thing for grumbling rather than
for gladness. However, for the sake of all, it must

be attended to, and with as fair a show of spirit and
alacrity as might be.   For otherwise the rest would
drag, and drop their hands and idle, being quicker to
take infection of dulness than of diligence.   And the
harvest was a heavy one, even heavier than the year
before, although of poorer quality.   Therefore was I
forced to work as hard as any horse could, during all
the daylight hours, and defer till night the brooding
upon my misfortune.   But the darkness always found
me stiff with work, and weary, and less able to think
than to dream, may be, of Lorna.   And now the house
was so dull and lonesome, wanting Annie's pretty
presence, and the light of Lorna's eyes, that a man
had no temptation, after supper-time, even to sit and
smoke a pipe.

For Lizzie, though so learned, and pleasant when
it suited her, never had taken very kindly to my love
for Lorna, and being of a proud and slightly upstart
nature, could not bear to be eclipsed in bearing, looks,
and breeding, and even in clothes, by the stranger.
For one thing I will say of the Doones, that whether
by purchase or plunder, they had always dressed my
darling well, with her own sweet taste to help them.
And though Lizzie's natural hate of the maid (as a
Doone and burdened with father's death) should have
been changed to remorse, when she learned of Lorna's
real parentage ; it was only altered to sullenness, and
discontent with herself, for frequent rudeness to an
innocent person, and one of such high descent.   Moreover the child had imbibed strange ideas as to our

aristocracy, partly perhaps from her own way of thinking, and partly from reading of history. For while from one point of view she looked up at them very demurely, as commissioned by God for the country's good; from another sight she disliked them, as ready to sacrifice their best and follow their worst members.

Now why should this wench dare to judge upon a matter so far beyond her, and form opinions which she knew better than to declare before mother? But with me she had no such scruple; for I had no authority over her; and my intellect she looked down upon, because I praised her own so. Thus she made herself very unpleasant to me; by little jags and jerks of sneering, sped as though unwittingly; which I (who now considered myself allied to the aristocracy, and perhaps took airs on that account) had not wit enough to parry, yet had wound enough to feel.

Now any one who does not know exactly how mothers feel and think, would have expected my mother (than whom could be no better one) to pet me, and make much of me, under my sad trouble; to hang with anxiety on my looks, and shed her tears with mine (if any), and season every dish of meat put by for her John's return. And if the whole truth must be told, I did expect that sort of thing, and thought what a plague it would be to me; yet not getting it, was vexed, as if by some new injury. For mother was a special creature (as I suppose we all are), being the warmest of the warm, when fired at the proper corner; and yet, if taken at the wrong point, you would say she was incombustible.

Hence it came to pass that I had no one even to speak to, about Lorna and my grievances ; for Captain Stickles was now gone southward ; and John Fry of course was too low for it, although a married man, and well under his wife's management.   But finding myself unable at last to bear this any longer, upon the first day when all the wheat was cut, and the stooks set up in every field, yet none quite fit for carrying, I saddled good Kickums at five in the morning, and without a word to mother (for a little anxiety might do her good) off I set for Molland parish, to have the counsel and the comfort of my darling Annie.

The horse took me over the ground so fast (there being few better to go, when he liked), that by nine o'clock Annie was in my arms, and blushing to the colour of Winnie's cheeks, with sudden delight and young happiness.

" You precious little soul !" I cried :  " how does Tom behave to you ? "

" Hush ! " said Annie :  " how dare you ask ?   He is the kindest, and the best, and the noblest of all men, John ; not even setting yourself aside.   Now look not jealous, John : so it is.   We all have special gifts, you know.   You are as good as you can be, John ; but my husband's special gift is nobility of character."   Here she looked at me, as one who has discovered something quite unknown.

" I am devilish glad to hear it," said I, being

touched at going down so: "keep him to that mark, my dear; and cork the whisky bottle."

"Yes, darling John," she answered quickly, not desiring to open that subject, and being too sweet to resent it: "and how is lovely Lorna? What an age it is since I have seen you! I suppose we must thank her for that."

"You may thank her for seeing me now," said I; "or rather,"—seeing how hurt she looked,—"you may thank my knowledge of your kindness, and my desire to speak of her to a soft-hearted dear little soul like you. I think all the women are gone mad. Even mother treats me shamefully. And as for Lizzie"——— Here I stopped, knowing no words strong enough, without shocking Annie.

"Do you mean to say that Lorna is gone?" asked Annie, in great amazement; yet leaping at the truth, as women do, with nothing at all to leap from.

"Gone. And I never shall see her again. It serves me right for aspiring so."

Being grieved at my manner, she led me in where none could interrupt us; and in spite of all my dejection, I could not help noticing how very pretty and even elegant all things were around. For we upon Exmoor have little taste; all we care for is warm comfort, and plenty to eat and to give away, and a hearty smack in everything. But Squire Faggus had seen the world, and kept company with great people; and the taste he had first displayed in the shoeing of farmers' horses (which led almost to his ruin, by bringing him into jealousy, and flattery, and dashing ways) had now been cultivated in London, and by moonlight, so that none could help admiring it.

"Well!" I cried, for the moment dropping care and woe in astonishment: "we have nothing like this at Plover's Barrows; nor even Uncle Reuben. I do hope it is honest, Annie?"

"Would I sit in a chair that was not my own?" asked Annie, turning crimson, and dropping defiantly, and with a whisk of her dress which I never had seen before, into the very grandest one: "would I lie on a couch, brother John, do you think, unless good money was paid for it? Because other people are clever, John, you need not grudge them their earnings."

"A couch!" I replied: "why what can you want with a couch in the day-time, Annie? A couch is a small bed, set up in a room without space for a good four-poster. What can you want with a couch downstairs? I never heard of such nonsense. And you ought to be in the dairy."

"I won't cry, brother John, I won't; because you want to make me cry"—and all the time she was crying—"you always were so nasty, John, sometimes. Ah, you have no nobility of character, like my husband. And I have not seen you for two months, John: and now you come to scold me!"

"You little darling," I said, for Annie's tears always conquered me; "if all the rest ill use me, I will not quarrel with you, dear. You have always been true to me; and I can forgive your vanity. Your things are very pretty, dear; and you may couch ten times a day, without my interference. No doubt your husband has paid for all this, with the ponies he stole from Exmoor. Nobility of character is a thing beyond my understanding; but when my sister loves a man, and he does well and flourishes, who am I to find fault with him? Mother ought to see these things: they would turn her head almost: look at the pimples on the chairs!"

"They are nothing," Annie answered, after kissing me for my kindness: "they are only put in for the time indeed; and we are to have much better, with gold all round the bindings, and double plush at the corners; so soon as ever the King repays the debt he owes to my poor Tom."

I thought to myself that our present King had been most unlucky in one thing—debts all over the kingdom. Not a man who had struck a blow for the King, or for his poor father, or even said a good word for him, in the time of his adversity, but expected at least a baronetcy, and a grant of estates to support it. Many have called King Charles ungrateful: and he may have been so. But some indulgence is due to a man, with entries few on the credit side, and a terrible column of debits.

"Have no fear for the chair," I said; for it creaked under me very fearfully, having legs not so large as my finger; "if the chair breaks, Annie, your fear should be, lest the tortoise-shell run into me. Why it is striped like a viper's loins! I saw some

hundreds in London; and very cheap they are.
They are made to be sold to the country people,
such as you and me, dear; and carefully kept they
will last for almost half-a-year. Now will you come
back from your furniture, and listen to my story?"

Annie was a hearty dear, and she knew that half
my talk was joke, to make light of my worrying.
Therefore she took it in good part, as I well knew that
she would do; and she led me to a good honest chair;
and she sate in my lap and kissed me.

"All this is not like you, John. All this is not one
bit like you: and your cheeks are not as they ought
to be. I shall have to come home again, if the women
worry my brother so. We always held together,
John; and we always will, you know."

"You dear," I cried, "there is nobody who understands me as you do. Lorna makes too much of me:
and the rest they make too little."

"Not mother; oh not mother, John!"

"No, mother makes too much, no doubt: but wants
it all for herself alone; and reckons it as a part of her.
She makes me more wroth than any one: as if not only
my life, but all my head and heart must seek from
hers, and have no other thought or care."

Being sped of my grumbling thus, and eased into
better temper, I told Annie all the strange history
about Lorna and her departure, and the small chance
that now remained to me of ever seeing my love again.
To this Annie would not hearken twice, but judging
women by her faithful self, was quite vexed with

me for speaking so. And then, to my surprise and sorrow, she would deliver no opinion, as to what I ought to do, until she had consulted darling Tom.

Now Tom knew much of the world, no doubt, especially the dark side of it. But to me it scarcely seemed becoming that my course of action with regard to the Lady Lorna Dugal should be referred to Tom Faggus, and depend upon his decision. However, I would not grieve Annie again by making light of her husband; and so when he came in to dinner, the matter was laid before him.

Now this man never confessed himself surprised, under any circumstances; his knowledge of life being so profound, and his charity universal. And in the present case he vowed that he had suspected it all along, and could have thrown light upon Lorna's history, if we had seen fit to apply to him. Upon further inquiry I found that this light was a very dim one, flowing only from the fact that he had stopped her mother's coach, at the village of Bolham, on the Bampton road, the day before I saw them. Finding only women therein, and these in a sad condition, Tom with his usual chivalry (as he had no scent of the necklace) allowed them to pass; with nothing more than a pleasant exchange of courtesies, and a testimonial forced upon him, in the shape of a bottle of Burgundy wine. This the poor countess handed him; and he twisted the cork out with his teeth, and drank her health with his hat off.

"A lady she was, and a true one: and I am a

pretty good judge," said Tom : " ah, I do like a high
lady !"

Our Annie looke d  rather queer at this having no
pretensions to be one : but she conquered herself, and
said, " Yes, Tom ; and many of them liked you."

With this, Tom went on the brag at once, being but
a shallow fellow, and not of settled principles, though
steadier than he used to be ; until I felt myself almost
bound to fetch him back a little ; for of all things I do
hate brag the most ; as any reader of this tale must by
this time know.    Therefore I said to Squire Faggus,
" Come back from your highway days.    You have
married the daughter of an honest man ; and such talk
is not fit for her.    If you were right in robbing people,
I am right in robbing you.    I could bind you to your
own mantel-piece, as you know thoroughly well, Tom ;
and drive away with your own horses, and all your
goods behind them, but for the sense of honesty.    And
should I not do as fine a thing as any you did on the
highway ?    If everything is of public right, how does
this chair belong to you ?    Clever as you are, Tom
Faggus, you are nothing but a fool to mix your felony
with your farmership.    Drop the one, or drop the
other ; you cannot maintain them both."

As I finished very sternly a speech which had
exhausted me more than ten rounds of wrestling—but
I was carried away by the truth, as sometimes happens
to all of us—Tom had not a word to say ; albeit his
·mind was so much more nimble and rapid than ever
mine was.  He leaned against the mantel-piece (a

newly-invented affair in his house) as if I had corded
him to it, even as I spoke of doing.   And he laid one
hand on his breast in a way which made Annie creep
softly to him, and look at me not like a sister.

" You have done me good, John," he said at last,
and the hand he gave me was trembling : " there is no
other man on God's earth would have dared to speak
to me as you have done.   From no other would I have
taken it.   Nevertheless, every word is true ; and I
shall dwell on it when you are gone.   If you never did
good in your life before, John, my brother, you have
done it now."

He turned away, in bitter pain, that none might see
his trouble : and Annie, going along with him, looked
as if I had killed our mother.   For my part, I was so
upset, for fear of having gone too far, that without a
word to either of them, but a message on the title-page
of King James his Prayer-book, I saddled Kickums,
and was off, and glad of the moorland air again.

## CHAPTER IX.

It was for poor Annie's sake, that I had spoken my mind to her husband so freely, and even harshly. For we all knew she would break her heart, if Tom took to evil ways again. And the right mode of preventing this was, not to coax, and flatter, and make a hero of him (which he did for himself, quite sufficiently), but to set before him the folly of the thing, and the ruin to his own interests.

They would both be vexed with me, of course, for having left them so hastily, and especially just before dinner-time; but that would soon wear off; and most likely they would come to see mother, and tell her that I was hard to manage, and they could feel for her about it.

Now with a certain yearning, I know not what, for softness; and for one who could understand me—for simple as a child though being, I found few to do that last, at any rate in my love-time—I relied upon Kickums' strength to take me round by Dulverton. It would make the journey some eight miles

longer, but what was that to a brisk young horse, even
with my weight upon him. And having left Squire
Faggus and Annie much sooner than had been
intended, I had plenty of time before me, and too
much, ere a prospect of dinner. Therefore I struck
to the right, across the hills, for Dulverton. .

Pretty Ruth was in the main street of the town, with
a basket in her hand, going home from the market.

"Why, Cousin Ruth, you are grown," I exclaimed;
"I do believe you are, Ruth. And you were almost
too tall, already."

At this the little thing was so pleased, that she
smiled through her blushes beautifully, and must needs
come to shake hands with me; though I signed to her
not to do it, because of my horse's temper. But
scarcely was her hand in mine, when Kickums turned
like an eel upon her, and caught her by the left arm
with his teeth, so that she screamed with agony. I
saw the white of his vicious eye, and struck him there
with all my force, with my left hand over her right
arm, and he never used that eye again; none the less
he kept his hold on her. Then I smote him again on
the jaw, and caught the little maid up by her right
hand, and laid her on the saddle in front of me; while
the horse being giddy and staggered with blows, and
foiled of his spite, ran backward. Ruth's wits were
gone; and she lay before me, in such a helpless and
senseless way, that I could have killed vile Kickums.
I struck the spurs into him past the rowels, and away
he went at full gallop; while I had enough to do

to hold on, with the little girl lying in front of me.
But I called to the men who were flocking around, to
send up a surgeon, as quick as could be, to Master
Reuben Huckaback's.

The moment I brought my right arm to bear, the
vicious horse had no chance with me; and if ever a
horse was well paid for spite, Kickums had his change
that day. The bridle would almost have held a whale
and I drew on it so that his lower jaw was well-nigh
broken from him; while with both spurs I tore his
flanks, and he learned a little lesson. There are times
when a man is more vicious than any horse may vie with.
Therefore by the time we had reached Uncle Reuben's
house at the top of the hill, the bad horse was only too
happy to stop; every string of his body was trembling,
and his head hanging down with impotence. I leaped
from his back at once, and carried the maiden into her
own sweet room.

Now Cousin Ruth was recovering softly from her
fright and faintness; and the volley of the wind from
galloping so had made her little ears quite pink, and
shaken her locks all round her. But any one who might
wish to see a comely sight and a moving one, need only
have looked at Ruth Huckaback, when she learned
(and imagined yet more than it was) the manner of her
little ride with me. Her hair was of a hazel-brown,
and full of waving readiness; and with no conceal-
ment of the trick, she spread it over her eyes and face.
Being so delighted with her, and so glad to see her
safe, I kissed her through the thick of it, as a cousin

has a right to do ; yea, and ought to do, with gravity.

"Darling," I said ; "he has bitten you dreadfully : show me your poor arm, dear."

She pulled up her sleeve in the simplest manner, rather to look at it herself, than to show me where the wound was. Her sleeve was of dark blue Taunton staple ; and her white arm shone, coming out of it, as round and plump and velvety, as a stalk of asparagus, newly fetched out of ground. But above the curved soft elbow, where no room was for one cross word (according to our proverb*), three sad gashes, edged with crimson, spoiled the flow of the pearly flesh. My presence of mind was lost altogether ; and I raised the poor sore arm to my lips, both to stop the bleeding and to take the venom out, having heard how wise it was, and thinking of my mother. But Ruth, to my great amazement, drew away from me in bitter haste, as if I had been inserting instead of extracting poison. For the bite of a horse is most venomous ; especially when he sheds his teeth ; and far more to be feared than the bite of a dog, or even of a cat. And in my haste, I had forgotton that Ruth might not know a word about this, and might doubt about my meaning, and the warmth of my osculation. But knowing her danger, I durst not heed her childishness, or her feelings.

"Don't be a fool, Cousin Ruth," I said, catching her so that she could not move ; "the poison is

---

* "A maid with an elbow sharp, or knee,
    Hath cross words two, out of every three."

soaking into you. Do you think that· I do it for pleasure ? "

The spread of shame on her face was such, when she saw her own misunderstanding, that I was ashamed to look at her ; and occupied myself with drawing all the risk of glanders forth from the white limb, hanging helpless now, and left entirely to my will. Before I was quite sure of having wholly exhausted suction, and when I had made the holes in her arm look like the gills of a lamprey, in came the doctor, partly drunk, and in haste to get through his business.

"Ha, ha ! I see," he cried ; "bite of a horse, they tell me. Very poisonous ; must be burned away. Sally, the iron in the fire. If you have a fire, this weather."

"Crave your pardon, good sir," I said ; for poor little Ruth was fainting again at his savage orders : "but my cousin's arm shall not be burned ; it is a great deal too pretty ; and I have sucked all the poison out. Look, sir, how clean and fresh it is."

"Bless my heart ! And so it is ! No need at all for cauterizing. The epidermis will close over, and the cutis and the pellis. John Ridd, you ought to have studied medicine, with your healing powers. Half my virtue lies in touch. A clean and wholesome body, sir ; I have taught you the Latin grammar. I leave you in excellent hands, my dear, and they wait for me at shovel-board. Bread and water poultice cold, to be renewed, *tribus horis*. John Ridd, I was at school with you, and you beat me very lamentably,

when I tried to fight with you. You remember me
not? It is likely enough; I am forced to take strong
waters, John, from infirmity of the liver. Attend to my
directions; and I will call again in the morning."

And in that melancholy plight, caring nothing for
business, went one of the cleverest fellows ever known
at Tiverton. He could write Latin verses a great
deal faster than I could ever write English prose, and
nothing seemed too great for him. We thought that
he would go to Oxford and astonish every one, and
write in the style of Buchanan; but he fell all abroad
very lamentably; and now, when I met him again,
was come down to push-pin and shovel-board, with
a wager of spirits pending.

When Master Huckaback came home, he looked at
me very sulkily; not only because of my refusal to
become a slave to the gold-digging, but also because
he regarded me as the cause of a savage broil between
Simon Carfax and the men who had cheated him as to
his Gwenny. However, when Uncle Ben saw Ruth,
and knew what had befallen her, and she with tears in
her eyes declared that she owed her life to Cousin
Ridd, the old man became very gracious to me; for if
he loved any one on earth, it was his little grand-
daughter.

I could not stay very long, because, my horse being
quite unfit to travel from the injuries which his violence
and vice had brought upon him, there was nothing for
me but to go on foot, as none of Uncle Ben's horses
could take me to Plover's Barrows, without downright

cruelty: and though there would be a harvest-moon, Ruth agreed with me that I must not keep my mother waiting, with no idea where I might be, until a late hour of the night. I told Ruth all about our Annie, and her noble furniture; and the little maid was very lively (although her wounds were paining her so, that half her laughter came "on the wrong side of her mouth," as we rather coarsely express it); especially she laughed about Annie's new-fangled closet for clothes, or standing-press as she called it. This had frightened me so that I would not come without my stick to look at it; for the front was inlaid with two fiery dragons, and a glass which distorted everything, making even Annie look hideous; and when it was opened, a woman's skeleton, all in white, revealed itself, in the midst of three standing women. "It is only to keep my best frocks in shape," Annie had explained to me; "hanging them up does ruin them so. But I own that I was afraid of it, John, until I had got all my best clothes there, and then I became very fond of it. But even now it frightens me sometimes in the moonlight."

Having made poor Ruth a little cheerful, with a full account of all Annie's frocks, material, pattern, and fashion (of which I had taken a list for my mother, and for Lizzie, lest they should cry out at man's stupidity about anything of real interest), I proceeded to tell her about my own troubles, and the sudden departure of Lorna; concluding with all the show of indifference which my pride could muster, that now I never should see her again, and must do my best to forget her, as being so far above me. I had not intended to speak of this, but Ruth's face was so kind and earnest, that I could not stop myself.

"You must not talk like that, Cousin Ridd," she said, in a low and gentle tone, and turning away her eyes from me; "no lady can be above a man, who is pure, and brave, and gentle. And if her heart be worth having, she will never let you give her up, for her grandeur, and her nobility."

She pronounced those last few words, as I thought, with a little bitterness, unperceived by herself perhaps, for it was not in her appearance. But I, attaching great importance to a maiden's opinion about a maiden (because she might judge from experience), would have led her further into that subject. But she declined to follow, having now no more to say in a matter so removed from her. Then I asked her full and straight, and looking at her in such a manner that she could not look away, without appearing vanquished by feelings of her own—which thing was very vile of me; but all men are so selfish—

"Dear cousin, tell me, once for all, what is your advice to me?"

"My advice to you," she answered bravely, with her dark eyes full of pride, and instead of flinching, foiling me,—"is to do what every man must do, if he would win fair maiden. Since she cannot send you token, neither is free to return to you; follow her, pay your court to her; show that you will not be forgotten; and perhaps she will look down—I mean, she will relent to you."

"She has nothing to relent about. I have never vexed, nor injured her. My thoughts have never strayed from her. There is no one to compare with her."

"Then keep her in that same mind about you. See now, I can advise no more. My arm is swelling painfully, in spite of all your goodness, and bitter task of surgeonship. I shall have another poultice on, and go to bed, I think, Cousin Ridd; if you will not hold me ungrateful. I am so sorry for your long walk. Surely it might be avoided. Give my love to dear Lizzie: oh, the room is going round so."

And she fainted into the arms of Sally, who was come just in time to fetch her: no doubt she had been suffering agony, all the time she talked to me. Leaving word that I would come again to inquire for her, and fetch Kickums home, so soon as the harvest permitted me, I gave directions about the horse, and striding away from the ancient town, was soon upon the moorlands.

Now, through the whole of that long walk—the latter part of which was led by starlight, till the moon arose —I dwelt, in my young and foolish way, upon the ordering of our steps by a Power beyond us. But as I could not bring my mind to any clearness upon this matter, and the stars shed no light upon it, but rather confused me with wondering how their Lord could attend to them all, and yet to a puny fool like me; it

came to pass that my thoughts on the subject were not
worth ink, if I knew them.

But it is perhaps worth ink to relate, so far as I can
do so, mother's delight at my return, when she had
almost abandoned hope, and concluded that I was gone
to London, in disgust at her behaviour. And now she
was looking up the lane, at the rise of the harvest-
moon, in despair, as she said afterwards. But if she
had despaired in truth, what use to look at all? Yet
according to the epigram, made by a good Blundellite,

> " Despair was never yet so deep,
> In sinking, as in seeming;
> Despair is hope just dropped asleep,
> For better chance of dreaming."

And mother's dream was a happy one, when she
knew my step at a furlong distant; for the night was
of those that carry sound, thrice as far as day can.
She recovered herself, when she was sure, and even
made up her mind to scold me, and felt as if she could
do it. But when she was in my arms, into which she
threw herself, and I by the light of the moon descried
the silver gleam on one side of her head (now spreading
since Annie's departure), bless my heart and yours
therewith, no room was left for scolding. She hugged
me, and she clung to me; and I looked at her, with
duty made tenfold, and discharged by love. We said
nothing to one another: but all was right between us.

Even Lizzie behaved very well, so far as her nature
admitted; not even saying a nasty thing, all the time
she was getting my supper ready, with a weak imita-

tion of Annie. She knew that the gift of cooking was not vouchsafed by God to her; but sometimes she would do her best, by intellect, to win it. Whereas it is no more to be won by intellect, than is divine poetry. An amount of strong quick heart is needful, and the understanding must second it, in the one art, as in the other. Now my fare was very choice, for the next three days or more; yet not turned out like Annie's. They could do a thing well enough on the fire; but they could not put it on table so; nor even have plates all piping hot. This was Annie's special gift; born in her, and ready to cool with her; like a plate borne away from the fire-place. I sighed sometimes about Lorna, and they thought it was about the plates. And mother would stand and look at me, as much as to say, "No pleasing him:" and Lizzie would jerk up one shoulder, and cry, "He had better have Lorna to cook for him:" while the whole truth was that I wanted not to be plagued about any cookery; but just to have something good and quiet; and then smoke and think about Lorna.

Nevertheless the time went on, with one change and another; and we gathered all our harvest in; and Parson Bowden thanked God for it, both in church and out of it; for his tithes would be very goodly. The unmatched cold of the previous winter, and general fear of scarcity, and our own talk about our ruin, had sent prices up to a grand high pitch; and we did our best to keep them there. For nine Englishmen out of every ten believe that a bitter winter must breed a sour summer, and explain away topmost prices. While according to my experience, more often it would be otherwise, except for the publick thinking so. However, I have said too much; and if any farmer reads my book, he will vow that I wrote it, for nothing else, except to rob his family.

## CHAPTER X.

ALL our neighbourhood was surprised that the Doones
had not ere now attacked, and probably made an end
of us.   For we lay almost at their mercy now, having
only Serjeant Bloxham, and three men, to protect us,
Captain Stickles having been ordered southwards with
all his force; except such as might be needful for collecting toll, and watching the imports at Lynmouth,
and thence to Porlock.  The Serjeant, having now
imbibed a taste for writing reports (though his first
great effort had done him no good, and only offended
Stickles), reported  weekly from  Plover's Barrows,
whenever he could find a messenger.   And though we
fed not Serjeant Bloxham at our own table, with the
best we had (as in the case of Stickles, who repre-
sented His Majesty), yet we treated him so well, that
he reported very highly of us, as loyal and true-hearted
lieges, and most devoted to our lord the King.   And
indeed he could scarcely have done less, when Lizzie
wrote great part of his reports, and furbished up the
rest to such a pitch of lustre, that Lord Clarendon
himself need scarce have been ashamed of them.   And

though this cost a great deal of ale, and even of strong
waters (for Lizzie would have it the duty of a critic to
stand treat to the author), and though it was otherwise
a plague, as giving the maid such airs of patronage,
and such pretence to politics ; yet there was no stopping it, without the risk of mortal offence to both
writer and reviewer.   Our mother also, while disap-
proving Lizzie's long stay in the saddle-room on a
Friday night and a Saturday, and insisting that Betty
should be there, was nevertheless as proud as need be,
that the King should read our Eliza's writing—at least
so the innocent soul believed—and we all looked forward to something great as the fruit of all this history.
And something great did come of it, though not as we
expected ; for these reports, or as many of them as were
ever opened, stood us in good stead the next year ;
when we were accused of harbouring and comforting
guilty rebels.

Now the reason why the Doones did not attack us
was that they were preparing to meet another and more
powerful assault upon their fortress ; being assured that
their repulse of King's troops could not be looked
over when brought before the authorities.   And no
doubt they were right ; for although the conflicts in the
Government during that summer and autumn had de-
layed the matter ; yet positive orders had been issued
that these outlaws, and malefactors, should at any
price be brought to justice ; when the sudden death of
King Charles the Second threw all things into confusion,
and all minds into a panic.

We heard of it first in church, on Sunday, the eighth day of February, 1684–5, from a cousin of John Fry, who had ridden over on purpose from Porlock. He came in just before the anthem: splashed and heated from his ride, so that every one turned and looked at him. He wanted to create a stir (knowing how much would be made of him), and he took the best way to do it. For he let the anthem go by very quietly—or rather I should say very pleasingly, for our choir was exceeding proud of itself, and I sang bass twice as loud as a bull, to beat the clerk with the clarionet—and then just as Parson Bowden, with a look of pride at his minstrels, was kneeling down to begin the prayer for the King's Most Excellent Majesty (for he never read the litany, except upon Easter Sunday) up jumps young Sam Fry, and shouts,

"I forbid that there prai-er."

"What!" cried the parson, arising slowly, and looking for some one to shut the door: "have we a rebel in the congregation?" For the parson was growing short-sighted now, and knew not Sam Fry at that distance.

"No," replied Sam, not a whit abashed by the staring of all the parish; "no rebel, parson; but a man who mislaiketh popery and murder. That there prai-er be a prai-er for the dead."

"Nay," cried the parson, now recognising and knowing him to be our John's first cousin: "you do not mean to say, Sam, that His Gracious Majesty is dead!"

" Dead as a sto-un : poisoned by they Papishers."
And Sam rubbed his hands with enjoyment, at the
effect he had produced.

" Remember where you are, Sam," said Parson
Bowden, solemnly; " when did this most sad thing
happen ?  The King is the head of the Church; Sam
Fry, when did he leave her ? "

" Day afore yesterday.  Twelve o' clock.  Warn't
us quick to hear of 'un ? "

" Can't be," said the minister : " the tidings can
never have come so soon.  Any how, he will want it
all the more.  Let us pray for His Gracious Majesty."

And with that he proceeded as usual; but nobody
cried " Amen," for fear of being entangled with
popery.  But after giving forth his text, our parson
said a few words out of book, about the many virtues
of His Majesty, and self-denial, and devotion, compar-
ing his pious mirth to the dancing of the patriarch
David, before the ark of the covenant; and he added,
with some severity, that if his flock would not join
their pastor (who was much more likely to judge
aright) in praying for the King, the least they could do
on returning home was to pray that the King might not
be dead, as his enemies had asserted.

Now when the service was over, we killed the King,
and we brought him to life, at least fifty times in the
churchyard : and Sam Fry was mounted on a high
gravestone, to tell every one all he knew of it.  But he
knew no more than he had told us, in the church, as
before repeated : upon which we were much disap-

pointed with him, and inclined to disbelieve him : until
he happily remembered that His Majesty had died in
great pain, with blue spots on his breast and black
spots all across his back, and these in the form of a
cross, by reason of papists having poisoned him.   When
Sam called this to his remembrance (or to his imagina-
tion) he was overwhelmed, at once, with so many invi-
tations to dinner, that he scarce knew which of them to
accept; but decided in our favour.

Grieving much for the loss of the King, however
greatly it might be (as the parson had declared it
was, while telling us to pray against it) for the royal
benefit, I resolved to ride to Porlock myself, directly
after dinner ; and make sure whether he were dead, or
not.   For it was not by any means hard to suppose that
Sam Fry, being John's first cousin, might have inherited
either from grandfather or grandmother some of those
gifts which had made our John so famous for mendacity.
At Porlock, I found that it was too true ; and the
women of the town were in great distress, for the King
had always been popular with them : the men on the other
hand were forecasting what would be likely to ensue.

And I myself was of this number, riding sadly
home again ; although bound to the King as churchwarden now ; which dignity, next to the parson's in
rank, is with us (as it ought to be in every good
parish) hereditary.   For who can stick to the church,
like the man whose father stuck to it before him ; and
who knows all the little ins, and great outs, which
must in these troublous times come across ?

But though appointed at last, by virtue of being best
farmer in the parish (as well as by vice of mismanage-
ment on the part of my mother, and Nicholas Snowe,
who had thoroughly muxed up everything, being too
quick-headed); yet, while I dwelled with pride upon
the fact that I stood in the King's shoes, as the manager
and promoter of the Church of England; and I knew
that we must miss His Majesty (whose arms were above
the Commandments), as the leader of our thoughts in
church, and handsome upon a guinea; nevertheless I
kept on thinking how his death would act on me.

And here I saw it, many ways. In the first place,
troubles must break out; and we had eight-and-twenty
ricks; counting grain, and straw, and hay. Moreover
mother was growing weak, about riots, and shooting,
and burning; and she gathered the bed-clothes around
her ears, every night, when her feet were tucked up;
and prayed not to awake until morning. In the next
place, much rebellion (though we would not own it; in
either sense of the verb, to " own ") was whispering,
and plucking skirts, and making signs, among us. And
the terror of the Doones helped greatly; as a fruitful
tree of lawlessness, and a good excuse for everybody.
And after this—or rather before it, and first of all
indeed (if I must state the true order)—arose upon
me the thought of Lorna, and how these things would
affect her fate.

And indeed I must admit that it had occurred to me
sometimes, or been suggested by others, that the Lady
Lorna had not behaved altogether kindly, since her

departure from among us. For although in those days
the post (as we call the service of letter-carrying,
which now comes within twenty miles of us) did not
extend to our part of the world; yet it might have
been possible to procure for hire a man who would ride
post, if Lorna feared to trust the pack-horses, or the
troopers, who went to and fro. Yet no message whatever had reached us; neither any token even of her
safety in London. As to this last however we had no
misgivings, having learned from the orderlies, more
than once, that the wealth, and beauty, and adventures
of young Lady Lorna Dugal, were greatly talked of,
both at court, and among the common people.

Now riding sadly homewards, in the sunset of the
early spring, I was more than ever touched with
sorrow, and a sense of being, as it were, abandoned.
And the weather growing quite beautiful, and so mild
that the trees were budding, and the cattle full of
happiness, I could not but think of the difference
between the world of to-day, and the world of this day
twelvemonth. Then all was howling desolation, all
the earth blocked up with snow, and all the air with
barbs of ice, as small as splintered needles, yet glittering, in and out, like stars, and gathering so upon a
man (if long he stayed among them) that they began
to weigh him down to sleepiness and frozen death.
Not a sign of life was moving; nor was any change of
view; unless the wild wind struck the crest of some
cold drift, and bowed it.

Now, on the other hand, all was good. The open

palm of spring was laid upon the yielding of the hills;
and each particular valley seemed to be the glove for a
finger.  And although the sun was low, and dipping in
the western clouds, the grey light of the sea came up,
and took, and taking, told the special tone of everything.  All this lay upon my heart, without a word of
thinking, spreading light and shadow there, and the soft
delight of sadness.  Nevertheless, I would it were the
savage snow around me, and the piping of the restless
winds, and the death of everything.  For in those days
I had Lorna.

Then I thought of promise fair; such as glowed
around me, where the red rocks held the sun, when he
was departed; and the distant crags endeavoured to
retain his memory.  But as evening spread across
them, shading with a silent fold; all the colour stole
away; all remembrance waned and died.

"So has it been with love," I thought; "and with
simple truth and warmth.  The maid has chosen the
glittering stars, instead of the plain daylight."

Nevertheless I would not give in, although in deep
despondency (especially when I passed the place where
my dear father had fought in vain), and I tried to see
things right and then judge aright about them.  This
however was more easy to attempt than to achieve;
and by the time I came down the hill, I was none the
wiser.  Only I could tell my mother that the King was
dead for sure; and she would have tried to cry, but
for thought of her mourning.

There was not a moment for lamenting.  All the

mourning must be ready (if we cared to beat the
Snowes) in eight-and-forty hours : and, although it was
Sunday night, mother now feeling sure of the thing,
sate up with Lizzie, cutting patterns, and stitching
things on brown paper, and snipping, and laying the
fashions down, and requesting all opinions, yet when
given scorning them ; insomuch that I grew weary even
of tobacco (which had comforted me, since Lorna) and
prayed her to go on, until the King should be alive
again.

The thought of that so flurried her—for she never
yet could see a joke—that she laid her scissors on the
table and said, "The Lord forbid, John ! after what I
have cut up !"

"It would be just like him ; " I answered, with a
knowing smile : "Mother, you had better stop.
Patterns may do very well ; but don't cut up any
more good stuff."

" Well, good lack, I am a fool ! Three tables pegged
with needles !   The Lord in his mercy keep His
Majesty, if ever he hath gotten him ! "

By this device, we went to bed ; and not another
stitch was struck, until the troopers had office-tidings
that the King was truly dead.   Hence the Snowes beat
us by a day ; and both old Betty and Lizzie laid the
blame upon me, as usual.

Almost before we had put off the mourning, which
as loyal subjects we kept for the King three months and
a week ; rumours of disturbances, of plottings, and of
outbreak, began to stir among us.   We heard of fight-

ing in Scotland, and buying of ships on the continent,
and of arms in Dorset and Somerset; and we kept our
beacon in readiness to give signals of a landing; or
rather the soldiers did.　For we, having trustworthy
reports that the King had been to high mass himself in
the Abbey of Westminster, making all the bishops go
with him, and all the guards in London, and then tor-
tured all the Protestants who dared to wait outside,
moreover had received from the Pope a flower grown in
the Virgin Mary's garden, and warranted to last for ever,
we of the moderate party, hearing all this and ten times
as much, and having no love for this sour James, such
as we had for the lively Charles, were ready to wait
for what might happen, rather than care about stopping
it.　Therefore we listened to rumours gladly, and shook
our heads with gravity, and predicted, every man something, but scarce any two the same.　Nevertheless, in
our part, things went on as usual, until the middle of
June was nigh.　We ploughed the ground, and sowed
the corn, and tended the cattle, and heeded every one
his neighbour's business, as carefully as heretofore;
and the only thing that moved us much was that Annie
had a baby.　This being a very fine child with blue
eyes, and christened "John" in compliment to me,
and with me for his godfather, it is natural to suppose
that I thought a good deal about him; and when
mother or Lizzie would ask me, all of a sudden, and
treacherously, when the fire flared up at supper-time
(for we always kept a little wood just alight in summer-
time, and enough to make the pot boil), then when they

would say to me, "John, what are you thinking of?
At a word, speak!" I would always answer, "Little
John Faggus;" and so they made no more of me.

But when I was down, on Saturday the thirteenth of
June, at the blacksmith's forge by Brendon town, where
the Lynn-stream runs so close that he dips his horse-
shoes in it, and where the news is apt to come first of
all our neighbourhood (except upon a Sunday), while
we were talking of the hay-crop, and of a great sheep-
stealer, round the corner came a man upon a pie-bald
horse looking flagged and weary. But seeing half-a-
dozen of us, young, and brisk, and hearty, he made
a flourish with his horse, and waved a blue flag
vehemently, shouting with great glory—

"Monmouth and the Protestant faith! Monmouth
and no Popery! Monmouth, the good King's eldest
son! Down with the poisoning murderer! Down
with the black usurper, and to the devil with all
papists!"

"Why so, thou little varlet?" I asked very quietly;
for the man was too small to quarrel with: yet knowing
Lorna to be a "papist" as we choose to call them—
though they might as well call us "kingists," after
the head of our church—I thought that this scurvy
scampish knave might show them the way to the place
he mentioned, unless his courage failed him.

"Papist yourself, be you?" said the fellow, not
daring to answer much: "then take this, and read
it."

And he handed me a long rigmarole, which he called

a "Declaration ;" I saw that it was but a heap of lies, and thrust it into the blacksmith's fire, and blew the bellows thrice at it. No one dared attempt to stop me, for my mood had not been sweet of late; and of course they knew my strength.

The man rode on with a muttering noise, having won no recruits from us, by force of my example; and he stopped at the alehouse further down, where the road goes away from the Lynn-stream. Some of us went thither after a time, when our horses were shodden and rasped, for although we might not like the man, we might be glad of his tidings, which seemed to be something wonderful. He had set up his blue flag in the tap-room, and was teaching every one.

"Here coom'th Maister Jan Ridd," said the landlady, being well pleased with the call for beer and cider : "her hath been to Lunnon-town, and live within a maile of me. Arl the news coom from them now-a-days, instead of from here, as her ought to do. If Jan Ridd say it be true, I will try a'most to belave it. Hath the good Duke landed, sir ? " And she looked at me over a foaming cup, and blew the froth off, and put more in.

"I have no doubt it is true enough ;" I answered, before drinking; "and too true, Mistress Pugsley. Many a poor man will die; but none shall die from our parish, nor from Brendon, if I can help it."

And I knew that I could help it: for every one in those little places would abide by my advice; not only from the fame of my schooling and long sojourn in

M 2

London, but also because I had earned repute, for
being very "slow and sure:" and with nine people out
of ten, this is the very best recommendation.  For they
think themselves much before you in wit, and under
no obligation; but rather conferring a favour, by doing
the thing that you do.   Hence, if I cared for influence
—which means, for the most part, making people do
one's will, without knowing it—my first step toward
it would be to be called, in common parlance, "slow,
but sure."

For the next fortnight we were daily troubled with
conflicting rumours, each man relating what he desired,
rather than what he had right, to believe.   We were
told that the Duke had been proclaimed King of
England in every town of Dorset and of Somerset;
that he had won a great battle at Axminster, and
another at Bridport, and another somewhere else; that
all the western counties had risen as one man for him,
and all the militia joined his ranks; that Taunton, and
Bridgewater, and Bristowe, were all mad with delight,
the two former being in his hands, and the latter craving
to be so.   And then, on the other hand, we heard that
the Duke had been vanquished, and put to flight, and
upon being apprehended had confessed himself an
impostor, and a papist as bad as the King was.

We longed for Colonel Stickles (as he always
became in time of war; though he fell back to Captain, and even Lieutenant, directly the fight was over),
for then we should have won trusty news, as well as
good consideration.   But even Serjeant Bloxham,

much against his will, was gone, having left his heart
with our Lizzie, and a collection of all his writings.
All the soldiers had been ordered away at full speed
for Exeter, to join the Duke of Albemarle, or if he
were gone to follow him. As for us, who had fed them
so long (although not quite for nothing) we must take
our chance of Doones, or any other enemies.

•Now all these tidings moved me a little; not enough
to spoil appetite, but enough to make things lively, and
to teach me that look of wisdom, which is bred of practice only, and the hearing of many lies. Therefore I
withheld my judgment, fearing to be triumphed over,
if it should happen to miss the mark. But mother and
Lizzie, ten times in a day, predicted all they could
imagine; and their prophecies increased in strength
according to contradiction. Yet this was not in the
proper style for a house like ours, which knew the news,
or at least had known it; and still was famous, all
around, for the last advices. Even from Lynmouth,
people sent up to Plover's Barrows, to ask how things
were going on: and it was very grievous to answer
that in truth we knew not, neither had heard for days
and days; and our reputation was so great, especially
since the death of the King had gone abroad from
Oare parish, that many inquirers would only wink,
and lay a finger on the lip; as if to say, "you know
well enough, but see not fit to tell me." And before
the end arrived, those people believed that they had
been right all along, and that we had concealed the
truth from them.

For I myself became involved (God knows how much
against my will and my proper judgment) in the
troubles, and the conflict, and the cruel work coming
afterwards.   If ever I had made up my mind to anything in all my life, it was at this particular time, and
as stern and strong as could be.   I had resolved to let
things pass,—to hear about them gladly, to encourage
all my friends to talk, and myself to express opinion
upon each particular point, when in the fulness of time
no further doubt could be.   But all my policy went for
nothing, through a few touches of feeling.

One day at the beginning of July, I came home
from mowing about noon, or a little later, to fetch
some cider for all of us, and to eat a morsel of bacon.
For mowing was no joke that year, the summer being
wonderfully wet (even for our wet country) and the
swathe falling heavier over the scythe than ever I
could remember it.   We were drenched with rain
almost every day; but the mowing must be done
somehow;   and we must trust to God for the hay-
making.

In the courtyard I saw a little cart, with iron breaks
underneath it, such as fastidious people use to deaden
the jolting of the road; but few men under a lord or
baronet would be so particular.   Therefore I wondered
who our noble visitor could be.   But when I entered
the kitchen-place, brushing up my hair for somebody,
behold it was no one greater than our Annie, with my
godson in her arms, and looking pale and tear-begone.
And at first she could not speak to me.   But presently

having sate down a little, and received much praise
for her baby, she smiled, and blushed, and found her
tongue as if she had never gone from us.

"How natural it all looks again! Oh, I love this
old kitchen so! Baby dear, only look at it wid him
pitty pitty eyes, and him tongue out of his mousy!
But who put the flour-riddle up there? And look
at the pestle and mortar, and rust I declare in the
patty pans! And a book, positively a dirty book,
where the clean skewers ought to hang! Oh, Lizzie,
Lizzie, Lizzie!"

"You may just as well cease lamenting," I said,
"for you can't alter Lizzie's nature, and you will only
make mother uncomfortable, and perhaps have a quarrel
with Lizzie; who is proud as Punch of her house-
keeping."

"She!" cried Annie, with all the contempt that
could be compressed in a syllable. "Well, John, no
doubt you are right about it. I will try not to notice
things. But it is a hard thing, after all my care, to
see everything going to ruin. But what can be
expected of a girl who knows all the kings of Carthage?"

"There were no kings of Carthage, Annie. They
were called, why let me see—they were called—oh,
something else."

"Never mind what they were called;" said Annie;
"will they cook our dinner for us? But now, John, I
am in such trouble. All this talk is make-believe."

"Don't you cry, my dear; don't cry, my darling

sister;" I answered, as she dropped into the worn place of the settle, and bent above her infant, rocking as if both their hearts were one: "don't you know, Annie, I cannot tell, but I know, or at least I mean, I have heard the men of experience say, it is so bad for the baby."

"Perhaps I know that as well as you do, John," said Annie, looking up at me, with a gleam of her old laughing: "but how can I help crying? I am in such trouble."

"Tell me what it is, my dear. Any grief of yours will vex me greatly: but I will try to bear it."

"Then, John, it is just this. Tom has gone off with the rebels: and you must, oh, you must go after him."

## CHAPTER XI.

MOVED as I was by Annie's tears, and gentle style of coaxing, and most of all by my love for her, I yet declared that I could not go, and leave our house and homestead, far less my dear mother and Lizzie, at the mercy of the merciless Doones.

"Is that all your objection, John?" asked Annie, in her quick panting way: "would you go but for that, John?"

"Now," I said, "be in no such hurry"—for while I was gradually yielding, I liked to pass it through my fingers, as if my fingers shaped it: "there are many things to be thought about, and many ways of viewing it."

"Oh, you never can have loved Lorna! No wonder you gave her up so! John, you can love nobody, but your oat-ricks, and your hay-ricks."

"Sister mine, because I rant not, neither rave of what I feel, can you be so shallow as to dream that I feel nothing? What is your love for Tom Faggus? What is your love for your baby (pretty darling as he is) to compare with such a love as for ever dwells with me? Because I do not prate of it; because it is beyond me, not only to express, but even form to my own heart in thoughts; because I do not shape my face, and would scorn to play to it, as a thing of acting, and lay it out before you, are you fools enough to think"——but here I stopped, having said more than was usual with me.

"I am very sorry, John. Dear John, I am so sorry. What a shallow fool I am!"

"I will go seek your husband," I said, to change the subject: for even to Annie I would not lay open all my heart about Lorna: "but only upon condition, that you ensure this house and people from the Doones meanwhile. Even for the sake of Tom, I cannot leave all helpless. The oat-ricks and the hay-ricks, which are my only love, they are welcome to make cinders of. But I will not have mother treated so: nor even little Lizzie, although you scorn your sister so."

"Oh, John, I do think you are the hardest, as well as the softest, of all the men I know. Not even a woman's bitter word but what you pay her out for. Will you never understand that we are not like you, John? We say all sorts of spiteful things, without a bit of meaning. John, for God's sake fetch Tom home; and then revile me as you please, and I will kneel and thank you."

"I will not promise to fetch him home," I answered, being ashamed of myself for having lost command so: "but I will promise to do my best, if we can only hit on a plan for leaving mother harmless."

Annie thought for a little while, trying to gather her

smooth clear brow into maternal wrinkles, and then she looked at her child, and said, "I will risk it, for daddy's sake, darling; you precious soul, for daddy's sake." I asked her what she was going to risk. She would not tell me; but took upper hand, and saw to my cider-cans and bacon, and went from corner to cupboard, exactly as if she had never been married; only without an apron on. And then she said, "Now to your mowers, John; and make the most of this fine afternoon: kiss your godson, before you go." And I, being used to obey her, in little things of that sort, kissed the baby, and took my cans, and went back to my scythe again.

By the time I came home it was dark night, and pouring again with a foggy rain, such as we have in July, even more than in January. Being soaked all through and through, and with water quelching in my boots, like a pump with a bad bucket, I was only too glad to find Annie's bright face, and quick figure, flitting in and out the firelight, instead of Lizzie sitting grandly, with a feast of literature, and not a drop of gravy. Mother was in the corner also, with her cherry-coloured ribbons glistening very nice by candle-light, looking at Annie now and then, with memories of her babyhood; and then at her having a baby: yet half afraid of praising her much, for fear of that young Lizzie. But Lizzie showed no jealousy: she truly loved our Annie (now that she was gone from us), and she wanted to know all sorts of things, and she adored the baby. Therefore Annie was allowed to attend to me, as she used to do.

"Now, John, you must start the first thing in the morning," she said, when the others had left the room, but somenow she stuck to the baby; "to fetch me back my rebel, according to your promise."

"Not so," I replied, misliking the job: "all I promised was to go, if this house were assured against any onslaught of the Doones."

"Just so; and here is that assurance." With these words, she drew forth a paper, and laid it on my knee with triumph, enjoying my amazement. This, as you may suppose, was great; not only at the document, but also at her possession of it. For in truth it was no less than a formal undertaking, on the part of the Doones, not to attack Plover's Barrows farm, or molest any of the inmates, or carry off any chattels, during the absence of John Ridd upon a special errand. This document was signed not only by the Counsellor, but by many other Doones: whether Carver's name were there, I could not say for certain; as of course he would not sign it under his name of "Carver," and I had never heard Lorna say to what (if any) he had been baptised.

In the face of such a deed as this, I could no longer refuse to go; and having received my promise, Annie told me (as was only fair) how she had procured that paper. It was both a clever and courageous act; and would have seemed to me, at first sight, far beyond Annie's power. But none may gauge a woman's power, when her love and faith are moved.

The first thing Annie had done was this: she made

herself look ugly. This was not an easy thing; but
she had learned a great deal from her husband, upon
the subject of disguises. It hurt her feelings not a
little, to make so sad a fright of herself; but what
could it matter?—if she lost Tom, she must be a far
greater fright in earnest, than now she was in seeming.
And then she left her child asleep, under Betty Muxworthy's tendance—for Betty took to that child, as if
there never had been a child before—and away she
went in her own "spring-cart" (as the name of that
engine proved to be), without a word to any one, except the old man who had driven her from Molland
parish that morning; and who coolly took one of our
best horses, without "by your leave" to any one.

Annie made the old man drive her within easy reach
of the Doone-gate, whose position she knew well enough,
from all our talk about it. And there she bade the old
man stay, until she should return to him. Then with
her comely figure hidden by a dirty old woman's cloak,
and her fair young face defaced by patches and by
liniments, so that none might covet her, she addressed
the young man at the gate in a cracked and trembling
voice; and they were scarcely civil to the "old hag,"
as they called her. She said that she bore important
tidings for Sir Counsellor himself, and must be conducted to him. To him accordingly she was led,
without even any hood-winking; for she had spectacles
over her eyes, and made believe not to see ten yards.

She found Sir Counsellor at home, and when the
rest were out of sight, threw off all disguise to him,

flashing forth as a lovely young woman, from all her
wraps and disfigurements. She flung her patches on
the floor, amid the old man's laughter, and let her
tucked-up hair come down; and then went up and
kissed him:

"Worthy and reverend Counsellor, I have a favour
to ask"—she began.

"So I should think from your proceedings,"—
the old man interrupted—"ah, if I were half my
age "——

"If you were, I would not sue so. But most
excellent Counsellor, you owe me some amends, you
know, for the way in which you robbed me."

"Beyond a doubt, I do, my dear. You have put it
rather strongly; and it might offend some people.
Nevertheless I own my debt, having so fair a
creditor."

"And do you remember how you slept, and how
much we made of you, and would have seen you home,
sir; only you did not wish it?"

"And for excellent reasons, child. My best escort
was in my cloak, after we made the cream to rise.
Ha, ha! The unholy spell. My pretty child, has
it injured you?"

"Yes, I fear it has," said Annie; "or whence can
all my ill luck come?" And here she showed some
signs of crying, knowing that Counsellor hated it.

"You shall not have ill luck, my dear. I have
heard all about your marriage to a very noble
highwayman. Ah, you made a mistake in that;

you were worthy of a Doone, my child; your frying was a blessing meant for those who can appreciate."

" My husband can appreciate;" she answered very proudly; " but what I wish to know is this, will you try to help me?"

The Counsellor answered that he would do so, if her needs were moderate; whereupon she opened her meaning to him, and told of all her anxieties. Considering that Lorna was gone, and her necklace in his possession, and that I (against whom alone of us the Doones could bear any malice) would be out of the way all the while; the old man readily undertook that our house should not be assaulted, nor our property molested, until my return. And to the promptitude of his pledge, two things perhaps contributed, namely, that he knew not how we were stripped of all defenders, and that some of his own forces were away in the rebel camp. For (as I learned thereafter) the Doones being now in direct feud with the present Government, and sure to be crushed if that prevailed, had resolved to drop all religious questions, and cast in their lot with Monmouth. And the turbulent youths, being long restrained from their wonted outlet for vehemence, by the troopers in the neighbourhood, were only too glad to rush forth upon any promise of blows and excitement.

However Annie knew little of this, but took the Counsellor's pledge as a mark of especial favour in her behalf (which it may have been, to some extent) and thanked him for it most heartily, and felt that he had earned the necklace; while he, like an ancient gentleman, disclaimed all obligation, and sent her under an escort safe to her own cart again. But Annie, repassing the sentinels, with her youth restored and blooming with the flush of triumph, went up to them very gravely, and said, "The old hag wishes you good evening, gentlemen;" and so made her best courtesy.

Now, look at it as I would, there was no excuse left for me, after the promise given. Dear Annie had not only cheated the Doones, but also had gotten the best of me, by a pledge to a thing impossible. And I bitterly said, "I am not like Lorna: a pledge once given, I keep it."

"I will not have a word against Lorna;" cried Annie: "I will answer for her truth as surely as I would for my own or yours, John." And with that she vanquished me.

But when my poor mother heard that I was committed, by word of honour, to a wild-goose chase, among the rebels, after that runagate Tom Faggus, she simply stared, and would not believe it. For lately I had joked with her, in a little style of jerks, as people do when out of sorts; and she, not understanding this, and knowing jokes to be out of my power, would only look, and sigh, and toss, and hope that I meant nothing. At last, however, we convinced her that I was in earnest, and must be off in the early morning, and leave John Fry with the hay-crop.

Then mother was ready to fall upon Annie, as not content with disgracing us, by wedding a man of new honesty (if indeed of any), but laying traps to catch her brother, and entangle him perhaps to his death, for the sake of a worthless fellow; and "felon"— she was going to say, as by the shape of her lips I knew. But I laid my hand upon dear mother's lips; because what must be, must be; and if mother and daughter stayed at home, better in love than in quarrelling.

Right early in the morning, I was off, without word to any one; knowing that mother and sister mine had cried, each her good self to sleep; relenting when the light was out, and sorry for hard words and thoughts; and yet too much alike in nature to understand each other. Therefore I took good Kickums, who (although with one eye spoiled) was worth ten sweet-tempered horses, to a man who knew how to manage him; and being well charged both with bacon and powder, forth I set on my wild-goose chace.

For this I claim no bravery. I cared but little what came of it; save for mother's sake, and Annie's, and the keeping of the farm, and discomfiture of the Snowes, and lamenting of Lorna at my death, if die I must in a lonesome manner, not found out till afterwards, and bleaching bones left to weep over. However I had a little kettle, and a pound and a half of tobacco, and two dirty pipes and a clean one; also a bit of clothes for change, also a brisket of hung venison, and four loaves of farm-house bread, and of

arned the necklace; a
m, disclaimed all o
n escort safe to h
repassing the sentine
oming with the flu
ry gravely, and s
d evening, gentle

f.

, look at it as I
after the prom
eated the Do
, by a pledg
y said, " I
I keep it."
will not h
: "I will
for my
nquishe
when
, by
the
aply
h
le

to consult the maps and plans in Uncle Reuben's parlour. Therefore I drew the off-hand rein, at the cross-road on the hills, and made for the town; expecting perhaps to have breakfast with Master Huckaback, and Ruth to help and encourage us. This little maiden was now become a very great favourite with me, having long outgrown, no doubt, her childish fancies and follies, such as my mother and Annie had planted under her soft brown hair. It had been my duty, as well as my true interest (for Uncle Ben was more and more testy, as he went on gold-digging), to ride thither, now and again, to inquire what the doctor thought of her. Not that her wounds were long in healing, but that people can scarcely be too careful and too inquisitive, after a great horse-bite. And she always let me look at the arm, as I had been first doctor; and she held it up in a graceful manner, curving at the elbow, and with a sweep of white round-ness going to a wrist the size of my thumb or so, and without any thimble-top standing forth, such as even our Annie had. But gradually all I could see, above the elbow, where the bite had been, was very clear transparent skin, with very firm sweet flesh below, and three little blue marks as far asunder as the prongs of a toasting-fork, and no deeper than where a twig has chafed the peel of a waxen apple. And then I used to say in fun, as the children do, "Shall I kiss it, to make it well, dear?"

Now Ruth looked very grave indeed, upon hearing of this my enterprise; and crying, said she could

almost cry, for the sake of my dear mother. Did
I know the risks and chances, not of the battle-field
alone, but of the havoc afterwards ; the swearing away
of innocent lives, and the hurdle, and the hanging ?
And if I would please not to laugh (which was so
unkind of me), had I never heard of imprisonments,
and torturing with the cruel boot, and selling into
slavery, where the sun and the lash outvied one another
in cutting a man to pieces ? I replied that of all
these things I had heard, and would take especial care
to steer me free of all of them. My duty was all that
I wished to do ; and none could harm me for doing
that. And I begged my cousin to give me good-
speed, instead of talking dolefully. Upon this she
changed her manner wholly, becoming so lively and
cheerful that I was convinced of her indifference, and
surprised even more than gratified.

"Go and earn your spurs, Cousin Ridd," she said :
"you are strong enough for anything. Which side is
to have the benefit of your doughty arm ? "

"Have I not told you, Ruth," I answered, not
being fond of this kind of talk, more suitable for
Lizzie : "that I do not mean to join either side, that
is to say, until "——

"Until, as the common proverb goes, you know
which way the cat will jump. Oh, John Ridd ! Oh,
John Ridd ! "

"Nothing of the sort," said I : "what a hurry you
are in ! I am for the King of course."

"But not enough to fight for him. Only enough

to vote, I suppose, or drink his health, or shout for him."

"I can't make you out to-day, Cousin Ruth; you are nearly as bad as Lizzie. You do not say any bitter things; but you seem to mean them."

"No, cousin, think not so of me. It is far more likely that I say them, without meaning them."

"Anyhow, it is not like you. And I know not what I can have done in any way, to vex you."

"Dear me, nothing, Cousin Ridd; you never do anything to vex me."

"Then I hope I shall do something now, Ruth, when I say good-bye. God knows if we ever shall meet again, Ruth: but I hope we may."

"To be sure we shall," she answered in her brightest manner. "Try not to look wretched, John: you are as happy as a May-pole."

"And you as a rose in May," I said; "and pretty nearly as pretty. Give my love to Uncle Ben; and I trust him to keep on the winning side."

"Of that you need have no misgiving. Never yet has he failed of it. Now, Cousin Ridd, why go you not? You hurried me so at breakfast time?"

"My only reason for waiting, Ruth, is that you have not kissed me, as you are almost bound to do, for the last time perhaps of seeing me."

"Oh, if that is all, just fetch the stool; and I will do my best, cousin."

"I pray you be not so vexatious: you always used to do it nicely, without any stool, Ruth."

"Ah, but you are grown since then, and become a famous man, John Ridd, and a member of the nobility. Go your way, and win your spurs. I want no lip-service."

Being at the end of my wits, I did even as she ordered me. At least I had no spurs to win, because there were big ones on my boots, paid for in the Easter bill, and made by a famous saddler, so as never to clog with marsh-weed, but prick as hard as any horse, in reason, could desire. And Kickums never wanted spurs; but always went tail-foremost, if anybody offered them for his consideration.

## CHAPTER XII.

WE rattled away, at a merry pace, out of the town of
Dulverton; my horse being gaily fed; and myself
quite fit again for going. Of course I was puzzled about
Cousin Ruth; for her behaviour was not at all such as
I had expected; and indeed I had hoped for a far
more loving and moving farewell, than I got from her.
But I said to myself, "It is useless ever to count upon
what a woman will do; and I think that I must have
vexed her, almost as much as she vexed me. And
now to see what comes of it." So I put my horse
across the moorland; and he threw his chest out
bravely.

Now if I tried to set down at length all the things
that happened to me, upon this adventure, every in
and out, and up and down, and to and fro, that
occupied me, together with the things I saw, and the
things I heard of; however much the wiser people
might applaud my narrative, it is likely enough that
idle readers might exclaim, "What ails this man?
Knows he not that men of parts, and of real under-

standing, have told us all we care to hear of that
miserable business ?   Let him keep to his farm, and
his bacon, and his wrestling, and constant feeding."

Fearing to meet with such rebuffs (which after my
death would vex me), I will try to set down only
what is needful for my story, and the clearing of my
character, and the good name of our parish.   But the
manner in which I was bandied about, by false information from pillar to post, or at other times driven quite
out of my way by the presence of King's soldiers, may
be known by the names of the following towns, to which
I was sent in succession, Bath, Frome, Wells, Win-
canton, Glastonbury, Shepton, Bradford, Axbridge,
Somerton, and Bridgewater.

This last place I reached on a Sunday night, the
fourth or fifth of July, I think—or it might be the
sixth, for that matter ; inasmuch as I had been too
much worried to get the day of the month at church.
Only I know that my horse and myself were glad to
come to a decent place, where meat and corn could
be had for money ; and being quite weary of wander-
ing about, we hoped to rest there a little.

Of this, however, we found no chance, for the town
was full of the good Duke's soldiers ; if men may be
called so, the half of whom had never been drilled, nor
had fired a gun.   And it was rumoured among them,
that the "popish army," as they called it, was to be
attacked that very night, and with God's assistance
beaten.   However by this time I had been taught to pay
little attention to rumours ; and having sought vainly

for Tom Faggus among these poor rustic warriors, I
took to my hostel, and went to bed, being as weary as
weary can be.

Falling asleep immediately, I took heed of nothing;
although the town was all alive, and lights had come
glancing, as I lay down, and shouts making echo all
round my room. But all I did was to bolt the door;
not an inch would I budge, unless the house, and even
my bed were on fire. And so for several hours I lay,
in the depth of the deepest slumber, without even a
dream on its surface; until I was roused and awakened
at last by a pushing, and pulling, and pinching, and a
plucking of hair out by the roots. And at length, being
able to open mine eyes, I saw the old landlady, with a
candle, heavily wondering at me.

"Can't you let me alone?" I grumbled: "I have
paid for my bed, mistress; and I won't get up for any
one."

"Would to God, young man," she answered, shaking
me as hard as ever, "that the popish soldiers may
sleep, this night, only half as strong as thou dost!
Fie on thee, fie on thee! Get up, and go fight; we
can hear the battle already; and a man of thy size
mought stop a cannon."

"I would rather stop a-bed," said I; "what have I
to do with fighting? I am for King James, if any."

"Then thou mayest even stop a-bed," the old woman
muttered sulkily. "A would never have laboured
half-an-hour to awake a papisher. But hearken you
one thing, young man; Zummerzett thou art, by thy

brogue; or at least by thy understanding of it; no
Zummerzett maid will look at thee, in spite of thy size
and stature, unless thou strikest a blow this night."

"I lack no Zummerzett maid, mistress: I have a
fairer than your brown things; and for her alone
would I strike a blow."

At this, the old woman gave me up, as being beyond
correction: and it vexed me a little that my great
fame had not reached so far as Bridgewater; when I
thought that it went to Bristowe. But those people in
East Somerset know nothing about wrestling. Devon
is the head-quarters of the art; and Devon is the
county of my chief love. Howbeit, my vanity was
moved, by this slur upon it—for I had told her my
name was "John Ridd," when I had a gallon of ale
with her, ere ever I came upstairs; and she had
nodded, in such a manner, that I thought she knew
both name and fame—and here was I, not only shaken,
pinched, and with many hairs pulled out, in the midst
of my first good sleep for a week, but also abused,
and taken amiss and (which vexed me most of all)
unknown.

Now there is nothing like vanity to keep a man
awake at night, however he be weary; and most of all,
when he believes that he is doing something great—
this time, if never done before—yet other people will
not see, except what they may laugh at; and so be
far above him, and sleep themselves the happier.
Therefore their sleep robs his own; for all things play
so, in and out (with the godly and ungodly ever

moving in a balance, as they have done in my time, almost every year or two), all things have such nice reply of produce to the call for it, and such a spread across the world, giving here and taking there, yet on the whole pretty even, that haply sleep itself has but a certain stock, and keeps in hand, and sells to flattered (which can pay) that which flattened vanity cannot pay, and will not sue for.

Be that as it may, I was by this time wide awake, though much aggrieved at feeling so, and through the open window heard the distant roll of musketry, and the beating of drums, with a quick rub-a-dub, and the "come round the corner" of trumpet-call. And perhaps Tom Faggus might be there, and shot at any moment, and my dear Annie left a poor widow, and my godson Jack an orphan, without a tooth to help him.

Therefore I reviled myself for all my heavy laziness; and partly through good honest will, and partly through the stings of pride, and yet a little perhaps by virtue of a young man's love of riot, up I arose, and dressed myself, and woke Kickums (who was snoring) and set out to see the worst of it. The sleepy hostler scratched his poll, and could not tell me which way to take; what odds to him who was King, or Pope, so long as he paid his way, and got a bit of bacon on Sunday? And would I please to remember that I had roused him up at night, and the quality always made a point of paying four times over for a man's loss of his beauty-sleep. I replied that his loss of beauty-sleep was rather improving to a man of so

high complexion ; and that I, being none of the quality,
must pay half-quality prices : and so I gave him double
fee, as became a good farmer ; and he was glad to be
quit of Kickums ; as I saw by the turn of his eye, while
going out at the archway.

All this was done by lanthorn light, although the
moon was high and bold ; and in the northern heaven,
flags and ribbons of a jostling pattern ; such as we
often have in Autumn, but in July very rarely. Of
these Master Dryden has spoken somewhere, in his
courtly manner ; but of him I think so little—because
by fashion preferred to Shakespeare—that I cannot
remember the passage ; neither is it a credit to him.

Therefore I was guided mainly by the sound of
guns and trumpets, in riding out of the narrow ways,
and into the open marshes. And thus I might have
found my road, in spite of all the spread of water, and
the glaze of moonshine ; but that, as I followed sound
(far from hedge or causeway), fog (like a chestnut-
tree in blossom, touched with moonlight) met me.
Now fog is a thing that I understand, and can do
with well enough, where I know the country : but
here I had never been before. It was nothing to our
Exmoor fogs ; not to be compared with them ; and all
the time one could see the moon ; which we cannot do
in our fogs ; nor even the sun, for a week together.
Yet the gleam of water always makes a fog more
difficult : like a curtain on a mirror ; none can tell the
boundaries.

And here we had broad water-patches, in and out,

inlaid on land, like mother-of-pearl in brown Shittim wood. To a wild duck, born and bred there, it would almost be a puzzle to find her own nest amongst it; what chance then had I and Kickums, both unused to marsh and mere? Each time when we thought that we must be right, now at last, by track or passage, and approaching the conflict, with the sounds of it waxing nearer, suddenly a break of water would be laid before us, with the moon looking mildly over it, and the northern lights behind us, dancing down the lines of fog.

It was an awful thing, I say (and to this day I remember it), to hear the sounds of raging fight, and the yells of raving slayers, and the howls of poor men stricken hard, and shattered from wrath to wailing; then suddenly the dead low hush, as of a soul departing, and spirits kneeling over it. Through the vapour of the earth, and white breath of the water, and beneath the pale round moon (bowing as the drift went by), all this rush and pause of fear passed or lingered on my path.

At last, when I almost despaired of escaping from this tangle of spongy banks, and of hazy creeks, and reed-fringe, my horse heard the neigh of a fellow-horse, and was only too glad to answer it; upon which the other, having lost his rider, came up and pricked his ears at us, and gazed through the fog very stead-fastly. Therefore I encouraged him with a soft and genial whistle, and Kickums did his best to tempt him with a snort of inquiry. However, nothing would suit

that nag, except to enjoy his new freedom; and he
capered away with his tail set on high, and the stirrup-
irons clashing under him.   Therefore, as he might
know the way, and appeared to have been in the battle,
we followed him very carefully; and he led us to a
little hamlet, called (as I found afterwards) West
Zuyland, or Zealand, so named perhaps from its situation amid this inland sea.

Here the King's troops had been quite lately, and
their fires were still burning; but the men themselves
had been summoned away by the night-attack of the
rebels.   Here I procured for my guide a young man
who knew the district thoroughly, and who led me by
many intricate ways to the rear of the rebel army.
We came upon a broad open moor striped with sullen
water-courses, shagged with sedge, and yellow iris, and
in the drier part with bilberries.   For by this time it
was four o'clock, and the summer sun, arising wanly,
showed us all the ghastly scene.

Would that I had never been there!   Often in the
lonely hours, even now it haunts me: would, far more,
that the piteous thing had never been done in England!
Flying men, flung back from dreams of victory and
honour, only glad to have the luck of life and limbs to
fly with, mud-bedraggled, foul with slime, reeking both
with sweat and blood, which they could not stop to
wipe, cursing, with their pumped-out lungs, every stick
that hindered them, or gory puddle that slipped the
step, scarcely able to leap over the corses that had
dragged to die.   And to see how the corses lay; some,

as fair as death in sleep; with the smile of placid valour, and of noble manhood, hovering yet on the silent lips. These had bloodless hands put upwards, white as wax, and firm as death, clasped (as on a monument) in prayer for dear ones left behind, or in high thanksgiving. And of these men there was nothing in their broad blue eyes to fear. But others were of different sort; simple fellows unused to pain, accustomed to the bill-hook, perhaps, or rasp of the knuckles in a quickset hedge, or making some todo, at breakfast, over a thumb cut in sharpening a scythe, and expecting their wives to make more todo. Yet here lay these poor chaps, dead; dead, after a deal of pain, with little mind to bear it, and a soul they had never thought of; gone, their God alone knows whither; but to mercy we may trust. Upon these things I cannot dwell; and none, I trow would ask me: only if a plain man saw, what I saw that morning, he (if God had blessed him with the heart which is in most of us) must have sickened of all desire to be great among mankind.

Seeing me riding to the front (where the work of death went on among the men of true English pluck; which, when moved, no further moves), the fugitives called out to me, in half a dozen dialects, to make no utter fool of myself; for the great guns were come, and the fight was over; all the rest was slaughter.

"Arl oop wi Moonmo'," shouted one big fellow, a miner of the Mendip hills, whose weapon was a pick-axe: "na oose to vaight na moor. Wend thee hame, yoong mon agin."

Upon this I stopped my horse; desiring not to be
shot for nothing; and eager to aid some poor sick people,
who tried to lift their arms to me.   And this I did to
the best of my power; though void of skill in the business; and more inclined to weep with them, than to
check their weeping.   While I was giving a drop of
cordial from my flask to one poor fellow, who sate up,
while his life was ebbing, and with slow insistence urged
me, when his broken voice would come, to tell his wife
(whose name I knew not) something about an apple-
tree, and a golden guinea stored in it, to divide among
six children—in the midst of this I felt warm lips laid
against my cheek quite softly, and then a little push;
and behold it was a horse leaning over me!   I arose in
haste, and there stood Winnie, looking at me with
beseeching eyes, enough to melt a heart of stone.
Then seeing my attention fixed, she turned her head,
and glanced back sadly towards the place of battle, and
gave a little wistful neigh: and then looked me full in
the face again, as much as to say, " Do you understand? "
while she scraped with one hoof impatiently.   If ever
a horse tried hard to speak, it was Winnie at that
moment.   I went to her side, and patted her; but that
was not what she wanted.   Then I offered to leap into the
empty saddle; but neither did that seem good to her:
for she ran away toward the part of the field at which
she had been glancing back, and then turned round,
and shook her mane, entreating me to follow her.

Upon this I learned from the dying man where to
find his apple-tree, and promised to add another guinea

to the one in store for his children; and so, commending him to God, I mounted my own horse again, and to Winnie's great delight, professed myself at her service. With her ringing silvery neigh, such as no other horse of all I ever knew could equal, she at once proclaimed her triumph, and told her master (or meant to tell, if death should not have closed his ears) that she was coming to his aid, and bringing one who might be trusted, of the higher race that kill.

A cannon-bullet (fired low, and ploughing the marsh slowly) met poor Winnie front to front; and she, being as quick as thought, lowered her nose to sniff at it. It might be a message from her master; for it made a mournful noise. But luckily for Winnie's life, a rise of wet ground took the ball, even under her very nose; and there it cut a splashy groove, missing her off hind-foot by an inch, and scattering black mud over her. It frightened me much more than Winnie; of that I am quite certain: because though I am firm enough, when it comes to a real tussle, and the heart of a fellow warms up and tells him that he must go through with it; yet I never did approve of making a cold pie of death.

Therefore, with those reckless cannons, brazen-mouthed, and bellowing, two furlongs off, or it might be more (and the more the merrier), I would have given that year's hay-crop for a bit of a hill, or a thicket of oaks, or almost even a badger's earth. People will call me a coward for this (especially when I had made up my mind, that life was not worth having, without any sign of Lorna), nevertheless, I cannot help it: those

were my feelings; and I set them down, because they
made a mark on me. At Glen Doone I had fought,
even against cannon, with some spirit and fury: but
now I saw nothing to fight about; but rather in every
poor doubled corpse, a good reason for not fighting.
So, in cold blood riding on, and yet ashamed that a
man should shrink where a horse went bravely, I cast
a bitter blame upon the reckless ways of Winnie.

Nearly all were scattered now. Of the noble countrymen (armed with scythe or pickaxe, blacksmth's
hammer, or fold-pitcher), who had stood their ground
for hours, against blazing musketry (from men whom
they could not get at, by reason of the water-dyke), and
then against the deadly cannon, dragged by the Bishop's
horses to slaughter his own sheep; of these sturdy
Englishmen, noble in their want of sense, scarce one
out of four remained for the cowards to shoot down.
"Cross the rhaine," they shouted out, "cross the
rhaine, and coom within rache:" but the other mongrel Britons, with a mongrel at their head, found it
pleasanter to shoot men who could not shoot in answer,
than to meet the chance of mischief from strong arms,
and stronger hearts.

The last scene of this piteous play was acting, just
as I rode up. Broad daylight, and upstanding sun,
winnowing fog from the eastern hills, and spreading
the moors with freshness; all along the dykes they
shone, glistened on the willow-trunks, and touched the
banks with a hoary grey. But alas, those banks were
touched more deeply with a gory red, and strewn with

fallen trunks, more woeful than the wreck of trees; while howling, cursing, yelling, and the loathsome reek of carnage, drowned the scent of new-mown hay, and the carol of the lark.

Then the cavalry of the King, with their horses at full speed, dashed from either side upon the helpless mob of countrymen. A few pikes feebly levelled met them; but they shot the pikemen, drew swords, and helter-skelter leaped into the shattered and scattering mass. Right and left, they hacked and hewed; I could hear the snapping of scythes beneath them, and see the flash of their sweeping swords. How it must end was plain enough, even to one like myself, who had never beheld such a battle before. But Winnie led me away to the left; and as I could not help the people, neither stop the slaughter, but found the cannon-bullets coming very rudely nigh me, I was only too glad to follow her.

## CHAPTER XIII.

THAT faithful creature, whom I began to admire as if she were my own (which is no little thing for a man to say of another man's horse), stopped in front of a low black shed, such as we call a "linhay." And here she uttered a little greeting, in a subdued and softened voice, hoping to obtain an answer, such as her master was wont to give in a cheery manner. Receiving no reply, she entered; and I (who could scarce keep up with her, poor Kickums being weary) leaped from his back, and followed. There I found her sniffing gently, but with great emotion, at the body of Tom Faggus. A corpse poor Tom appeared to be, if ever there was one in this world; and I turned away, and felt unable to keep altogether from weeping. But the mare either could not understand, or else would not believe it. She reached her long neck forth, and felt him with her under lip, passing it over his skin as softly as a mother would do to an infant; and then she looked up at me again; as much as to say, "he is all right."

Upon this I took courage, and handled poor Tom;

which being young I had feared at first to do. He
groaned very feebly, as I raised him up; and there
was the wound, a great savage one (whether from
pike-thrust or musket-ball), gaping and welling in his
right side, from which a piece seemed to be torn away.
I bound it up with some of my linen, so far as I knew
how; just to stanch the flow of blood, until we could
get a doctor. Then I gave him a little weak brandy
and water, which he drank with the greatest eagerness,
and made sign to me for more of it. But not knowing
how far it was right to give cordial under the circumstances, I handed him unmixed water that time;
thinking that he was too far gone to perceive the
difference. But herein I wronged Tom Faggus; for
he shook his head and frowned at me. Even at the
door of death, he would not drink what Adam drank:
by whom came death into the world. So I gave him
a little more eau-de-vie, and he took it most sub-
missively.

After that, he seemed better, and a little colour
came into his cheeks; and he looked at Winnie and
knew her; and would have her nose in his clammy hand,
though I thought it not good for either of them. With
the stay of my arm, he sate upright, and faintly looked
about him; as if at the end of a violent dream, too
much for his power of mind. Then he managed to
whisper, " Is Winnie hurt? "

" As sound as a roach," I answered. " Then so am
I;" said he: " put me upon her back, John; she and
I die together."

Surprised as I was, at this fatalism (for so it appeared to me), of which he had often shown symptoms before (but I took them for mere levity), now I knew not what to do ; for it seemed to me a murderous thing to set such a man on horseback ; where he must surely bleed to death, even if he could keep the saddle. But he told me, with many breaks and pauses, that unless I obeyed his orders, he would tear off all my bandages, and accept no further aid from me.

While I was yet hesitating, a storm of horse at full gallop went by, tearing, swearing, bearing away all the country before them. Only a little pollard hedge kept us from their blood-shot eyes. " Now is the time," said my Cousin Tom, so far as I could make out his words ; " on their heels, I am safe, John, if I only have Winnie under me. Winnie and I die together."

Seeing this strong bent of his mind, stronger than any pains of death, I even did what his feeble eyes sometimes implored, and sometimes commanded. With a strong sash, from his own hot neck, bound and twisted, tight as wax, around his damaged waist, I set him upon Winnie's back, and placed his trembling feet in stirrups, with a band from one to other, under the good mare's body ; so that no swerve could throw him out : and then I said, " Lean forward Tom ; it will stop your hurt from bleeding." He leaned almost on the neck of the mare ; which, as I knew, must close the wound ; and the light of his eyes was quite different, and the pain of his forehead unstrung itself, as he felt the undulous readiness of her volatile paces under him.

"God bless you, John; I am safe," he whispered, fearing to open his lungs much: "who can come near my Winnie mare? A mile of her gallop is ten years of life. Look out for yourself, John Ridd." He sucked his lips, and the mare went off, as easy and swift as a swallow.

"Well," thought I, as I looked at Kickums, ignobly cropping a bit of grass, "I have done a very good thing, no doubt, and ought to be thankful to God for the chance. But as for getting away unharmed, with all these scoundrels about me, and only a foundered horse to trust in—good and spiteful as he is—upon the whole, I begin to think that I have made a fool of myself, according to my habit. No wonder Tom said, 'Look out for yourself!' I shall look out from a prison window, or perhaps even out of a halter. And then, what will Lorna think of me?"

Being in this wistful mood, I resolved to abide awhile, even where fate had thrown me; for my horse required good rest no doubt, and was taking it even while he cropped, with his hind legs far away stretched out, and his forelegs gathered under him, and his muzzle on the mole-hills; so that he had five supportings from his mother earth. Moreover the linhay itself was full of very ancient cow-dung; than which there is no balmier and more maiden soporific. Hence I resolved, upon the whole, though grieving about breakfast, to light a pipe, and go to sleep; or at least until the hot sun should arouse the flies.

I may have slept three hours, or four, or it might be even five—for I never counted time, while sleeping —when a shaking, more rude than the old landlady's, brought me back to the world again. I looked up, with a mighty yawn; and saw twenty, or so, of foot-soldiers.

"This linhay is not yours," I said, when they had quite aroused me, with tongue, and hand, and even sword-prick: "what business have you here, good fellows?"

"Business bad for you," said one; "and will lead you to the gallows."

"Do you wish to know the way out again?" I asked, very quietly; as being no braggadocio.

"We will show thee the way out," said one: "and the way out of the world," said another: "but not the way to heaven," said one chap, most unlikely to know it: and thereupon they all fell wagging, like a bed of clover leaves in the morning, at their own choice humour.

"Will you pile your arms outside," I said, "and try a bit of fair play with me?"

For I disliked these men sincerely, and was fain to teach them a lesson; they were so unchristian in appearance, having faces of a coffee colour, and dirty beards half over them. Moreover their dress was outrageous, and their address still worse. However I had wiser let them alone, as will appear afterwards. These savage-looking fellows laughed at the idea of my having any chance against some twenty of them: but I knew that the place was in my favour; for my part of it had been fenced off (for weaning a calf most likely), so that only two could come at me at once; and I must be very much out of training, if I could not manage two of them. Therefore I laid aside my carbine, and the two horse-pistols; and they with many coarse jokes at me went a little way outside, and set their weapons against the wall, and turned up their coat-sleeves jauntily; and then began to hesitate.

"Go you first, Bob," I heard them say; "you are the biggest man of us; and Dick the wrestler along of you. Us will back you up, boy."

"I'll warrant I'll draw the badger," said Bob; "and not a tooth will I leave him. But mind, for the honour of Kirke's lambs, every man stands me a glass of gin." Then he, and another man, made a rush, and the others came double-quick-march on their heels. But as Bob ran at me most stupidly, not even knowing how to place his hands, I caught him with my knuckles at the back of his neck, and with all the sway of my right arm sent him over the heads of his comrades. Meanwhile Dick the wrestler had grappled me, expecting to show off his art, of which indeed he had some small knowledge; but being quite of the light weights, in a second he was flying after his companion Bob.

Now these two men were hurt so badly, the light one having knocked his head against the lintel of the outer gate, that the rest had no desire to encounter the like misfortune. So they hung back whispering; and before they had made up their minds, I rushed into the midst of them. The suddenness and the weight of my onset took them wholly by surprise; and for once in their lives perhaps, Kirke's lambs were worthy of their name. Like a flock of sheep at a dog's attack, they fell away, hustling one another, and my only difficulty was not to tumble over them.

I had taken my carbine out with me, having a fondness for it; but the two horse-pistols I left behind; and therefore felt good title to take two from the magazine of the lambs. And with these, and my carbine, I leaped upon Kickums, who was now quite glad of a gallop again; and I bade adieu to that mongrel lot; yet they had the meanness to shoot at me. Thanking God for my deliverance (inasmuch as those men would have strung me up, from a pollard ash without trial, as I heard them tell one another, and saw the tree they had settled upon), I ventured to go rather fast on my way, with doubt and uneasiness urging me. And now my way was home again. Nobody could say but what I had done my duty, and rescued Tom (if he could be rescued) from the mischief into which his own perverseness and love of change (rather than deep religious convictions, to which our Annie ascribed his outbreak) had led, or seemed likely to lead him. And how proud would my mother be; and—ah well, there was nobody else to be proud of me now.

But while thinking these things, and desiring my breakfast, beyond any power of describing, and even beyond my remembrance, I fell into another fold of lambs, from which there was no exit. These, like true crusaders, met me, swaggering very heartily, and with their barrels of cider set, like so many cannon, across the road, over against a small hostel.

"We have won the victory, my lord king, and we mean to enjoy it. Down from thy horse, and have a stoup of cider, thou big rebel."

"No rebel am I. My name is John Ridd. I belong to the side of the King: and I want some breakfast."

These fellows were truly hospitable; that much I will say for them. Being accustomed to Arab ways, they could toss a grill, or fritter, or the inner meaning of an egg, into any form they pleased, comely and very good to eat; and it led me to think of Annie. So I made the rarest breakfast any man might hope for, after all his troubles; and getting on with these brown fellows better than could be expected, I craved permission to light a pipe, if not disagreeable. Hearing this, they roared at me, with a superior laughter, and asked me, whether or not, I knew the tobacco-leaf from the chick-weed; and when I was forced to answer no, not having gone into the subject, but being content with anything brown, they clapped me on the back and swore they had never seen any one like me. Upon the whole, this pleased me much; for I do not wish to be taken always, as of the common pattern: and so we smoked admirable tobacco—for they would not have any of mine, though very courteous concerning it—and I was beginning to understand a little of what they

told me; when up came those confounded lambs, who
had shown more tail than head to me, in the linhay,
as I mentioned.

Now these men upset everything. Having been
among wrestlers so much as my duty compelled me to
be, and having learned the necessity of the rest which
follows the conflict, and the right of discussion which
all people have who pay their sixpence to enter; and
how they obtrude this right, and their wisdom, upon
the man who has laboured, until he forgets all the
work he did, and begins to think that they did it;
having some knowledge of this sort of thing, and the
flux of minds swimming in liquor, I foresaw a brawl,
as plainly as if it were Bear Street in Barnstaple.

And a brawl there was, without any error, except of
the men who hit their friends, and those who defended
their enemies. My partners in breakfast and beer-can
swore that I was no prisoner, but the best and most
loyal subject, and the finest-hearted fellow they had
ever the luck to meet with. Whereas the men from
the linhay swore that I was a rebel miscreant; and
have me they would, with a rope's-end ready, in spite
of every [violent language] who had got drunk at my
expense, and been misled by my [strong word] lies.

While this fight was going on (and its mere occur-
rence shows, perhaps, that my conversation in those
days was not entirely despicable—else why should my
new friends fight for me, when I had paid for the ale,
and therefore won the wrong tense of gratitude?), it
was in my power at any moment to take horse and go.

And this would have been my wisest plan, and a very great saving of money; but somehow I felt as if it would be a mean thing to slip off so. Even while I was hesitating, and the men were breaking each other's heads, a superior officer rode up, with his sword drawn, and his face on fire.

"What, my lambs, my lambs!" he cried, smiting with the flat of his sword; "is this how you waste my time and my purse, when you ought to be catching a hundred prisoners, worth ten pounds apiece to me? Who is this young fellow we have here? Speak up, sirrah; what are thou, and how much will thy good mother pay for thee?"

"My mother will pay nought for me," I answered; while the lambs fell back, and glowered at one another: "so please your worship, I am no rebel; but an honest farmer, and well-proved of loyalty."

"Ha, ha; a farmer art thou? Those fellows always pay the best. Good farmer, come to yon barren tree; thou shalt make it fruitful."

Colonel Kirke made a sign to his men, and before I could think of resistance, stout new ropes were flung around me; and with three men on either side I was led along very painfully. And now I saw, and repented deeply of my careless folly, in stopping with those boon-companions, instead of being far away. But the newness of their manners to me, and their mode of regarding the world (differing so much from mine own), as well as the flavour of their tobacco, had made me quite forget my duty to the farm and to myself.

Yet methought they would be tender to me, after all
our speeches: how then was I disappointed, when the
men who had drunk my beer, drew on those grievous
ropes, twice as hard as the men I had been at strife
with! Yet this may have been from no ill will; but
simply that having fallen under suspicion of laxity,
they were compelled, in self-defence, now to be over-
zealous.

Nevertheless, however pure and godly might be
their motives, I beheld myself in a grievous case, and
likely to get the worst of it. For the face of the
Colonel was hard and stern as a block of bogwood oak;
and though the men might pity me and think me
unjustly executed, yet they must obey their orders, or
themselves be put to death. Therefore I addressed
myself to the Colonel, in a most ingratiating manner;
begging him not to sully the glory of his victory, and
dwelling upon my pure innocence, and even good service to our lord the King. But Colonel Kirke only
gave command that I should be smitten in the mouth;
which office Bob, whom I had flung so hard out of the
linhay, performed with great zeal and efficiency. But
being aware of the coming smack, I thrust forth a
pair of teeth; upon which the knuckles of my good
friend made a melancholy shipwreck.

It is not in my power to tell half the thoughts that
moved me, when we came to the fatal tree, and saw
two men hanging there already, as innocent perhaps as
I was, and henceforth entirely harmless. Though
ordered by the Colonel to look stedfastly upon them, I

could not bear to do so : upon which he called me a paltry coward, and promised my breeches to any man who would spit upon my countenance. This vile thing Bob, being angered perhaps by the smarting wound of his knuckles, bravely stepped forward to do for me, trusting no doubt to the rope I was led with. But, unluckily as it proved for him, my right arm was free for a moment ; and therewith I dealt him such a blow, that he never spake again. For this thing I have often grieved ; but the provocation was very sore to the pride of a young man ; and I trust that God has forgiven me. At the sound and sight of that bitter stroke, the other men drew back ; and Colonel Kirke, now black in the face with fury and vexation, gave orders for to shoot me, and cast me into the ditch hard by. The men raised their pieces, and pointed at me, waiting for the word to fire ; and I being quite overcome by the hurry of these events, and quite unprepared to die yet, could only think all upside down about Lorna, and my mother, and wonder what each would say to it. I spread my hands before my eyes, not being so brave as some men ; and hoping, in some foolish way, to cover my heart with my elbows. I heard the breath of all around, as if my skull were a sounding-board ; and knew even how the different men were fingering their triggers. And a cold sweat broke all over me, as the Colonel, prolonging his enjoyment, began slowly to say, " Fire."

But while he was yet dwelling on the " F," the hoofs of a horse dashed out on the road, and horse and horse-

man flung themselves betwixt me and the gun-muzzles.
So narrowly was I saved that one man could not check
his trigger : his musket went off, and the ball struck
the horse on the withers, and scared him exceedingly.
He began to lash out with his heels all around, and the
Colonel was glad to keep clear of him ; and the men
made excuse to lower their guns, not really wishing to
shoot me.

"How now, Captain Stickles?" cried Kirke, the
more angry because he had shown his cowardice ;
"dare you, sir, to come betwixt me and my lawful
prisoner ?"

"Nay, hearken one moment, Colonel," replied my
old friend Jeremy ; and his damaged voice was the
sweetest sound I had heard for many a day ; "for your
own sake hearken." He looked so full of momentous
tidings, that Colonel Kirke made a sign to his men,
not to shoot me till further orders ; and then he went
aside with Stickles, so that in spite of all my anxiety
I could not catch what passed between them. But I
fancied that the name of the Lord Chief-Justice
Jeffreys was spoken more than once, and with emphasis
and deference.

"Then I leave him in your hands, Captain Stickles,"
said Kirke at last, so that all might hear him ; and
though the news was so good for me, the smile of
baffled malice made his dark face look most hideous ;
"and I shall hold you answerable for the custody of
this prisoner."

"Colonel Kirke, I will answer for him," Master

Stickles replied, with a grave bow, and one hand on his breast: "John Ridd, you are my prisoner. Follow me, John Ridd."

Upon that, those precious lambs flocked away, leaving the rope still around me ; and some were glad, and some were sorry, not to see me swinging. Being free of my arms again, I touched my hat to Colonel Kirke, as became his rank and experience ; but he did not condescend to return my short salutation, having espied in the distance a prisoner, out of whom he might make money.

I wrung the hand of Jeremy Stickles, for his truth and goodness; and he almost wept (for since his wound he had been a weakened man) as he answered, "Turn for turn, John. You saved my life from the Doones ; and by the mercy of God, I have saved you from a far worse company. Let your sister Annie know it."

## CHAPTER XIV.

Now Kickums was not like Winnie, any more than a man is like a woman; and so he had not followed my fortunes, except at his own distance. No doubt but what he felt a certain interest in me; but his interest was not devotion; and man might go his way and be hanged, rather than horse would meet hardship. Therefore seeing things to be bad, and his master involved in trouble, what did this horse do but start for the ease and comfort of Plover's Barrows, and the plentiful ration of oats abiding in his own manger? For this I do not blame him. It is the manner of mankind.

But I could not help being very uneasy at the thought of my mother's discomfort and worry, when she should spy this good horse coming home, without any master, or rider, and I almost hoped that he might be caught, (although he was worth at least twenty pounds), by some of the King's troopers, rather than find his way home, and spread distress among our people. Yet, knowing his nature, I doubted if any could catch, or catching would keep him.

Jeremy Stickles assured me, as we took the road to
Bridgewater, that the only chance for my life (if I still
refused to fly) was to obtain an order forthwith, for
my dispatch to London, as a suspected person indeed,
but not found in open rebellion, and believed to be
under the patronage of the great Lord Jeffreys.
"For," said he, "in a few hours' time, you would fall
into the hands of Lord Feversham, who has won this
fight, without seeing it, and who has returned to bed
again, to have his breakfast more comfortably. Now
he may not be quite so savage perhaps as Colonel Kirke,
nor find so much sport in gibbeting; but he is equally
pitiless, and his price no doubt would be higher."

"I will pay no price whatever," I answered;
"neither will I fly. An hour agone I would have
fled for the sake of my mother, and the farm. But
now that I have been taken prisoner, and my name is
known; if I fly, the farm is forfeited; and my mother
and sister must starve. Moreover, I have done no
harm; I have borne no weapons against the King, nor
desired the success of his enemies. I like not that the
son of a bona-roba should be King of England; neither
do I count the papists any worse than we are. If they
have aught to try me for, I will stand my trial."

"Then to London thou must go, my son. There is
no such thing as trial here: we hang the good folk
without it, which saves them much anxiety. But
quicken thy step, good John; I have influence with
Lord Churchill, and we must contrive to see him,
ere the foreigner falls to work again. Lord Churchill

is a man of sense, and imprisons nothing but his money."

We were lucky enough to find this nobleman, who has since become so famous by his foreign victories. He received us with great civility; and looked at me with much interest, being a tall and fine young man himself; but not to compare with me in size; although far better favoured. I liked his face well enough; but thought there was something false about it. He put me a few keen questions, such as a man not assured of honesty might have found hard to answer; and he stood in a very upright attitude, making the most of his figure.

I saw nothing to be proud of, at the moment, in this interview; but since the great Duke of Marlborough rose to the top of glory, I have tried to remember more about him than my conscience quite backs up. How should I know that this man would be foremost of our kingdom, in five-and-twenty years or so; and not knowing, why should I heed him, except for my own pocket? Nevertheless, I have been so cross-questioned—far worse than by young Lord Churchill—about His Grace the Duke of Marlborough, and what he said to me, and what I said then, and how His Grace replied to that, and whether he smiled like another man, or screwed up his lips like a button (as our parish tailor said of him), and whether I knew from the turn of his nose that no Frenchman could stand before him; all these inquiries have worried me so, ever since the battle of Blenheim, that if tailors would only print upon waistcoats, I would give double price for a vest bearing this inscription, "No information can be given about the Duke of Marlborough."

Now this good Lord Churchill—for one might call him good, by comparison with the very bad people around him—granted without any long hesitation the order for my safe deliverance to the Court of King's Bench at Westminster; and Stickles, who had to report in London, was empowered to convey me, and made answerable for producing me. This arrangement would have been entirely to my liking, although the time of year was bad for leaving Plover's Barrows so; but no man may quite choose his times, and on the whole I would have been quite content to visit London, if my mother could be warned that nothing was amiss with me, only a mild, and as one might say, nominal captivity. And to prevent her anxiety, I did my best to send a letter through good Serjeant Bloxham, of whom I heard as quartered with Dumbarton's regiment at Chedzuy. But that regiment was away in pursuit; and I was forced to entrust my letter to a man who said that he knew him, and accepted a shilling to see to it.

For fear of any unpleasant change, we set forth at once for London; and truly thankful may I be, that God in his mercy spared me the sight of the cruel and bloody work with which the whole country reeked and howled during the next fortnight. I have heard things that set my hair on end, and made me loathe good meat for days; but I make a point of setting down only the things which I saw done; and in this particular case, not many will quarrel with my decision. Enough, therefore, that we rode on (for Stickles had found me a horse at last) as far as Wells, where we slept that night; and being joined in the morning by several troopers and orderlies, we made a slow but safe journey to London, by way of Bath and Reading.

The sight of London warmed my heart with various emotions, such as a cordial man must draw from the heart of all humanity. Here there are quick ways and manners, and the rapid sense of knowledge, and the power of understanding, ere a word be spoken. Whereas at Oare, you must say a thing, three times, very slowly, before it gets inside the skull of the good man you are addressing. And yet we are far more clever there, than in any parish for fifteen miles.

But what moved me most, when I saw again the noble oil and tallow of the London lights, and the dripping torches at almost every corner, and the handsome sign-boards, was the thought that here my Lorna lived, and walked, and took the air, and perhaps thought now and then of the old days in the good farm-house. Although I would make no approach to her, any more than she had done to me (upon which grief I have not dwelt, for fear of seeming selfish), yet there must be some large chance, or the little chance might be enlarged, of falling in with the maiden somehow, and learning how her mind was set. If against me, all should be over. I was not the man to sigh and cry for love, like a Romeo: none should even guess my grief, except my sister Annie.

But if Lorna loved me still—as in my heart of hearts I hoped—then would I for no one care, except her own delicious self. Rank and title, wealth and grandeur, all should go to the winds, before they scared me from my own true love.

Thinking thus, I went to bed in the centre of London town; and was bitten so grievously by creatures, whose name is "legion," mad with the delight of getting a wholesome farmer among them, that verily I was ashamed to walk in the Courtly parts of the town next day, having lumps upon my face of the size of a pickling walnut. The landlord said that this was nothing; and that he expected, in two days at the utmost, a very fresh young Irishman, for whom they would all forsake me. Nevertheless, I declined to wait, unless he could find me a hayrick to sleep in; for the insects of grass only tickle. He assured me that no hayrick could now be found in London; upon which I was forced to leave him, and with mutual esteem we parted.

The next night I had better luck, being introduced to a decent widow, of very high Scotch origin. That house was swept and garnished so, that not a bit was left to eat, for either man or insect. The change of air having made me hungry, I wanted something after supper; being quite ready to pay for it, and showing my purse as a symptom. But the face of Widow MacAlister, when I proposed to have some more food, was a thing to be drawn (if it could be drawn further) by our new carickaturist.

Therefore I left her also ; for liefer would I be eaten
myself, than have nothing to. eat ; and so I came back
to my old furrier; the which was a thoroughly hearty
man, and welcomed me to my room again, with two
shillings added to the rent, in the joy of his heart at
seeing me.   Being under parole to Master Stickles, I
only went out betwixt certain hours ; because I was
accounted as liable to be called upon ; for what purpose I knew not ; but hoped it might be a good one.
I felt it a loss, and a hinderance to me, that I was so
bound to remain at home during the session of the
courts of law ; for thereby the chance of ever beholding
Lorna was very greatly contracted; if not altogether
annihilated.   For these were the very hours, in which
the people of fashion, and the high world, were wont
to appear to the rest of mankind, so as to encourage
them.   And of course by this time, the Lady Lorna
was high among people of fashion, and was not
likely to be seen out of fashionable hours.   It is true
that there were some places of expensive entertain-
ment, at which the better sort of mankind might be
seen and studied, in their hours of relaxation, by those
of the lower order, who could pay sufficiently.   But
alas, my money was getting low ; and the privilege of
seeing my betters was more and more denied to me, as
my cash drew shorter.   For a man must have a good
coat at least, and the pockets not wholly empty, before
he can look at those whom God has created for his
ensample.

Hence, and from many other causes—part of which

was my own pride—it happened that I abode in London, betwixt a month and five weeks' time, ere ever I saw Lorna. It seemed unfit that I should go, and waylay her, and spy on her, and say (or mean to say), "Lo, here is your poor faithful farmer, a man who is unworthy of you, by means of his common birth; and yet who dares to crawl across your path, that you may pity him. For God's sake, show a little pity, though you may not feel it." Such behaviour might be comely in a love-lorn boy, a page to some grand princess; but I, John Ridd, would never stoop to the lowering of love so.

Nevertheless I heard of Lorna, from my worthy furrier, almost every day, and with a fine exaggeration. This honest man was one of those who in virtue of their trade, and nicety of behaviour, are admitted into noble life, to take measurements, and show patterns. And while so doing, they contrive to acquire what is to the English mind at once the most important and most interesting of all knowledge,—the science of being able to talk about the titled people. So my furrier (whose name was Ramsack), having to make robes for peers, and cloaks for their wives and otherwise, knew the great folk, sham or real, as well as he knew a fox or skunk from a wolverine skin.

And when, with some fencing and foils of inquiry, I hinted about Lady Lorna Dugal, the old man's face became so pleasant that I knew her birth must be wondrous high. At this, my own countenance fell, I suppose,—for the better she was born, the harder she

would be to marry—and mistaking my object, he took
me up:

"Perhaps you think, Master Ridd, that because her
ladyship, Lady Lorna Dugal, is of Scottish origin,
therefore her birth is not as high as of our English
nobility. If you think so, you are wrong, sir. She
comes not of the sandy Scotch race, with high cheek-
bones, and raw shoulder-blades, who set up pillars in
their court-yards. But she comes of the very best
Scotch blood, descended from the Norsemen. Her
mother was of the very noblest race, the Lords of
Lorne; higher even than the great Argyle, who has
lately made a sad mistake, and paid for it most sadly.
And her father was descended from the King Dugal,
who fought against Alexander the Great. No, no,
Master Ridd; none of your promiscuous blood, such
as runs in the veins of half our modern peerage."

"Why should you trouble yourself about it, Master
Ramsack?" I replied: "let them all go their own
ways: and let us all look up to them, whether they
come by hook or crook."

"Not at all, not at all, my lad. That is not the
way to regard it. We look up at the well-born men;
and sideways at the base-born."

"Then we are all base-born ourselves. I will look
up to no man, except for what himself has done."

"Come, Master Ridd, you might be lashed from
Newgate to Tyburn and back again, once a week, for a
twelvemonth, if some people heard you. Keep your
tongue more close, young man; or here you lodge no

longer; albeit I love your company, which smells to me of the hay-field. Ah, I have not seen a hay-field for nine-and-twenty years, John Ridd. The cursed moths keep me at home, every day of the summer."

"Spread your furs on the haycocks," I answered very boldly: "the indoor moth cannot abide the presence of the outdoor ones."

"Is it so?" he answered: "I never thought of that before. And yet I have known such strange things happen in the way of fur, that I can well believe it. If you only knew, John Ridd, the way in which they lay their eggs, and how they work tail-foremost"——

"Tell me nothing of the kind," I replied, with equal confidence: "they cannot work tail-foremost; and they have no tails to work with." For I knew a little about grubs, and the ignorance concerning them, which we have no right to put up with. However not to go into that (for the argument lasted a fortnight; and then was only come so far as to begin again), Master Ramsack soon convinced me of the things I knew already; the excellence of Lorna's birth, as well as her lofty place at Court, and beauty, and wealth, and elegance. But all these only made me sigh, and wish that I were born to them.

From Master Ramsack I discovered that the nobleman, to whose charge Lady Lorna had been committed, by the Court of Chancery, was Earl Brandir of Lochawe, her poor mother's uncle. For the Countess of Dugal was daughter, and only child, of the last Lord

Lorne, whose sister had married Sir Ensor Doone ; while he himself had married the sister of Earl Brandir. This nobleman had a country house near the village of Kensington ; and here his niece dwelled with him, when she was not in attendance on Her Majesty the Queen, who had taken a liking to her. Now since the King had begun to attend the celebration of mass, in the chapel at Whitehall—and not at Westminster Abbey, as our gossips had averred—he had given order that the doors should be thrown open, so that all who could make interest to get into the antechamber, might see this form of worship. Master Ramsack told me that Lorna was there, almost every Sunday ; their Majesties being most anxious to have the presence of all the nobility of the Catholic persuasion, so as to make a goodly show. And the worthy furrier, having influence with the door-keepers, kindly obtained admittance for me, one Sunday, into the antechamber.

Here I took care to be in waiting, before the Royal procession entered ; but being unknown, and of no high rank, I was not allowed to stand forward among the better people, but ordered back into a corner very dark and dismal ; the verger remarking, with a grin, that I could see over all other heads, and must not set my own so high. Being frightened to find myself among so many people of great rank and gorgeous apparel, I blushed at the notice drawn upon me by this uncourteous fellow ; and silently fell back into the corner by the hangings.

You may suppose that my heart beat high, when the King and Queen appeared, and entered, followed by the Duke of Norfolk bearing the sword of state, and by several other noblemen, and people of repute. Then the doors of the chapel were thrown wide open; and though I could only see a little, being in the corner so, I thought that it was beautiful. Bowers of rich silk were there, and plenty of metal shining, and polished wood with lovely carving, flowers too of the noblest kind, and candles made by somebody who had learned how to clarify tallow. This last thing amazed me more than all; for our dips never will come clear: melt the mutton-fat how you will. And methought that this hanging of flowers about was a very pretty thing; for if a man can worship God best of all beneath a tree, as the natural instinct is; surely when by fault of climate, the tree would be too apt to drip, the very best make-believe is to have enough and to spare of flowers; which to the dwellers in London seem to have grown on the tree denied them.

Be that as it may; when the King and Queen crossed the threshold, a mighty flourish of trumpets arose, and a waving of banners. The Knights of the Garter (who-ever they be) were to attend that day in state; and some went in, and some stayed out, and it made me think of the difference betwixt the ewes and the wethers. For the ewes will go wherever you lead them; but the wethers will not, having strong opinions, and meaning to abide by them. And one man I noticed was of the wethers, to wit the Duke of Norfolk; who stopped outside with the sword of state, like a beadle with a rapping-rod. This has taken more to tell than the time it happened in. For after all the men were gone, some to this side, some to that, according to their feelings, a number of ladies, beautifully dressed, being of the Queen's retinue, began to enter, and were stared at three times as much as the men had been. And indeed they were worth looking at (which men never are to my ideas, when they trick themselves with gew-gaws), but none was so well worth eye-service, as my own beloved Lorna. She entered modestly and shyly, with her eyes upon the ground, knowing the rudeness of the gallants, and the large sum she was priced at. Her dress was of the purest white, very sweet and simple, without a line of ornament, for she herself adorned it. The way she walked, and touched her skirt (rather than seemed to hold it up), with a white hand bearing one red rose, this, and her stately supple neck, and the flowing of her hair, would show, at a distance of a hundred yards, that she could be none but Lorna Doone. Lorna Doone of my early love; in the days when she blushed for her name before me, by reason of dishonesty; but now the Lady Lorna Dugal; as far beyond reproach, as above my poor affection. All my heart, and all my mind, gathered themselves upon her. Would she see me, or would she pass? Was there in-stinct in our love?

By some strange chance, she saw me. Or was it through our destiny? While with eyes kept sedulously on the marble floor, to shun the weight of admiration

thrust too boldly on them, while with shy quick steps
she passed, some one (perhaps with purpose) trod on
the skirt of her clear white dress,—with the quickness
taught her by many a scene of danger, she looked up;
and her eyes met mine.

As I gazed upon her, steadfastly, yearningly, yet
with some reproach, and more of pride than humility,
she made me one of the Courtly bows, which I do so
much detest; yet even that was sweet and graceful,
when my Lorna did it. But the colour of her pure
clear cheeks was nearly as deep as that of my own,
when she went on for the religious work. And the
shining of her eyes was owing to an unpaid debt of
tears.

Upon the whole I was satisfied. Lorna had seen
me; and had not (according to the phrase of the high
world then) even tried to "cut" me. Whether this
low phrase is born of their own stupid meanness, or
whether it comes of necessity exercised on a man
without money; I know not and I care not. But one
thing I know right well; any man who "cuts" a man
(except for vice or meanness) should be quartered
without quarter.

All these proud thoughts rose within me, as the lovely
form of Lorna went inside, and was no more seen. And
then I felt how coarse I was; how apt to think strong
thoughts, and so on; without brains to bear me out:
even as a hen's egg layed, without enough of lime, and
looking only a poor jelly.

Nevertheless, I waited on; as my usual manner is.

For to be beaten, while running away, is ten times worse than to face it out, and take it, and have done with it. So at least, I have, always found, because of reproach of conscience : and all the things those clever people carried on inside, at large, made me long for our Parson Bowden that he might know how to act.

While I stored up, in my memory, enough to keep our parson going through six pipes on a Saturday night—to have it as right as could be next day—a lean man with a yellow beard, too thin for a good Catholic (which religion always fattens), came up to me, working sideways, in the manner of a female crab.

"This is not to my liking," I said : "if aught thou hast, speak plainly; while they make that horrible noise inside."

Nothing had this man to say; but with many sighs, because I was not of the proper faith, he took my reprobate hand to save me; and with several religious tears, looked up at me, and winked with one eye. Although the skin of my palms was thick, I felt a little suggestion there, as of a gentle leaf in spring, fearing to seem too forward. I paid the man; and he went happy; for the standard of heretical silver is purer than that of the Catholics.

Then I lifted up my little billet; and in that dark corner read it, with a strong rainbow of colours coming from the angled light. And in mine eyes there was enough to make rainbow of strongest sun, as my anger clouded off.

Not that it began so well; but that in my heart I

knew (ere three lines were through me) that I was with all heart loved—and beyond that, who may need? The darling of my life went on, as if I were of her own rank, or even better than she was; and she dotted her " i's," and crossed her " t's," as if I were at least a school-master. All of it was done in pencil; but as plain as plain could be. In my coffin it shall lie, with my ring, and something else. Therefore will I not expose it to every man who buys this book, and haply thinks that he has bought me to the bottom of my heart. Enough for men of gentle birth (who never are inquisitive) that my love told me, in her letter, just to come and see her.

I ran away, and could not stop. To behold even her, at the moment, would have dashed my fancy's joy. Yet my brain was so amiss, that I must do something. Therefore to the river Thames, with all speed, I hurried ; and keeping all my best clothes on (indued for sake of Lorna), into the quiet stream I leaped, and swam as far as London Bridge, and ate noble dinner afterwards.

## CHAPTER XV.

ALTHOUGH a man may be as simple as the flowers of
the field; knowing when, but scarcely why, he closes to
the bitter wind; and feeling why, but scarcely when,
he opens to the genial sun; yet without his questing
much into the capsule of himself—to do which is a
misery—he may have a general notion how he happens
to be getting on.

I felt myself to be getting on better than at any
time since the last wheat-harvest, as I took the lane
to Kensington upon the Monday evening. For although
no time was given in my Lorna's letter, I was not
inclined to wait more than decency required. And
though I went and watched the house, decency would
not allow me to knock on the Sunday evening, especially when I found at the corner that his lordship was
at home.

The lanes and fields between Charing Cross and the
village of Kensington, are, or were at that time, more
than reasonably infested with footpads and with highwaymen. However my stature and holly club kept

these fellows from doing more than casting sheeps' eyes at me. For it was still broad daylight, and the view of the distant villages, Chelsea, Battersea, Tyburn, and others, as well as a few large houses, among the hams and towards the river, made it seem less lonely. Therefore I sang a song in the broadest Exmoor dialect, which caused no little amazement in the minds of all who met me.

When I came to Earl Brandir's house, my natural modesty forbade me to appear at the door for guests; therefore I went to the entrance for servants and retainers. Here, to my great surprise, who should come and let me in, but little Gwenny Carfax, whose very existence had almost escaped my recollection. Her mistress, no doubt, had seen me coming, and sent her to save trouble. But when I offered to kiss Gwenny, in my joy and comfort to see a farmhouse face again, she looked ashamed, and turned away, and would hardly speak to me.

I followed her to a little room, furnished very daintily; and there she ordered me to wait, in a most ungracious manner. " Well," thought I, "if the mistress and the maid are alike in temper, better it had been for me to abide at Master Ramsack's." But almost ere my thought was done, I heard the light quick step which I knew as well as 'Watch,' my dog, knew mine; and my breast began to tremble, like the trembling of an arch, ere the keystone is put in.

Almost ere I hoped—for fear and hope were so entangled, that they hindered one another—the velvet

hangings of the doorway parted, with a little doubt,
and then a good face put on it. Lorna, in her
perfect beauty, stood before the crimson folds, and her
dress was all pure white, and her cheeks were rosy
pink, and her lips were scarlet.

Like a maiden, with skill and sense checking violent
impulse, she stayed there for one moment only, just to
be admired: and then like a woman, she came to me,
seeing how alarmed I was. The hand she offered me I
took, and raised it to my lips with fear, as a thing too
good for me. "Is that all?" she whispered; and
then her eyes gleamed up at me: and in another
instant, she was weeping on my breast.

"Darling Lorna, Lady Lorna," I cried, in astonishment; yet unable but to keep her closer to me, and
closer; "surely, though I love you so, this is not as it
should be."

"Yes it is, John. Yes, it is. Nothing else should
ever be. Oh why have you behaved so?"

"I am behaving," I replied, "to the very best of
my ability. There is no other man in the world could
hold you so, without kissing you."

"Then why don't you do it, John?" asked Lorna,
looking up at me, with a flash of her old fun.

Now this matter, proverbially, is not for discussion,
and repetition. Enough that we said nothing more
than, "Oh John, how glad I am!" and "Lorna, Lorna,
Lorna!" for about five minutes. Then my darling
drew back proudly; with blushing cheeks, and tear-
bright eyes, she began to cross-examine me.

"Master John Ridd, you shall tell the truth, the whole truth, and nothing but the truth. I have been in Chancery, sir; and can detect a story. Now why have you never, for more than a twelvemonth, taken the smallest notice of your old friend, Mistress Lorna Doone?" Although she spoke in this lightsome manner, as if it made no difference, I saw that her quick heart was moving, and the flash of her eyes controuled.

"Simply for this cause," I answered, "that my old friend, and true love, took not the smallest heed of me. Nor knew I where to find her."

"What!" cried Lorna; and nothing more; being overcome with wondering; and much inclined to fall away, but for my assistance. I told her, over and over again, that not a single syllable of any message from her, or tidings of her welfare, had reached me, or any one of us, since the letter she left behind: except by soldiers' gossip.

"Oh, you poor dear John!" said Lorna, sighing at thought of my misery: "how wonderfully good of you, thinking of me as you must have done, not to marry that little plain thing (or perhaps I should say that lovely creature, for I have never seen her), Mistress Ruth—I forget her name; but something like a towel."

"Ruth Huckaback is a worthy maid;" I answered with some dignity: "and she alone of all our world, except indeed poor Annie, has kept her confidence in you, and told me not to dread your rank, but trust your heart, Lady Lorna."

"Then Ruth is my best friend," she answered, "and

is worthy of you, John. And now remember one thing, dear; if God should part us, as may be by nothing short of death, try to marry that little Ruth, when you cease to remember me. And now for the head-traitor. I have often suspected it: but she looks me in the face, and wishes—fearful things, which I cannot repeat."

With these words, she moved an implemeut such as I had not seen before, and which made a ringing noise at a serious distance. And before I had ceased wondering—for if such things go on, we might ring the church bells, while sitting in our back-kitchen—little Gwenny Carfax came, with a grave and sullen face.

"Gwenny," began my Lorna, in a tone of high rank and dignity: "go and fetch the letters which I gave you at various times, for dispatch to Mistress Ridd."

"How can I fetch them, when they are gone? It be no use for him to tell no lies "——

"Now, Gwenny, can you look at me?" I asked very sternly; for the matter was no joke to me, after a year's unhappiness.

"I don't want to look at 'ee. What should I look at a young man for, although he did offer to kiss me?"

I saw the spite and impudence of this last remark; and so did Lorna, although she could not quite refrain from smiling.

"Now, Gwenny, not to speak of that," said Lorna, very demurely: "if you thought it honest to keep the letters, was it honest to keep the money?"

At this the Cornish maiden broke into a rage of

honesty: "A putt the money by for 'ee. 'Ee shall have every farden of it." And so she flung out of the room.

"And, Gwenny," said Lorna very softly, following under the door-hangings; "if it is not honest to keep the money, it is not honest to keep the letters, which would have been worth more than any gold to those who were so kind to you. Your father shall know the whole, Gwenny, unless you tell the truth."

"Now, a will tell all the truth;" this strange maiden answered, talking to herself at least as much as to her mistress, while she went out of sight and hearing. And then I was so glad at having my own Lorna once again, cleared of all contempt for us, and true to me through all of it, that I would have forgiven Gwenny, for treason, or even forgery.

"I trusted her so much," said Lorna, in her old ill-fortuned way; "and look how she has deceived me! That is why I love you John (setting other things aside), because you never told me falsehood: and you never could, you know."

"Well, I am not so sure of that. I think I could tell any lie, to have you, darling, all my own."

"Yes. And perhaps it might be right. To other people besides us two. But you could not do it to me, John. You never could do it to me, you know."

Before I quite perceived my way to the bottom of this distinction—although beyond doubt a valid one—Gwenny came back with a leathern bag, and tossed it upon the table. Not a word did she vouchsafe to us; but stood there, looking injured.

"Go, and get your letters, John;" said Lorna very gravely; "or at least your mother's letters, made of messages to you. As for Gwenny, she shall go before Lord Justice Jeffreys." I knew that Lorna meant it not; but thought that the girl deserved a frightening; as indeed she did. But we both mistook the courage of this child of Cornwall. She stepped upon a little round thing, in the nature of a stool, such as I never had seen before, and thus delivered her sentiments.

"And you may take me, if you please, before the great Lord Jefferays. I have done no more than duty, though I did it crookedly, and told a heap of lies, for your sake. And pretty gratitude I gets."

"Much gratitude you have shown," replied Lorna, "to Master Ridd, for all his kindness and his goodness to you. Who was it that went down, at the peril of his life, and brought your father to you, when you had lost him for months and months? Who was it? Answer me, Gwenny?"

"Girt Jan Ridd;" said the handmaid, very sulkily.

"What made you treat me so, little Gwenny?" I asked, for Lorna would not ask lest the reply should vex me.

"Because 'ee be'est below her so. Her shanna' have a poor farmering chap, not even if her were a Carnishman. All her land, and all her birth—and who be you, I'd like to know?"

"Gwenny, you may go," said Lorna, reddening quiet anger; "and remember that you come not

near me for the next three days. It is the only
way to punish her," she continued to me, when the
maid was gone, in a storm of sobbing and weeping.
" Now for the next three days, she will scarcely touch
a morsel of food, and scarcely do a thing but cry.
Make up your mind to one thing, John; if you mean
to take me, for better for worse, you will have to take
Gwenny with me."

" I would take you with fifty Gwennies," said I,
" although every one of them hated me, which I do
not believe this little maid does, in the bottom of her
heart."

" No one can possibly hate you, John," she answered
very softly ; and I was better pleased with this, than
if she had called me the most noble and glorious man
in the kingdom.

After this, we spoke ot ourselves and the way
people would regard us, supposing that when Lorna
came to be her own free mistress (as she must do in
the course of time) she were to throw her rank aside,
and refuse her title, and caring not a fig for folk who
cared less than a fig-stalk for her, should shape her
mind to its native bent, and to my perfect happiness.
It was not my place to say much, lest I should appear
to use an improper and selfish influence. And of
course to all men of common sense, and to everybody
of middle age (who must know best what is good
for youth), the thoughts which my Lorna entertained
would be enough to prove her madness.

Not that we could not keep her well ; comfortably,

and with nice clothes, and plenty of flowers, and fruit, and landscape, and the knowledge of our neighbours' affairs, and their kind interest in our own. Still this would not be as if she were the owner of a county, and a haughty title; and able to lead the first men of the age, by her mind, and face, and money.

Therefore was I quite resolved not to have a word to say, while this young queen of wealth and beauty, and of noblemen's desire, made her mind up how to act for her purest happiness. But to do her justice, this was not the first thing she was thinking of; the test of her judgment was only this, "How will my love be happiest?"

"Now, John," she cried: for she was so quick that she always had my thoughts beforehand; "why will you be backward, as if you cared not for me? Do you dream that I am doubting? My mind has been made up, good John, that you must be my husband, for—well, I will not say how long, lest you should laugh at my folly. But I believe it was ever since you came, with your stockings off, and the loaches. Right early for me to make up my mind; but you know that you made up yours, John; and, of course, I knew it; and that had a great effect on me. Now, after all this age of loving, shall a trifle sever us?"

I told her that it was no trifle, but a most important thing, to abandon wealth, and honour, and the brilliance of high life, and be despised by every one for such abundant folly. Moreover that I should appear a knave, for taking advantage of her youth, and bound-

less generosity, and ruining (as men would say) a
noble maid by my selfishness. And I told her
outright, having worked myself up by my own conversation, that she was bound to consult her guardian ;
and that without his knowledge, I would come no more
to see her. Her flash of pride at these last words
made her look like an empress; and I was about to
explain myself better; but she put forth her hand, and
stopped me.

"I think that condition should rather have proceeded
from me. You are mistaken, Master Ridd, in supposing that I would think of receiving you in secret.
It was a different thing in Glen Doone, where all
except yourself were thieves, and when I was but a
simple child, and oppressed with constant fear. You
are quite right in threatening to visit me thus no
more ; but I think you might have waited for an
invitation, sir."

"And you are quite right, Lady Lorna, in pointing
out my presumption. It is a fault that must ever be
found in any speech of mine to you."

This I said so humbly, and not with any bitterness
—for I knew that I had gone too far—and made her
so polite a bow, that she forgave me in a moment, and
we begged each other's pardon.

"Now, will you allow me just to explain my own
view of this matter, John?" said she, once more my
darling. "It may be a very foolish view, but I shall
never change it. Please not to interrupt me, dear,
until you have heard me to the end. In the first place

it is quite certain that neither you, nor I, can be happy
without the other.    Then what stands between us?
Worldly position, and nothing else.    I have no more
education than you have, John Ridd: nay, and not so
much.    My birth and ancestry are not one whit more
pure than yours, although they may be better known.
Your descent from ancient freeholders, for five-and-
twenty generations of good, honest men, although you
bear no coat of arms, is better than the lineage of nine
proud English noblemen, out of every ten I meet with.
In manners, though your mighty strength, and hatred
of any meanness, sometimes break out in violence—
of which I must try to cure you, dear—in manners, if
kindness, and gentleness, and modesty are the true
things wanted, you are immeasurably above any of our
Court-gallants; who indeed have very little.    As for
difference.of religion, we allow for one another, neither
having been brought up in a bitterly pious manner."

Here, though the tears were in my eyes, at the
loving things love said of me, I could not help a little
laugh at the notion of any bitter piety being found
among the Doones; or even in mother, for that matter.
Lorna smiled, in her slyest manner, and went on
again:

"Now, you see, I have proved my point; there is
nothing between us but worldly position—if you can
defend me against the Doones, for which, I trow, I may
trust you.    And wordly position means wealth, and
title, and the right to be in great houses, and the
pleasure of being envied.    I have not been here for a

year, John, without learning something. Oh, I hate
it; how I hate it! Of all the people I know, there
are but two, besides my uncle, who do not either covet,
or detest me. And who are those two, think you?"

"Gwenny, for one," I answered.

"Yes, Gwenny, for one. And the Queen, for the
other. The one is too far below me (I mean, in her
own opinion), and the other too high above: As for the
women who dislike me, without having even heard my
voice, I simply have nothing to do with them. As for
the men who covet me, for my land and money, I
merely compare them with you, John Ridd; and all
thought of them is over. Oh, John, you must never
forsake me, however cross I am to you. I thought you
would have gone, just now; and though I would not
move to stop you, my heart would have broken."

"You don't catch me go in a hurry," I answered
very sensibly; "when the loveliest maiden in the
world, and the best, and the dearest loves me. All my·
fear of you is gone, darling Lorna, all my fear"——

"Is it possible you could fear me, John, after all we
have been through together? Now you promised not
to interrupt me; is this fair behaviour? Well, let me
see where I left off—oh, that my heart would have
broken. Upon that point, I will say no more, lest you
should grow conceited, John; if anything could make
you so. But I do assure you that half London—however upon that point also, I will check my power of
speech, lest you think me conceited. And now to put
aside all nonsense; though I have talked none for a

year, John, having been so unhappy; and now it is
such a relief to me "——

"Then talk it for an hour," said I; "and let me sit
and watch you. To me it is the very sweetest of all
sweetest wisdom."

"Nay, there is no time," she answered, glancing at
a jewelled timepiece, scarcely larger than an oyster,
which she drew from near her waist-band; and then
she pushed it away, in confusion, lest its wealth should
startle me. "My uncle will come home in less than
half-an-hour, dear: and you are not the one to take a
side-passage, and avoid him. I shall tell him that you
have been here; and that I mean you to come again."

As Lorna said this, with a manner as confident as
need be, I saw that she had learned in town the power
of her beauty, and knew that she could do with most
men aught she set her mind upon. And as she stood
there, flushed with pride and faith in her own loveliness, and radiant with the love itself, I felt that she
must do exactly as she pleased with every one. For
now, in turn, and elegance, and richness, and variety,
there was nothing to compare with her face, unless it
were her figure. Therefore I gave in, and said,

"Darling, do just what you please. Only make no
rogue of me."

For that she gave me the simplest, kindest, and
sweetest of all kisses : and I went down the great stairs
grandly; thinking of nothing else but that.

## CHAPTER XVI.

It would be hard for me to tell the state of mind in which I lived, for a long time after this. I put away from me all torment, and the thought of future cares, and the sight of difficulty; and to myself appeared, which means that I became, the luckiest of lucky fellows, since the world itself began. I thought not of the harvest even, nor of the men who would get their wages without having earned them, nor of my mother's anxiety, and worry about John Fry's great fatness (which was growing upon him), and how she would cry fifty times in a day, "Ah, if our John would only come home, how different everything would look!"

Although there were no soldiers now quartered at Plover's Barrows, all being busied in harassing the country, and hanging the people, where the rebellion had thriven most; my mother, having received from me a message containing my place of abode, contrived to send me, by the pack-horses, as fine a maund as need be of provisions, and money, and other comforts. Therein I found addressed to Colonel Jeremiah

Stickles, in Lizzie's best handwriting, half a side of
the dried deer's flesh, in which he rejoiced so greatly.
Also, for Lorna, a fine green goose, with a little salt
towards the tail, and new-laid eggs inside it, as well as
a bottle of brandied cherries, and seven, or it may have
been eight, pounds of fresh home-made butter. Moreover to myself there was a letter full of good advice,
excellently well expressed, and would have been of the
greatest value, if I had cared to read it. But I read
all about the farm affairs, and the man who had offered
himself to our Betty for the five pounds in her stocking; as well as the antics of Sally Snowe, and how she
had almost thrown herself at Parson Bowden's head
(old enough to be her grandfather), because on the
Sunday after the hanging of a Countisbury man, he
had preached a beautiful sermon about Christian love;
which Lizzie with her sharp eyes found to be the work
of good Bishop Ken. Also I read that the Doones
were quiet; the parishes round about having united to
feed them well through the harvest-time, so that after
the day's hard work, the farmers might go to bed at
night. And this plan had been found to answer well,
and to save much trouble on both sides: so that everybody wondered it had not been done before. But
Lizzie thought that the Doones could hardly be expected much longer to put up with it; and probably
would not have done so now, but for a little adversity;
to wit, that the famous Colonel Kirke had, in the most
outrageous manner, hanged no less than six of them,
who were captured among the rebels; for he said that

men of their rank and breeding, and above all of their religion, should have known better than to join ploughboys, and carters, and pickaxe-men, against our lord the King, and his holy holiness the Pope. This hanging of so many Doones caused some indignation, among people who were used to them ; and it seemed for a while to check the rest from any spirit of enterprise.

Moreover, I found from this same letter (which was pinned upon the knuckle of a leg of mutton, for fear of being lost in straw) that good Tom Faggus was at home again, and nearly cured of his dreadful wound ; but intended to go to war no more, only to mind his family. And it grieved him more than anything he ever could have imagined, that his duty to his family, and the strong power of his conscience, so totally forbade him to come up and see after me. For now his design was to lead a new life, and be in charity with all men. Many better men than he had been hanged, he saw no cause to doubt; but by the grace of God he hoped himself to cheat the gallows.

There was no further news of moment in this very clever letter, except that the price of horses' shoes was gone up again, though already twopence-farthing each ; and that Betty had broken her lover's head with the stocking full of money ; and then in the corner it was written that the distinguished man of war, and worshipful scholar, Master Bloxham, was now promoted to take the tolls, and catch all the rebels around our part.

Lorna was greatly pleased with the goose, and

the butter, and the brandied cherries; and the Earl
Brandir himself declared that he never tasted better
than those last, and would beg the young man from
the country to procure him instructions for making
them.   This nobleman, being as deaf as a post, and of
a very solid mind, could never be brought to understand the nature of my thoughts towards Lorna.   He
looked upon me as an excellent youth, who had
rescued the maiden from the Doones, whom he cordially
detested; and learning that I had thrown two of them
out of window (as the story was told him), he patted
me on the back, and declared that his doors would
ever be open to me, and that I could not come too
often.

I thought this very kind of his lordship, especially
as it enabled me to see my darling Lorna, not indeed
as often as I wished, but at any rate very frequently;
and as many times as modesty (ever my leading
principle) would in common conscience approve of.
And I made up my mind, that if ever I could help
Earl Brandir, it would be—as we say, when with
brandy and water—the "proudest moment of my
life," when I could fulfil the pledge.

And I soon was able to help Lord Brandir, as
I think, in two different ways; first of all as regarded
his mind, and then as concerned his body: and the
latter perhaps was the greatest service, at his time
of life.   But not to be too nice about that; let me tell
how these things were.

Lorna said to me one day, being in a state of

excitement—whereto she was over prone, when reft of my slowness to steady her—

"I will tell him, John: I must tell him, John. It is mean of me to conceal it."

I thought that she meant all about our love, which we had endeavoured thrice to drill into his fine old ears; but could not make him comprehend, without risk of bringing the house down: and so I said, "By all means, darling: have another try at it."

Lorna, however, looked at me—for her eyes told more than tongue—as much as to say, "Well you are a stupid. We agreed to let that subject rest." And then she saw that I was vexed at my own want of quickness; and so she spoke very kindly:

"I meant about his poor son, dearest; the son of his old age almost; whose loss threw him into that dreadful cold—for he went, without hat, to look for him—which ended in his losing the use of his dear old ears. I believe if we could only get him to Plover's Barrows for a month, he would be able to hear again. And look at his age! he is not much over seventy, John, you know; and I hope that you will be able to hear me, long after you are seventy, John."

"Well," said I; "God settles that. Or at any rate, he leaves us time to think about those questions, when we are over fifty. Now let me know what you want, Lorna. The idea of my being seventy! But you would still be beautiful."

"To the one who loves me," she answered, trying to make wrinkles in her pure bright forehead: "but

if you will have common sense, as you always will,
John, whether I wish it or otherwise—I want to know
whether I am bound, in honour, and in conscience, to
tell my dear and good old uncle what I know about
his son."

"First let me understand quite clearly," said I,
never being in a hurry, except when passion moves
me, "what his lordship thinks at present; and how
far his mind is urged with sorrow and anxiety." This
was not the first time we had spoken of the matter.

"Why, you know John well enough," she answered,
wondering at my coolness, "that my poor uncle still
believes that his one beloved son will come to light
and life again. He has made all arrangements accordingly : all his property is settled on that supposition. He knows that young Alan always was what
he calls a 'feckless neer-doo-weel;' but he loves him
all the more for that. He cannot believe that he will
die, without his son coming back to him; and he
always has a bedroom ready, and a bottle of Alan's
favourite wine cool from out the cellar; he has made
me work him a pair of slippers from the size of a
mouldy boot; and if he hears of a new tobacco—
much as he hates the smell of it—he will go to the
other end of London to get some for Alan, Now you
know how deaf he is; but if any one say 'Alan,'
even in the place outside the door, he will make
his courteous bow to the very highest visitor, and
be out there in a moment, and search the entire
passage, and yet let no one know it."

"It is a piteous thing," I said; for Lorna's eyes were full of tears.

"And he means me to marry him. It is the pet scheme of his life. I am to grow more beautiful, and more highly taught, and graceful; until it pleases Alan to come back, and demand me. Can you understand this matter, John? Or do you think my uncle mad?"

"Lorna, I should be mad myself, to call any other man mad, for hoping."

"Then will you tell me what to do? It makes me very sorrowful. For I know that Alan Brandir lies below the sod in Doone-valley."

"And if you tell his father," I answered softly, but clearly, "in a few weeks he will lie below the sod in London: at least if there is any."

"Perhaps you are right, John," she replied: "to lose hope must be a dreadful thing, when one is turned of seventy. Therefore I will never tell him."

The other way in which I managed to help the good Earl Brandir, was of less true moment to him; but as he could not know of the first, this was the one which moved him. And it happened pretty much as follows—though I hardly like to tell, because it advanced me to such a height as I myself was giddy at; and which all my friends resented greatly (save those of my own family), and even now are sometimes bitter, in spite of all my humility. Now this is a matter of history, because the King was concerned in it; and being so strongly misunderstood, especially in my own neighbourhood, I will overcome (so far as I can) my diffidence in telling it.

The good Earl Brandir was a man of the noblest charity. True charity begins at home; and so did his; and was afraid of losing the way, if it went abroad. So this good nobleman kept his money in a handsome pewter box, with his coat of arms upon it, and a double lid and locks. Moreover, there was a heavy chain, fixed to a staple in the wall, so that none might carry off the pewter with the gold inside of it. Lorna told me the box was full, for she had seen him go to it, and she often thought that it would be nice for us to begin the world with. I told her that she must not allow her mind to dwell upon things of this sort; being wholly against the last commandment set up in our church at Oare.

Now, one evening towards September, when the days were drawing in, looking back at the house to see whether Lorna were looking after me, I espied (by a little glimpse, as it were) a pair of villainous fellows (about whom there could be no mistake) watching from the thicket-corner, some hundred yards or so behind the good Earl's dwelling. "There is mischief a-foot," thought I to myself, being thoroughly conversant with theft, from my knowledge of the Doones; "how will be the moon to-night, and when may we expect the watch?"

I found that neither moon, nor watch, could be looked for until the morning; the moon, of course, before the watch, and more likely to be punctual.

Therefore I resolved to wait, and see what those
two villains did, and save (if it were possible) the
Earl of Brandir's pewter box.    But inasmuch as
those bad men were almost sure to have seen me
leaving the house and looking back, and striking
out on the London road, I marched along at a
merry pace, until they could not discern me; and
then I fetched a compass round, and refreshed myself
at a certain inn, entitled "The Cross-bones and
Buttons."

Here I remained until it was very nearly as dark
as pitch; and the house being full of foot-pads and
cut-throats, I thought it right to leave them. One
or two came after me, in the hope of designing a
stratagem; but I dropped them in the darkness;
and knowing all the neighbourhood well, I took up
my position, two hours before midnight, among the
shrubs at the eastern end of Lord Brandir's mansion.
Hence, although I might not see, I could scarcely fail
to hear, if any unlawful entrance, either at back or
front, were made.

From my own observation, I thought it likely that
the attack would be in the rear; and so indeed it
came to pass.    For when all the lights were quenched,
and all the house was quiet, I heard a low and wily
whistle from a clump of trees close by; and then three
figures past between me and a whitewashed wall, and
came to a window which opened into a part of the
servants' basement.    This window was carefully raised
by some one inside the house; and after a little

whispering, and something which sounded like a kiss, all the three men entered.

"Oh, you villains!" I said to myself; "this is worse than any Doone job: because there is treachery in it." But without waiting to consider the subject from a moral point of view, I crept along the wall, and entered very quietly after them; being rather uneasy about my life, because I bore no fire-arms, and had nothing more than my holly staff, for even a violent combat.

To me this was matter of deep regret, as I followed these vile men inward. Nevertheless I was resolved that my Lorna should not be robbed again. Through us (or at least through our Annie) she had lost that brilliant necklace; which then was her only birthright: therefore it behoved me doubly, to preserve the pewter box; which must belong to her in the end, unless the thieves got hold of it.

I went along very delicately (as a man who has learned to wrestle can do, although he may weigh twenty stone), following carefully the light, brought by the traitorous maid, and shaking in her loose dishonest hand. I saw her lead the men into a little place called a pantry; and there she gave them cordials, and I could hear them boasting.

Not to be too long over it—which they were much inclined to be—I followed them from this drinking-bout, by the aid of the light they bore, as far as Earl Brandir's bed-room, which I knew, because Lorna had shown it to me that I might admire the tapestry. But I had said that no horse could ever be shod as the horses were shod therein, unless he had the foot of a frog, as well as a frog to his foot. And Lorna had been vexed at this (as taste and high art always are, at any small accurate knowledge), and so she had brought me out again, before I had time to admire things.

Now, keeping well away in the dark, yet nearer than was necessary to my own dear Lorna's room, I saw these fellows try the door of the good Earl Brandir, knowing from the maid, of course, that his lordship could hear nothing, except the name of Alan. They tried the lock, and pushed at it, and even set their knees upright; but a Scottish nobleman may be trusted to secure his door at night. So they were forced to break it open; and at this the guilty maid, or woman, ran away. These three rogues—for rogues they were, and no charity may deny it—burst into Earl Brandir's room, with a light, and a crow-bar, and fire-arms. I thought to myself that this was hard upon an honest nobleman; and if further mischief could be saved, I would try to save it.

When I came to the door of the room, being myself in shadow, I beheld two bad men trying vainly to break open the pewter box, and the third with a pistol-muzzle laid to the night-cap of his lordship. With foul face and yet fouler words, this man was demanding the key of the box, which the other men could by no means open, neither drag it from the chain.

"I tell you," said this aged Earl, beginning to understand at last what these rogues were up for; "I will give no key to you. It all belongs to my boy, Alan. No one else shall have a farthing."

"Then you may count your moments, lord. The key is in your old cramped hand. One, two; and at three, I shoot you."

. I saw that the old man was abroad; not with fear, but with great wonder, and the regrets of deafness. And I saw, that rather would he be shot, than let these men go rob his son, buried now, or laid to bleach in the tangles of the wood; three, or it might be four years agone, but still alive to his father. Hereupon my heart was moved; and I resolved to interfere. The thief with the pistol began to count, as I crossed the floor very quietly, while the old Earl fearfully gazed at the muzzle, but clenched still tighter his wrinkled hand. The villain, with hair all over his eyes, and the great horse-pistol levelled, cried "three," and pulled the trigger; but luckily at that very moment, I struck up the barrel with my staff, so that the shot pierced the tester, and then with a spin and a thwack, I brought the good holly down upon the rascal's head, in a manner which stretched him upon the floor.

Meanwhile the other two robbers had taken the alarm, and rushed at me, one with a pistol, and one with a hanger; which forced me to be very lively. Fearing the pistol most, I flung the heavy velvet curtain of the bed across, that he might not see where to aim at me; and then stooping very quickly I caught up the senseless robber, and set him up for a shield and target; whereupon he was shot immediately, without having the pain of knowing it; and a happy thing it was for him. Now the other two were at my mercy, being men below the average strength; and no hanger, except in most skilful hands, as well as firm and strong ones, has any chance to a powerful man armed with a stout cudgel, and thoroughly practised in single-stick.

So I took these two rogues, and bound them together; and leaving them under charge of the butler (a worthy and shrewd Scotchman), I myself went in search of the constables; whom, after some few hours, I found; neither were they so drunk but what they could take roped men to prison. In the morning, these two men were brought before the Justices of the Peace : and now my wonderful luck appeared ; for the merit of having defeated, and caught them, would never have raised me one step in the State, or in public consideration ; if they had only been common robbers, or even notorious murderers. But when these fellows were recognized, by some one in the court, as Protestant witnesses out of employment, companions and understrappers to Oates, and Bedloe, and Carstairs, and hand in glove with Dangerfield, Turberville, and Dugdale—in a word, the very men against whom His Majesty the King bore the bitterest rancour, but whom he had hitherto failed to catch—when this was laid before the public (with emphasis and admiration), at least a dozen men came up, whom I had never seen before, and prayed me to accept their congratulations, and to be sure to remember them: for all were of neglected merit, and required no more than a piece of luck.

I answered them very modestly, and each according to his worth, as stated by himself, who of course could judge the best. The magistrates made me many compliments, ten times more than I deserved, and took good care to have them copied, that His Majesty might see them. And ere the case was thoroughly heard, and those poor fellows were committed, more than a score of generous men had offered to lend me a hundred pounds, wherewith to buy a new Court suit, when called before His Majesty.

Now this may seem very strange to us who live in a better and purer age—or say at least that we do so —and yet, who are we to condemn our fathers for teaching us better manners, and at their own expense? With these points any virtuous man is bound to deal quite tenderly, making allowance for corruption, and not being too sure of himself. And to tell the truth, although I had seen so little of the world as yet, that which astonished me in the matter, was not so much that they paid me court, as that they found out so soon the expediency of doing it.

In the course of that same afternoon, I was sent for by His Majesty. He had summoned first the good Earl Brandir, and received the tale from him, not without exaggeration, although my lord was a Scotchman. But the chief thing His Majesty cared to know was that, beyond all possible doubt, these were the very precious fellows from perjury turned to robbery.

Being fully assured at last of this, His Majesty had rubbed his hands, and ordered the boots of a stricter pattern (which he himself had invented) to be brought at once, that he might have them in the best possible order. And he oiled them himself, and expressed his fear that there was no man in London quite competent to work them. Nevertheless he would try one or two, rather than wait for his pleasure, till the torturer came from Edinburgh.

The next thing he did was to send for me; and in great alarm and flurry I put on my best clothes, and hired a fashionable hair-dresser, and drank half-a-gallon of ale, because both my hands were shaking. Then forth I set, with my holly staff, wishing myself well out of it. I was shown at once, and before I desired it, into His Majesty's presence, and there I stood most humbly, and made the best bow I could think of.

As I could not advance any further—for I saw that the Queen was present, which frightened me tenfold— His Majesty, in the most gracious manner, came down the room to encourage me. And as I remained with my head bent down, he told me to stand up, and look at him.

"I have seen thee before, young man," he said; "thy form is not one to be forgotten. Where was it? Thou art most likely to know."

"May it please Your Most Gracious Majesty the

King," I answered, finding my voice in a manner
·which surprised myself : " it was in the Royal Chapel."

Now I meant no harm whatever by this. I ought
to have said the " Ante-chapel," but I could not
remember the word, and feared to keep the King
looking at me.

" I am well-pleased," said His Majesty, with a smile
which almost made his dark and stubborn face look
pleasant, " to find that our greatest subject, greatest
I mean in the bodily form, is also a good Catholic.
Thou needest not say otherwise. The time shall be,
and that right soon, when men shall be proud of the
one true faith." Here he stopped, having gone rather
far ; but the gleam of his heavy eyes was such that I
durst not contradict.

" This is that great Johann Reed," said Her Majesty,·
coming forward, because the King was in meditation ;
" for whom I have so much heard, from the dear, dear
Lorna. Ah, she is not of this black countree, she of
the breet Italie."

I have tried to write it, as she said it : but it wants
a better scholar to express her mode of speech.

" Now John Ridd," said the King, recovering from
his thoughts about the true Church, and thinking that
his wife was not to take the lead upon me : " thou
hast done great service to the realm, and to religion.
It was good to save Earl Brandir, a loyal and Catholic
nobleman ; but it was great service to catch two of the
vilest bloodhounds ever laid on by heretics. And to
⁻ake them shoot another : it was rare ; it was rare,

my lad. Now ask us anything in reason: thou canst
carry any honours, on thy club, like Hercules. What
is thy chief ambition, lad?"

"Well," said I, after thinking a little, and meaning
to make the most of it, for so the Queen's eyes conveyed
to me: "my mother always used to think that having
been schooled at Tiverton, with thirty marks a year to
pay, I was worthy of a coat of arms. And that is what
she longs for."

"A good lad! A very good lad!" said the King,
and he looked at the Queen, as if almost in joke:
"but what is thy condition in life?"

"I am a freeholder," I answered, in my confusion;
"ever since the time of King Alfred. A Ridd was
with him in the isle of Athelney; and we hold our
farm by gift from him; or at least people say so. We
have had three very good harvests running, and might
support a coat of arms; but for myself I want it not."

"Thou shalt have a coat my lad," said the King,
smiling at his own humour: "but it must be a large
one to fit thee. And more than that shalt thou have,
John Ridd, being of such loyal breed, and having done
such service."

And while I wondered what he meant, he called to
some of the people in waiting at the further end of the
room, and they brought him a little sword, such as
Annie would skewer a turkey with. Then he signified
to me to kneel, which I did (after dusting the board,
for the sake of my best breeches), and then he gave me
a little tap very nicely upon my shoulder, before I

knew what he was up to; and said, "Arise, Sir John
Ridd!"

This astonished, and amazed me; to such extent of
loss of mind, that when I got up I looked about, and
thought what the Snowes would think of it. And I
said to the King, without forms of speech,

"Sir, I am very much obliged. But what be I to do
with it?"

## CHAPTER XVII.

THE coat of arms, devised for me by the Royal heralds, was of great size, and rich colours, and full of bright imaginings. They did me the honour to consult me first, and to take no notice of my advice. For I begged that there might be a good-sized cow on it, so as to stamp our pats of butter, before they went to market: also a horse on the other side,. and a flock snowed up at the bottom. But the gentlemen would not hear of this ; and to find something more appropriate, they inquired strictly into the annals of our family. I told them, of course, all about King Alfred ; upon which they settled that one quarter should be, three cakes on a bar, with a lion regardant, done upon a field of gold. Also I told them that very likely there had been a Ridd in the battle fought, not very far from Plover's Barrows, by the Earl of Devon against the Danes, when Hubba their chief was killed, and the sacred standard taken. As some of the Danes are said to be buried, even upon land of ours, and we call their graves (if such they be) even to this day "barrows," the heralds quite agreed with me that a Ridd might

have been there, or thereabouts; and if he was there, he
was almost certain to have done his best, being in sight
of hearth and home; and it was plain that he must
have had good legs to be at the same time both there
and in Athelney; and good legs are an argument for
good arms: and supposing a man of this sort to have
done his utmost (as the manner of the Ridds is), it was
next to certain that he himself must have captured the
standard. Moreover the name of our farm was pure
proof; a plover being a wild bird, just the same as a
raven is. Upon this chain of reasoning, and without
any weak misgiving, they charged my growing escucheon
with a black raven on a ground of red. And the next
thing which I mentioned possessing absolute certainty,
to wit, that a pig with two heads had been born upon
our farm, not more than two hundred years agone
(although he died within a week), my third quarter was
made at once, by a two-headed boar with noble tusks,
sable upon silver. All this was very fierce and fine;
and so I pressed for a peaceful corner in the lower
dexter, and obtained a wheat-sheaf set upright, gold
upon a field of green.

Here I was inclined to pause, and admire the effect;
for even De Whichehalse could not show a bearing so
magnificent. But the heralds said that it looked a
mere sign-board, without a good motto under it; and
the motto must have my name in it. They offered me
first " Ridd non ridendus," but I said, " for God's sake,
gentlemen, let me forget my Latin." Then they proposed " Ridd readeth riddles:" but I begged them not

to set down such a lie; for no Ridd ever had made, or made out, such a thing as a riddle, since Exmoor itself began. Thirdly they gave me "Ridd never be ridden," and fearing to make any further objections, I let them inscribe it in bronze upon blue. The heralds thought that the King would pay for this noble achievement; but His Majesty, although graciously pleased with their ingenuity, declined in the most decided manner to pay a farthing towards it; and as I had now no money left, the heralds became as blue as azure, and as red as gules; until Her Majesty the Queen came forward very kindly, and said that if His Majesty gave me a coat of arms, I was not to pay for it; therefore she herself did so quite handsomely, and felt good will towards me in consequence.

Now being in a hurry—so far at least as it is in my nature to hurry—to get to the end of this narrative, is it likely that I would have dwelled so long upon my coat of arms, but for some good reason? And this good reason is that Lorna took the greatest pride in it, and thought (or at any rate said) that it quite threw into the shade, and eclipsed, all her own ancient glories. And half in fun, and half in earnest, she called me "Sir John" so continually, that at last I was almost angry with her; until her eyes were bedewed with tears; and then I was angry with myself.

Beginning to be short of money, and growing anxious about the farm, longing also to show myself and my noble escucheon to mother, I took advantage of Lady Lorna's interest with the Queen, to obtain my acquit

tance and full discharge from even nominal custody.
It had been intended to keep me in waiting, until the
return of Lord Jeffreys, from that awful circuit of
shambles, through which his name is still used by
mothers to frighten their children into bed. And right
glad was I—for even London shrank with horror at
the news—to escape a man so blood-thirsty, savage,
and even to his friends (among whom I was reckoned),
malignant.

Earl Brandir was greatly pleased with me, not only
for having saved his life, but for saving that which he
valued more, the wealth laid by for Lord Alan. And
he introduced me to many great people, who quite
kindly encouraged me, and promised to help me in
every way, when they heard how the King had spoken.
As for the furrier, he could never have enough of my
society; and this worthy man, praying my commendation, demanded of me one thing only—to speak of him
as I found him. As I had found him many a Sunday,
furbishing up old furs for new, with a glaze to conceal
the moths' ravages, I begged him to reconsider the
point, and not to demand such accuracy. He said,
"Well, well; all trades had tricks; especially the
trick of business: and I must take him—if I were
his true friend—according to his own description."
This I was glad enough to do; because it saved so
much trouble, and I had no money to spend with
him. But still he requested the use of my name; and
I begged him to do the best with it, as I never had
kept a banker. And the "John Ridd cuffs," and the
"Sir John mantles," and the "Holly-staff capes," he put

into his window, as the winter was coming on, ay and sold (for everybody was burning with gossip about me), must have made this good man's fortune; since the excess of price over value is the true test of success in life.

To come away from all this stuff, which grieves a man in London—when the brisk air of the autumn cleared its way to Ludgate Hill, and clever prentices ran out, and sniffed at it, and fed upon it (having little else to eat); and when the horses from the country were a goodly sight to see, with the rasp of winter bristles rising through and among the soft summer-coat; and when the new straw began to come in, golden with the harvest-gloss, and smelling most divinely, at those strange livery-stables, where the nags are put quite tail to tail; and when all the London folk themselves were asking about white frost (from recollections of childhood); then, I say, such a yearning seized me for moory crag, and for dewy blade, and even the grunting of our sheep (when the sun goes down) that nothing but the new wisps of Sampson could have held me in London town.

Lorna was moved with equal longing towards the country, and country ways; and she spoke quite as much of the glistening dew, as she did of the smell of our oven. And here let me mention—although the two are quite distinct and different—that both the dew and the bread of Exmoor may be sought, whether high or low, but never found elsewhere. The dew is so crisp, and pure, and pearly, and in such abundance: and the bread is so sweet, so kind, and homely, you can eat a loaf, and then another.

Now while I was walking daily, in and out great
crowds of men (few of whom had any freedom from
the cares of money; and many of whom were even
morbid with a worse pest, called "politics") I could
not be quit of thinking how we jostle one another.
God has made the earth quite large, with a spread of
land enough for all to live on, without fighting. Also
a mighty spread of water, laying hands on sand and
cliff with a solemn voice in storm-time; and in the
gentle weather moving men to thoughts of equity.
This, as well, is full of food.; being two-thirds of the
world, and reserved for devouring knowledge; by the
time the sons of men have fed away the dry land.
Yet before the land itself has acknowledged touch
of man, upon one in a hundred acres; and before one
mile in ten thousand of the exhaustless ocean has ever
felt the plunge of hook, or combing of the haul-nets;
lo we crawl, in flocks together, upon the hot ground
that stings us; even as the black grubs crowd upon the
harried nettle! Surely we are too much given to follow
the tracks of each other.

However, for a moralist I never set up, and never
shall; while common sense abides with me. Such a
man must be very wretched in this pure dearth of
morality; like a fisherman where no fish be: and most
of us have enough to do, to attend to our own morals.
Enough that I resolved to go: and as Lorna could
not come with me, it was even worse' than stopping.
Nearly everybody vowed that I was a great fool indeed,
to neglect so rudely—which was the proper word, they

said—the pushing of my fortunes. But I answered that to push was rude, and I left it to people who had no room; and thought that my fortune must be heavy, if it would not move without pushing.

Lorna cried, when I came away (which gave me great satisfaction), and she sent a whole trunkful of things for mother, and Annie, and even Lizzie. And she seemed to think, though she said it not, that I made my own occasion for going, and might have stayed on till the winter. Whereas I knew well that my mother would think (and every one on the farm the same) that here I had been in London, lagging, and taking my pleasure, and looking at shops, upon pretence of King's business, and leaving the harvest to reap itself, not to mention the spending of money; while all the time there was nothing whatever, except my own love of adventure and sport, to keep me from coming home again. But I knew that my coat of arms, and title, would turn every bit of this grumbling into fine admiration.

And so it fell out, to a greater extent than even I desired: for all the parishes round about united in a sumptuous dinner, at the Mother Melldrum inn—for now that good lady was dead, and her name and face set on a sign-post—to which I was invited so, that it was as good as a summons. And if my health was no better next day, it was not from want of good wishes, any more than from stint of the liquor.

It is needless to say that the real gentry for a long time treated my new honours with contempt and ridicule;

but gradually as they found that I was not such a fool
as to claim any equality with them, but went about
my farm-work, and threw another man at wrestling,
and touched my hat to the magistrates, just the same
as ever; some gentlemen of the highest blood—of
which we think a great deal more than of gold, around
our neighbourhood—actually expressed a desire to
make my acquaintance. And when, in a manner
quite straightforward, and wholly free from bitterness,
I thanked them for this (which appeared to me the
highest honour yet offered me), but declined to go into
their company, because it would make me uncomfortable, and themselves as well, in a different way :
they did what nearly all Englishmen do, when a thing
is right and sensible. They shook hands with me;
and said, that they could not deny but that there was
reason in my view of the matter. And although they
themselves must be the losers—which was a handsome
thing to say—they would wait until I was a little older,
and more aware of my own value.

Now this reminds me how it is, that an English
gentleman is so far in front of foreign noblemen and
princes. I have seen, at times, a little, both of one
and of the other : and making more than due allowance for the difficulties of language, and the difference
of training ; upon the whole the balance is in favour of
our people. And this, because we have two weights,
solid and (even in scale of manners) outweighing all
light complaisance ; to wit, the inborn love of justice,
and the power of abiding.

Yet some people may be surprised that men with any love of justice, whether inborn or otherwise, could continue to abide the arrogance, and rapacity, and tyranny of the Doones.

For, now as the winter passed, the Doones were not keeping themselves at home, as in honour they were bound to do. Twenty sheep a week, and one fat ox, and two stout red deer (for wholesome change of diet) as well as three score bushels of flour, and two hogsheads and a half of cider, and a hundred weight of candles, not to mention other things of almost every variety, which they got by insisting upon it—surely these might have sufficed to keep the people in their place, with no outburst of wantonness. Nevertheless, it was not so : they had made complaint about something—too much ewe-mutton, I think it was—and in spite of all the pledges given, they had ridden forth, and carried away two maidens of our neighbourhood.

Now these two maidens were known, because they had served the beer at an ale-house ; and many men who had looked at them, over a pint or quart vessel (especially as they were comely girls), thought that it was very hard for them to go in that way, and perhaps themselves unwilling. And their mother (although she had taken some money, which the Doones were always full of) declared that it was a robbery : and though it increased for a while the custom, that must soon fall off again. And who would have her two girls now, clever as they were and good ?

Before we had finished meditating upon this loose

outrage—for so I at least would call it, though people accustomed to the law may take a different view of it—we had news of a thing far worse, which turned the hearts of our women sick. This I will tell in most careful language, so as to give offence to none, if skill of words may help it.*

Mistress Margery Badcock, a healthy and upright young woman, with a good rich colour, and one of the finest hen-roosts any where round our neighbourhood, was nursing her child about six of the clock, and looking out for her husband. Now this child was too old to be nursed; as everybody told her, for he could run, say two yards alone, and perhaps four or five, by holding to handles. And he had a way of looking round, and spreading his legs, and laughing, with his brave little body well fetched up, after a desperate journey to the end of the table, which his mother said nothing could equal. Nevertheless he would come to be nursed, as regular as a clock almost; and inasmuch as he was the first, both father and mother made much of him; for God only knew whether they could ever compass such another one.

Christopher Badcock was a tenant farmer, in the parish of Martinhoe, renting some fifty acres of land, with a right of common attached to them; and at this particular time, being now the month of February, and fine open weather, he was hard at work ploughing and preparing for spring corn. Therefore his wife was not

---

* The following story is strictly true; and true it is that the country-people rose, to a man, at this dastard cruelty, and did what the Goverment failed to do.—ED. L. D.

surprised, although the dusk was falling, that farmer
Christopher should be at work in "blind man's holiday," as we call it.

But she was surprised, nay astonished, when by the
light of the kitchen fire (brightened up for her husband) she saw six or seven great armed men burst into
the room upon her; and she screamed so that the
maid in the back-kitchen heard her, but was afraid to
come to help. Two of the strongest and fiercest men,
at once, seized poor young Margery; and though she
fought for her child, and home, she was but an infant
herself in their hands. In spite of tears, and shrieks,
and struggles, they tore the babe from the mother's
arms, and cast it on the lime-ash floor; then they bore
her away to their horses (for by this time she was
senseless), and telling the others to sack the house,
rode off with their prize to the valley. And from the
description of one of those two, who carried off the
poor woman, I knew beyond all doubt that it was
Carver Doone himself.

The other Doones being left behind, and grieved
perhaps in some respects, set to with a will to scour
the house, and to bring away all that was good to eat.
And being a little vexed herein (for the Badcocks were
not a rich couple), and finding no more than bacon,
and eggs, and cheese, and little items, and nothing to
drink but water; in a word, their taste being offended,
they came back to the kitchen, and stamped; and
there was the baby lying.

By evil luck, this child began to squeal about his

mother; having been petted hitherto, and wont to get all he wanted, by raising his voice but a little. Now the mark of the floor was upon his head; as the maid (who had stolen to look at him, when the rough men were swearing upstairs) gave evidence. And she put a dish-cloth under his head, and kissed him, and ran away again. Her name was Honour Jose, and she meant what was right by her master and mistress: but could not help being frightened. And many women have blamed her, and as I think unduly, for her mode of forsaking baby so. If it had been her own baby, instinct rather than reason might have had the day with her; but the child being born of her mistress, she wished him good luck, and left him, as the fierce men came downstairs. And being alarmed by their power of language (because they had found no silver), she crept away in a breathless hurry, and afraid how her breath might come back to her. For often-time, she had hiccoughs.

While this good maid was in the oven, by side of back-kitchen fire-place, with a faggot of wood drawn over her, and lying so that her own heart beat worse than if she were baking; the men (as I said before) came downstairs, and stamped around the baby.

"Rowland, is the bacon good?" one of them asked, with an oath or two: "it is too bad of Carver to go off with the only prize, and leave us in a starving cottage; and not enough to eat for two of us. Fetch down the staves of the rack, my boy. What was farmer to have for supper?"

"Nought but an onion or two, and a loaf, and a rasher of rasty bacon. These poor devils live so badly, they are not worth robbing."

"No game! Then let us have a game of loriot with the baby! It will be the best thing that could befall a lusty infant heretic. Ride a cock-horse to Banbury Cross. Bye, bye, baby Bunting; toss him up, and let me see if my wrist be steady."

The cruelty of this man is a thing it makes me sick to speak of; enough that when the poor baby fell (without attempt at cry or scream, thinking it part of his usual play, when they tossed him up, to come down again), the maid in the oven of the back-kitchen, not being any door between, heard them say as follows:

"If any man asketh who killed thee,
Say 'twas the Doones of Bagworthy." *

Now I think that when we heard this story, and poor Kit Badcock came all around, in a sort of half-crazy manner, not looking up at any one, but dropping his eyes, and asking whether we thought he had been well-treated; and seeming void of regard for life, if this were all the style of it: then, having known him a lusty man, and a fine singer in an alehouse, and much inclined to lay down the law, and show a high hand about women, I really think that it moved us more than if he had gone about ranting, and raving, and vowing revenge upon every one.

* Always pronounced 'Badgery.'

## CHAPTER XVIII.

THERE had been some trouble in our own home, during the previous autumn, while yet I was in London. For certain noted fugitives from the army of King Monmouth (which he himself had deserted, in a low and currish manner), having failed to obtain free shipment from the coast near Watersmouth, had returned into the wilds of Exmoor, trusting to lurk, and be comforted, among the common people. Neither were they disappointed, for a certain length of time; nor in the end was their disappointment caused by fault on our part. Major Wade was one of them; an active and well-meaning man; but prone to fail in courage, upon lasting trial; although in a moment ready. Squire John Whichehalse (not the baron) and Parson Powell* caught him (two or three months before my return) in Farley farm-house, near Brendon. He had been up at our house several times; and Lizzie thought a great deal of him. And well I know that if

---

* Not our Parson Bowden, nor any more a friend of his. Our Parson Bowden never had nought whatever to do with it: and never smoked a pipe with Parson Powell after it.—J. R.

at that time I had been in the neighbourhood, he
should not have been taken so easily.

John Birch, the farmer who had sheltered him, was
so fearful of punishment that he hanged himself, in a
few days' time, and even before he was apprehended.
But nothing was done to Grace Howe, of Bridgeball,
who had been Wade's greatest comforter; neither was
anything done to us; although Eliza added greatly to
mother's alarm and danger, by falling upon Rector
Powell, and most soundly rating him, for his meanness, and his cruelty, and cowardice as she called it, in
setting men with fire-arms upon a poor helpless fugitive,
and robbing all our neighbourhood of its fame for
hospitality. However by means of Serjeant Bloxham,
and his good report of us, as well as by virtue of
Wade's confession (which proved of use to the Government) my mother escaped all penalties.

It is likely enough that good folk will think it hard
upon our neighbourhood, to be threatened, and sometimes heavily punished, for kindness and humanity; and
yet to be left to help ourselves against tyranny, and
base rapine. And now at last our gorge was risen,
and our hearts in tumult. We had borne our troubles
long, as a wise and wholesome chastisement; quite
content to have some few things of our own unmeddled
with. But what could a man dare to call his own, or
what right could he have to wish for it; while he left
his wife and children at the pleasure of any stranger?

The people came flocking all around me, at the
blacksmith's forge, and the Brendon alehouse; and I

could scarce come out of church, but they got me
among the tombstones. They all agreed that I was
bound to take command and management. I bade them
go to the magistrates : but they said they had been too
often. Then I told them that I had no wits for ordering
of an armament, although I could find fault enough
with the one which had not succeeded. But they
would hearken to none of this. All they said was,
" Try to lead us ; and we will try not to run away."

This seemed to me to be common sense, and good
stuff, instead of mere bragging : moreover I myself was
moved by the bitter wrongs of Margery, having known
her at the Sunday-school, ere ever I went to Tiverton ;
and having, in those days, serious thoughts of making
her my sweetheart ; although she was three years my
elder. But now I felt this difficulty—the Doones had
behaved very well to our farm, and to mother, and all
of us, while I was away in London. Therefore would
it not be shabby, and mean, for me to attack them
now ?

Yet being pressed still harder and harder, as day
by day the excitement grew (with more and more
talking over it), and no one else coming forward to
undertake the business, I agreed at last to this ; that
if the Doones, upon fair challenge, would not endeavour
to make amends, by giving up Mistress Margery, as
well as the man who had slain the babe ; then I would
lead the expedition, and do my best to subdue them.
All our men were content with this, being thoroughly
ell assured, from experience, that the haughty

robbers would only shoot any man who durst approach them with such proposal.

And then arose a difficult question—who was to take the risk of making overtures so unpleasant? I waited for the rest to offer; and as none was ready, the burden fell on me, and seemed to be of my own inviting. Hence I undertook the task, sooner than reason about it; for to give the cause of everything is worse than to go through with it.

It may have been three of the afternoon, when leaving my witnesses behind (for they preferred the back-ground) I appeared with our Lizzie's white hand-kerchief upon a kidney-bean stick, at the entrance to the robbers' dwelling. Scarce knowing what might come of it, I had taken the wise precaution of fastening a Bible over my heart, and another across my spinal column, in case of having to run away, with rude men shooting after me. For my mother said that the Word of God would stop a two-inch bullet with three ounces of powder behind it. Now I took no weapons, save those of the Spirit, for fear of being misunderstood. But I could not bring myself to think that any of honourable birth would take advantage of an unarmed man coming in guise of peace to them.

And this conclusion of mine held good, at least for a certain length of time; inasmuch as two decent Doones appeared, and hearing of my purpose, offered, without violence, to go and fetch the Captain; if I would stop where I was, and not begin to spy about

anything. To this, of course, I agreed at once ; for I
wanted no more spying, because I had thorough knowledge of all ins and outs already. Therefore, I stood
waiting steadily, with one hand in my pocket feeling
a sample of corn for market ; and the other against the
rock, while I wondered to see it so brown already.

Those men came back in a little while, with a sharp
short message that Captain Carver would come out and
speak to me by-and-by, when his pipe was finished.
Accordingly, I waited long, and we talked about the
signs of bloom for the coming apple season, and the
rain that had fallen last Wednesday night, and the
principal dearth of Devonshire, that it will not grow
many cowslips—which we quite agreed to be the pret-
tiest of spring flowers ; and all the time I was wondering, how many black and deadly deeds these two
innocent youths had committed, even since last
Christmas.

At length, a heavy and haughty step sounded along
the stone roof of the way; and then the great Carver
Doone drew up, and looked at me rather scornfully.
Not with any spoken scorn, nor flash of strong con-
tumely ; but with that air of thinking little, and
praying not to be troubled, which always vexes a man
who feels that he ought not to be despised so, and yet
knows not how to help it.

"What is it you want, young man?" he asked, as
if he had never seen me before.

In spite of that strong loathing which I always felt
at sight of him, I commanded my temper moderately,

and told him that I was come for his good, and that of
his worshipful company, far more than for my own.
That a general feeling of indignation had arisen among
us at the recent behaviour of certain young men, for
which he might not be answerable, and for which we
would not condemn him, without knowing the rights of
the question. But I begged him clearly to understand
that a vile and inhuman wrong had been done, and
such as we could not put up with; but that if he
would make what amends he could by restoring the
poor woman, and giving up that odious brute who had
slain the harmless infant, we would take no further
motion; and things should go on as usual. As I put
this in the fewest words that would meet my purpose,
I was grieved to see a disdainful smile spread on his
sallow countenance. Then he made me a bow of mock
courtesy, and replied as follows :

"Sir John, your new honours have turned your poor
head, as might have been expected. We are not in
the habit of deserting anything that belongs to us;
far less our sacred relatives. The insolence of your
demand well-nigh outdoes the ingratitude. If there
be a man upon Exmoor who has grossly ill-used us,
kidnapped our young women, and slain half a dozen of
our young men, you are that outrageous rogue, Sir John.
And after all this, how have we behaved? We have
laid no hand upon your farm, we have not carried off
your women, we have even allowed you to take our
Queen, by creeping and crawling treachery; and we
have given you leave of absence to help your cousin

the highwayman, and to come home with a title.  And
now, how do you requite us?   By inflaming the
boorish indignation at a little frolic of our young men;
and by coming with insolent demands, to yield to which
would ruin us.   Ah, you ungrateful viper ! "

As he turned away in sorrow from me, shaking his
head at my badness, I became so overcome (never
having been quite assured, even by people's praises,
about my own goodness), moreover the light which he
threw upon things differed so greatly from my own,
that, in a word—not to be too long—I feared that I was
a villain.  And with many bitter pangs—for I have bad
things to repent of—I began at my leisure to ask
myself whether or not this bill of indictment against
John Ridd was true.   Some of it I knew to be (however much I condemned myself) altogether out of
reason ; for instance about my going away with Lorna
very quietly, over the snow, and to save my love from
being starved away from me.   In this there was no
creeping neither crawling treachery ; for all was done
with sliding : and yet I was so out of training for being
charged by other people beyond mine own conscience,
that Carver Doone's harsh words came on me, like
prickly spinach sown with raking.   Therefore I replied,
and said :

" It is true that I owe you gratitude, sir, for a certain
time of forbearance ; and it is to prove my gratitude,
that I am come here now.  I do not think that my evil
deeds can be set against your own ; although I cannot
speak flowingly upon my good deeds as you can.   I

took your Queen, because you starved her, having stolen her long before, and killed her mother and brother. This is not for me to dwell upon now; any more than I would say much about your murdering of my father. But how the balance hangs between us, God knows better than thou or I; thou low miscreant, Carver Doone."

I had worked myself up, as I always do, in the manner of heavy men; growing hot like an ill-washered wheel revolving, though I start with a cool axle; and I felt ashamed of myself for heat; and ready to ask pardon. But Carver Doone regarded me with a noble and fearless grandeur.

"I have given thee thy choice, John Ridd:" he said, in a lofty manner, which made me drop away under him: "I always wish to do my best with the worst people who come near me. And of all I have ever met with thou art the very worst, Sir John, and the most dishonest."

Now after all my labouring to pay every man to a penny, and to allow the women over, when among the couch-grass (which is a sad thing for their gowns), to be charged like this, I say, so amazed me that I stood, with my legs quite open, and ready for an earthquake. And the scornful way in which he said "Sir John," went to my very heart, reminding me of my littleness. But seeing no use in bandying words, nay, rather the chance of mischief, I did my best to look calmly at him, and to say with a quiet voice, "Farewell, Carver Doone, this time; our day of reckoning is nigh."

" Thou fool, it is come : " he cried, leaping aside into
the niche of rock by the doorway : " Fire ! "

Save for the quickness of spring, and readiness,
learned in many a wrestling bout, that knavish trick
must have ended me : but scarce was the word " fire ! "
out of his mouth, ere I was out of fire, by a single
bound behind the rocky pillar of the opening.  In this
jump I was so brisk, at impulse of the love of life (for
I saw the muzzles set upon me from the darkness of
the cavern), that the men who had trained their guns
upon me with good will and daintiness, could not
check their fingers crooked upon the heavy triggers :
and the volley sang with a roar behind it, down the
avenue of crags.

With one thing and another, and most of all the
treachery of this dastard scheme, I was so amazed that
I turned and ran, at the very top of my speed, away
from these vile fellows ; and luckily for me they had
not another charge to send after me.  And thus by good
fortune, I escaped ; but with a bitter heart, and mind,
at their treacherous usage.

Without any further hesitation, I agreed to take
command of the honest men who were burning to
punish, ay and destroy, those outlaws, as now beyond
all bearing.  One condition however I made, namely
that the Counsellor should be spared if possible ; not
because he was less a villain than any of the others ;
but that he seemed less violent ; and above all, had
been good to Annie.  And I found hard work to make
them listen to my wish upon this point ; for of all the

Doones, Sir Counsellor had made himself most hated, by his love of law and reason.

We arranged that all our men should come, and fall into order with pike and musket, over against our dung-hill; and we settled, early in the day, that their wives might come and look at them. For most of these men had good wives; quite different from sweethearts, such as the militia had; women indeed who could hold to a man, and see to him, and bury him—if his luck were evil—and perhaps have no one afterwards. And all these women pressed their rights upon their precious husbands, and brought so many children with them, and made such a fuss, and hugging, and racing after little legs, that our farm-yard might be taken for an out-door school for babies, rather than a review-ground.

I myself was to and fro among the children continually; for if I love anything in the world, foremost I love children. They warm, and yet they cool our hearts, as we think of what we were; and what in young clothes we hoped to be; and how many things have come across. And to see our motives moving in the little things that know not what their aim or object is, must almost, or ought at least, to lead us home, and soften us. For either end of life is home: both source and issue being God.

Nevertheless, I must confess that the children were a plague sometimes. They never could have enough of me—being a hundred to one, you might say—but I had more than enough of them; and yet was not contented. For they had so many ways of talking, and

of tugging at my hair, and of sitting upon my neck (not
even two with their legs alike) and they forced me to
jump so vehemently, seeming to court the peril of my
coming down neck-and-crop with them, and urging me
still to go faster, however fast I might go with them;
I assure you that they were sometimes so hard and
tyrannical over me, that I might almost as well have
been among the very Doones themselves.

Nevertheless the way in which the children made me
useful proved also of some use to me; for their mothers
were so pleased by the exertions of the "great Gee-gee"
—as all the small ones entitled me—that they gave me
unlimited power and authority over their husbands:
moreover they did their utmost among their relatives
round about, to fetch recruits for our little band. And
by such means, several of the yeomanry from Barnstaple, and from Tiverton, were added to our number;
and inasmuch as these were armed with heavy swords,
and short carabines, their appearance was truly for-
midable.

Tom Faggus also joined us heartily, being now quite
healed of his wound, except at times when the wind
was easterly. He was made second in command to
me; and I would gladly have had him first, as more
fertile in expedients; but he declined such rank, on
the plea that I knew most of the seat of war; besides
that I might be held in some measure to draw authority from the King. Also Uncle Ben came over to
help us, with his advice and presence, as well as with
a band of stout warehousemen, whom he brought from

Dulverton. For he had never forgiven the old outrage put upon him; and though it had been to his interest to keep quiet during the last attack, under Commander Stickles—for the sake of his secret gold mine—yet now he was in a position to give full vent to his feelings. For he and his partners when fully assured of the value of their diggings, had obtained from the Crown a license to adventure in search of minerals, by payment of a heavy fine and a yearly royalty. Therefore they had now no longer any cause for secrecy, neither for dread of the outlaws; having so added to their force as to be a match for them. And although Uncle Ben was not the man to keep his miners idle an hour more than might be helped, he promised that when we had fixed the moment for an assault on the valley, a score of them should come to aid us, headed by Simon Carfax, and armed with the guns which they always kept for the protection of their gold.

Now whether it were Uncle Ben, or whether it were Tom Faggus, or even my own self—for all three of us claimed the sole honour—is more than I think fair to settle without allowing them a voice. But at any rate, a clever thing was devised amongst us; and perhaps it would be the fairest thing, to say that this bright stratagem (worthy of the great Duke himself) was contributed, little by little, among the entire three of us, all having pipes, and schnapps-and-water, in the chimney-corner. However, the world, which always judges according to reputation, vowed that so fine a

stroke of war could only come from a highwayman:
and so Tom Faggus got all the honour, at less perhaps than a third of the cost.

Not to attempt to rob him of it—for robbers, more
than any other, contend for rights of property—let me
try to describe this grand artifice. It was known that
the Doones were fond of money, as well as strong
drink, and other things; and more especially fond of
gold, when they could get it pure and fine. Therefore
it was agreed, that in this way we should tempt them;
for we knew that they looked with ridicule upon our
rustic preparations: after repulsing King's troopers,
and the militia of two counties, was it likely that they
should yield their fortress to a set of ploughboys?
We, for our part, felt, of course, the power of this
reasoning, and that where regular troops had failed,
half-armed countrymen must fail, except by superior
judgment and harmony of action. Though perhaps
the militia would have sufficed, if they had only
fought against the foe, instead of against each other.
From these things we took warning: having failed
through over-confidence, was it not possible now to
make the enemy fail through the self-same cause?

Hence, what we devised was this, to delude from
home a part of the robbers, and fall by surprise on the
other part. We caused it to be spread abroad that a
large heap of gold was now collected at the mine of
the Wizard's Slough. And when this rumour must
have reached them, through women who came to and
fro, as some entirely faithful to them were allowed to

do, we sent Captain Simon Carfax, the father of little
Gwenny, to demand an interview with the Counsellor,
by night, and as it were secretly. Then he was to set
forth a list of imaginary grievances against the owners
of the mine; and to offer, partly through resentment,
partly through the hope of gain, to betray into their
hands, upon the Friday night, by far the greatest
weight of gold as yet sent up for refining. He was to
have one quarter part, and they to take the residue.
But inasmuch as the convoy across the moors, under
his command, would be strong, and strongly armed,
the Doones must be sure to send not less than a score
of men, if possible. He himself, at a place agreed
upon, and fit for an ambuscade, would call a halt, and
contrive in the darkness to pour a little water into the
priming of his company's guns.

It cost us some trouble and a great deal of money,
to bring the sturdy Cornishman into this deceitful
part; and perhaps he never would have consented
but for his obligation to me, and the wrongs (as he
said) of his daughter. However, as he was the man
for the task, both from his coolness and courage, and
being known to have charge of the mine, I pressed
him, until he undertook to tell all the lies we required.
And right well he did it too, having once made up
his mind to it; and perceiving that his own interests
called for the total destruction of the robbers.

## CHAPTER XIX.

HAVING resolved on a night-assault (as our undis-
ciplined men, three-fourths of whom had never been
shot at, could not fairly be expected to march up to
visible musket-mouths), we cared not much about
drilling our forces, only to teach them to hold a
musket, so far as we could supply that weapon to
those with the cleverest eyes; and to give them
familiarity with the noise it made in exploding. And
we fixed upon Friday night for our venture, because
the moon would be at the full; and our powder was
coming from Dulverton on the Friday afternoon.

Uncle Reuben did not mean to expose himself to
shooting; his time of life for risk of life being now
well over, and the residue too valuable. But his coun-
sels, and his influence, and above all his warehousemen, well practised in beating carpets, were of true
service to us. His miners also did great wonders,
having a grudge against the Doones; as indeed who
had not for thirty miles round their valley?

It was settled that the yeomen, having good horses

under them, should give account (with the miners'
help) of as many Doones as might be despatched to
plunder the pretended gold. And as soon as we knew
that this party of robbers, be it more or less, was out
of hearing from the valley, we were to fall to, osten-
sibly at the Doone-gate (which was impregnable now),
but in reality upon their rear, by means of my old
water-slide. For I had chosen twenty young fellows,
partly miners, and partly warehousemen, and sheep-
farmers, and some of other vocations, but all to be
relied upon for spirit and power of climbing. And
with proper tools to aid us, and myself to lead the
way, I felt no doubt whatever but that we could all
attain the crest, where first I had met with Lorna.

Upon the whole, I rejoiced that Lorna was not
present now. It must have been irksome to her feelings to have all her kindred and old associates (much
as she kept aloof from them) put to death without
ceremony, or else putting all of us to death. For all
of us were resolved this time to have no more shilly-
shallying; but to go through with a nasty business,
in the style of honest Englishmen, when the question
comes to "Your life, or mine."

There was hardly a man among us who had not
suffered bitterly from the miscreants now before us.
One had lost his wife perhaps; another had lost a
daughter—according to their ages—another had lost
his favourite cow; in a word, there was scarcely any
one who had not to complain of a hayrick: and what
surprised me then, not now, was that the men least

injured made the greatest push concerning it. But be the wrong too great to speak of, or too small to swear about, from poor Kit Badcock to rich Master Hucka-back, there was not one but went heart and soul for stamping out these firebrands.

The moon was lifting well above the shoulder of the uplands, when we, the chosen band, set forth, having the short cut along the valleys to foot of the Bagworthy water; and therefore having allowed the rest an hour, to fetch round the moors and hills. We were not to begin our climb, until we heard a musket fired from the heights, on the left hand side; where John Fry himself was stationed, upon his own and his wife's request; so as to keep out of action. And that was the place where I had been used to sit, and to watch for Lorna. And John Fry was to fire his gun, with a ball of wool inside it, so soon as he heard the hurly-burly at the Doone-gate begin-ning; which we, by reason of waterfall, could not hear, down in the meadows there.

We waited a very long time, with the moon marching up heaven steadfastly, and the white fog trembling in chords and columns, like a silver harp of the meadows. And then the moon drew up the fogs, and scarfed herself in white with them; and so being proud, gleamed upon the water, like a bride at her looking-glass; and yet there was no sound of either John Fry, or his blunderbuss.

I began to think that the worthy John, being out of all danger, and having brought a counterpane (ac-

cording to his wife's directions, because one of the
children had a cold) must veritably have gone to sleep;
leaving other people to kill, or be killed, as might
be to the will of God; so that he were comfortable.
But herein I did wrong to John, and am ready to
acknowledge it: for suddenly the most awful noise
that anything short of thunder could make, came
down among the rocks, and went and hung upon
the corners.

"The signal, my lads!" I cried, leaping up, and
rubbing my eyes; for even now, while condemning
John unjustly, I was giving him right to be hard upon
me. "Now hold on by the rope, and lay your quarter-
staffs across, my lads; and keep your guns pointing
to heaven, lest haply we shoot one another."

"Us shan't never shutt one anoother, wi' our goons
at that mark, I reckon," said an oldish chap, but
as tough as leather, and esteemed a wit for his
dryness.

"You come next to me, old Ike: you be enough to
dry up the waters: now, remember; all lean well
forward. If any man throws his weight back, down
he goes; and perhaps he may never get up again;
and most likely he will shoot himself."

I was still more afraid of their shooting me; for
my chief alarm in this steep ascent was neither of the
water, nor of the rocks, but of the loaded guns we
bore. If any man slipped, off might go his gun; and
however good his meaning, I being first was most
likely to take far more than I fain would apprehend.

For this cause, I had debated with Uncle Ben and
with Cousin Tom, as to the expediency of our climbing
with guns unloaded.      But they, not being in the way
themselves, assured me that there was nothing to fear,
except through uncommon clumsiness; and that as
for charging our guns at the top, even veteran troops
could scarce be trusted to perform it properly in the
hurry, and the darkness, and the noise of fighting
before them.

However, thank God, though a gun went off, no
one was any the worse for it; neither did the Doones
notice it, in the thick of the firing in front of them.
For the orders to those of the sham attack, conducted
by Tom Faggus, were to make the greatest possible
noise, without exposure of themselves ; until we, in the
rear, had fallen to; which John Fry was again to
give signal of.

Therefore we, of the chosen band, stole up the
meadow quietly, keeping in the blots of shade, and
hollow of the watercourse.      And the earliest notice
the Counsellor had, or any one else, of our presence,
was the blazing of the log-wood house, where lived
that villain Carver.      It was my especial privilege to
set this house on fire; upon which I had insisted,
exclusively, and conclusively.      No other hand but
mine should lay a brand, or strike steel on flint
for it; I had made all preparations carefully for a
goodly blaze.      And I must confess that I rubbed my
hands, with a strong delight and comfort, when I saw
the home of that man, who had fired so many houses,

having its turn of smoke, and blaze, and of crackling fury.

We took good care, however, to burn no innocent women or children in that most righteous destruction. For we brought them all out beforehand; some were glad, and some were sorry; according to their dispositions. For Carver had ten or a dozen wives; and perhaps that had something to do with his taking the loss of Lorna so easily. One child I noticed, as I saved him; a fair and handsome little fellow, whom (if Carver Doone could love anything on earth, beside his wretched self) he did love. The boy climbed on my back and rode; and much as I hated his father, it was not in my heart to say or do a thing to vex him.

Leaving these poor injured people, to behold their burning home, we drew aside, by my directions, into the covert beneath the cliff. But not before we had laid our brands to three other houses, after calling the women forth, and bidding them go for their husbands, to come and fight a hundred of us. In the smoke, and rush, and fire, they believed that we were a hundred; and away they ran, in consternation, to the battle at the Doone-gate.

"All Doone-town is on fire, on fire!" we heard them shrieking as they went: "a hundred soldiers are burning it, with a dreadful great man at the head of them!"

Presently, just as I expected, back came the warriors of the Doones; leaving but two or three at the gate, and burning with wrath to crush under foot the pre-

sumptuous clowns in their valley. Just then the
waxing fire leaped above the red crest of the cliffs,
and danced on the pillars of the forest, and lapped like
a tide on the stones of the slope. All the valley flowed
with light, and the limpid waters reddened, and the
fair young women shone; and the naked children
glistened.

But the finest sight of all, was to see those haughty
men striding down the causeway darkly, reckless of
their end, but resolute to have two lives for every one.
A finer dozen of young men could not have been found
in the world perhaps, nor a braver, nor a viler one.

Seeing how few there were of them, I was very loth
to fire, although I covered the leader, who appeared to
be dashing Charley; for they were at easy distance
now, brightly shown by the fire-light, yet ignorant
where to look for us. I thought that we might take
them prisoners—though what good that could be God
knows; as they must have been hanged thereafter—
anyhow I was loth to shoot, or to give the word
to my followers.

But my followers waited for no word: they saw
a fair shot at the men they abhorred, the men who had
robbed them of home or of love; and the chance was
too much for their charity. At a signal from old
Ikey, who levelled his own gun first, a dozen muskets
were discharged, and half of the Doones dropped
lifeless, like so many logs of firewood, or chopping-
blocks rolled over.

Although I had seen a great battle before, and a

hundred times the carnage, this appeared to me to be horrible; and I was at first inclined to fall upon our men for behaving so. But one instant showed me that they were right: for while the valley was filled with howling, and with shrieks of women, and the beams of the blazing houses fell, and hissed in the bubbling river; all the rest of the Doones leaped at us, like so many demons. They fired wildly, not seeing us well among the hazel bushes; and then they clubbed their muskets, or drew their swords, as might be; and furiously drove at us.'

For a moment, although we were twice their number, we fell back before their valorous fame, and the power of their onset. For my part, admiring their courage greatly, and counting it slur upon manliness that two should be down upon one so, I withheld my hand awhile; for I cared to meet none but Carver; and he was not among them. The whirl and hurry of this fight, and the hard blows raining down—for now all guns were empty—took away my power of seeing, or reasoning upon anything. Yet one thing I saw, which dwelled long with me; and that was Christopher Badcock spending his life to get Charley's.

How he had found out, none may tell; both being dead so long ago : but, at any rate, he had found out, that Charley was the man who had robbed him of his wife and honour. It was Carver Doone who took her away; but Charlesworth Doone was beside him; and, according to cast of dice, she fell to Charley's share. All this Kit Badcock (who was mad, according to

our measures) had discovered, and treasured up; and
now was his revenge-time.

He had come into the conflict without a weapon of
any kind; only begging me to let him be in the very
thick of it. For him, he said, life was no matter, after
the loss of his wife and child; but death was matter to
him, and he meant to make the most of it. Such a face
I never saw, and never hope to see again, as when poor
Kit Badcock spied Charley coming towards us.

We had thought this man a patient fool, a philosopher
of a little sort, or one who could feel nothing. And
his quiet manner of going about, and the gentleness of
his answers (when some brutes asked him where his
wife was, and whether his baby had been well-trussed)
these had misled us to think that the man would turn
the mild cheek to everything. But I, in the loneliness
of our barn, had listened, and had wept with him.

Therefore was I not surprised, so much as all the
rest of us, when, in the foremost of red light, Kit went
up to Charlesworth Doone, as if to some inheritance;
and took his seisin of right upon him, being himself a
powerful man; and begged a word aside with him.
What they said aside, I know not: all I know is that
without weapon, each man killed the other. And
Margery Badcock came, and wept, and hung upon her
poor husband; and died, that summer, of heart-disease.

Now for these and other things (whereof I could tell
a thousand) was the reckoning come that night; and
not a line we missed of it; soon as our bad blood was
up. I like not to tell of slaughter, though it might be

of wolves and tigers: and that was a night of fire and
slaughter, and of very long harboured revenge.
Enough that ere the day-light broke, upon that wan
March morning, the only Doones still left alive were
the Counsellor and Carver. And of all the dwellings
of the Doones (inhabited with luxury, and luscious
taste, and licentiousness) not even one was left; but
all made potash in the river.

This may seem a violent and unholy revenge upon
them. And I (who led the heart of it) have in these
my latter years, doubted how I shall be judged, not
of men—for God only knows the errors of man's judg-
ments—but by that great God himself, the front of
whose forehead is mercy.

## CHAPTER XX.

FROM that great confusion—for nothing can be
broken up, whether lawful or unlawful, without a
vast amount of dust, and many people grumbling, and
mourning for the good old times, when all the world
was happiness, and every man a gentleman, and the sun
himself far brighter than since the brassy idol upon
which he shone was broken—from all this loss of
ancient landmarks (as unrobbed men began to call our
clearance of those murderers) we returned on the
following day, almost as full of anxiety, as we were of
triumph.   In the first place, what could we possibly
do with all these women and children, thrown on our
hands, as one might say, with none to protect and care
for them?    Again, how should we answer to the
justices of the peace, or perhaps even to Lord Jeffreys,
for having, without even a warrant, taken the law into
our own hands, and abated our nuisance so forcibly?
And then, what was to be done with the spoil, which
was of great value; though the diamond necklace
came not to public light?   For we saw a mighty host

of claimants already leaping up for booty. Every man who had ever been robbed expected usury on his loss: the lords of the manors demanded the whole; and so did the King's Commissioner of Revenue at Porlock; and so did the men who had fought our battle; while even the parsons, both Bowden and Powell, and another who had no parish in it, threatened us with the just wrath of the Church, unless each had tithes of the whole of it.

Now this was not as it ought to be; and it seemed as if by burning the nest of robbers, we had but hatched their eggs: until being made sole guardian of the captured treasure (by reason of my known honesty) I hit upon a plan, which gave very little satisfaction; yet carried this advantage, that the grumblers argued against one another, and for the most part came to blows; which renewed their good-will to me, as being abused by the adversary.

And my plan was no more than this—not to pay a farthing to lord of manor, parson, or even King's Commissioner, but after making good some of the recent and proven losses—where the men could not afford to lose— to pay the residue (which might be worth some fifty thousand pounds) into the Exchequer at Westminster; and then let all the claimants file what bills they pleased in Chancery.

Now this was a very noble device; for the mere name of Chancery, and the high repute of the fees therein, and low repute of the lawyers, and the comfortable knowledge that the wool-sack itself is the golden fleece, absorbing gold for ever, if the standard

be but pure ; consideration of these things staved off
at once the lords of the manors, and all the little
farmers, and even those whom most I feared ; vide-
licet, the parsons.  And the King's Commissioner was ·
compelled to profess himself contented ; although of all
he was most aggrieved ; for his pickings would have
been goodly.

Moreover, by this plan I made—although I never
thought of that—a mighty friend worth all the enemies,
whom the loss of money moved.  The first man now in
the kingdom (by virtue perhaps of energy, rather than
of excellence), was the great Lord Jeffreys, appointed
the head of the Equity, as well as the law of the realm,
for his kindness in hanging five hundred people, without
the mere grief of trial.  Nine out of ten of these
people were innocent, it was true ; but that proved the
merit of the Lord Chief-Justice so much the greater
for hanging them, as showing what might be expected
of him, when he truly got hold of a guilty man.  Now
the King had seen the force of this argument ; and not
being without gratitude for a high-seasoned dish of
cruelty, had promoted the only man in England,
combining the gifts both of butcher and cook.

Nevertheless, I do beg you all to believe of me—and
I think that, after following me so long, you must
believe it—that I did not even know at the time of
Lord Jeffreys' high promotion.  Not that my knowledge of this would have led me to act otherwise in
the matter ; for my object was to pay into an office, and
not to any official ; neither if I had known the fact,

could I have seen its bearing upon the receipt of my money. For the King's Exchequer is, meseemeth, of the Common Law; while Chancery is of Equity, and well named for its many chances. But the true result of the thing was this—Lord Jeffreys being now head of the law, and almost head of the kingdom, got possession of that money, and was kindly pleased with it.

And this met our second difficulty; for the law having won and laughed over the spoil, must have injured its own title by impugning our legality.

Next, with regard to the women and children, we were long in a state of perplexity. We did our very best at the farm; and so did many others; to provide for them, until they should manage about their own subsistence. And after a while, this trouble went; as nearly all troubles go with time. Some of the women were taken back by their parents, or their husbands, or it may be their sweethearts: and those who failed of this, went forth, some upon their own account to the New World plantations, where the fairer sex is valuable; and some to English cities; and the plainer ones to field-work. And most of the children went with their mothers, or were bound apprentices; only Carver Doone's handsome child had lost his mother, and stayed with me.

This boy went about with me everywhere. He had taken as much of liking to me—first shown in his eyes by the firelight—as his father had of hatred; and I perceiving his noble courage, scorn of lies, and high spirit, became almost as fond of Ensie, as he was of

me. He told us that his name was "Ensie," meant
for "Ensor," I suppose, from his father's grandfather, the old Sir Ensor Doone. And this boy
appeared to be Carver's heir; having been born in
wedlock, contrary to the general manner and custom
of the Doones.

However, although I loved the poor child, I could
not help feeling very uneasy about the escape of his
father, the savage and brutal Carver. This man was
left to roam the country, homeless, foodless, and desperate, with his giant strength, and great skill in arms,
and the whole world to be revenged upon. For his
escape the miners, as I shall show, were answerable;
but of the Counsellor's safe departure the burden lay
on myself alone. And inasmuch as there are people
who consider themselves ill-used, unless one tells them
everything; straitened though I am for space, I will
glance at this transaction.

After the desperate charge of young Doones had
been met by us, and broken, and just as poor Kit
Badcock died in the arms of the dead Charley, I
happened to descry a patch of white on the grass of
the meadow, like the head of a sheep after washing-
day. Observing with some curiosity how carefully this
white thing moved along the bars of darkness betwixt
the panels of fire-light, I ran up to intercept it, before
it reached the little postern which we used to call
Gwenny's door. Perceiving me, the white thing
stopped, and was for making back again; but I ran up
at full speed; and lo, it was the flowing silvery hair of

that sage the Counsellor, who was scuttling away upon all fours; but now rose and confronted me.

"John," he said; "Sir John, you will not play falsely with your ancient friend, among these violent fellows. I look to you to protect me, John."

"Honoured sir, you are right," I replied; "but surely that posture was unworthy of yourself, and your many resources. It is my intention to let you go free."

"I knew it. I could have sworn to it. You are a noble fellow, John. I said so, from the very first; you are a noble fellow, and an ornament to any rank."

"But upon two conditions," I added, gently taking him by the arm; for instead of displaying any desire for commune with my nobility, he was edging away toward the postern: "the first is that you tell me truly (for now it can matter to none of you) who it was that slew my father?"

"I will tell you truly and frankly, John; however painful to me to confess it. It was my son, Carver."

"I thought as much, or I felt as much, all along," I answered: "but the fault was none of yours, sir; for you were not even present."

"If I had been there, it would not have happened. I am always opposed to violence. Therefore, let me haste away: this scene is against my nature."

"You shall go directly, Sir Counsellor, after meeting my other condition; which is that you place in my hands Lady Lorna's diamond necklace."

"Ah, how often I have wished," said the old man,

with a heavy sigh; "that it might yet be in my power to ease my mind in that respect; and to do a thoroughly good deed, by lawful restitution."

"Then try to have it in your power, sir. Surely, with my encouragement, you might summon resolution."

"Alas, John, the resolution has been ready long ago. But the thing is not in my possession. Carver, my son, who slew your father, upon him you will find the necklace. What are jewels to me, young man, at my time of life? Baubles and trash,—I detest them, from the sins they have led me to answer for. When you come to my age, good Sir John, you will scorn all jewels, and care only for a pure and bright conscience. Ah! ah! Let me go. I have made my peace with God."

He looked so hoary, and so silvery, and serene in the moonlight, that verily I must have believed him, if he had not drawn in his breast. But I happened to have noticed, that when an honest man gives vent to noble and great sentiments, he spreads his breast, and throws it out, as if his heart were swelling: whereas I had seen this old gentleman draw in his breast more than once, as if it happened to contain better goods than sentiment.

"Will you applaud me, kind sir," I said, keeping him very tight, all the while; "if I place it in your power to ratify your peace with God? The pledge is upon your heart, no doubt; for there it lies at this moment."

With these words, and some apology for having

recourse to strong measures, I thrust my hand inside his waistcoat, and drew forth Lorna's necklace, purely sparkling in the moonlight, like the dancing of new stars. The old man made a stab at me, with a knife which I had not espied; but the vicious onset failed; and then he knelt, and clasped his hands.

"Oh, for God's sake, John, my son, rob me not, in that manner. They belong to me; and I love them so; I would give almost my life for them. There is one jewel there, I can look at for hours, and see all the lights of heaven in it; which I never shall see elsewhere. All my wretched, wicked life—oh, John, I am a sad hypocrite—but give me back my jewels. Or else, kill me here: I am a babe in your hands: but I must have back my jewels."

As his beautiful white hair fell away from his noble forehead, like a silver wreath of glory, and his powerful face, for once, was moved with real emotion; I was so amazed and overcome by the grand contradictions of nature, that verily I was on the point of giving him back the necklace. But honesty, which is said to be the first instinct of all Ridds (though I myself never found it so) happened here to occur to me: and so, I said, without more haste than might be expected:

"Sir Counsellor, I cannot give you what does not belong to me. But if you will show me that particular diamond which is heaven to you, I will take upon myself the risk and the folly of cutting it out for you. And with that, you must go contented: and I beseech you not to starve with that jewel upon your lips."

Seeing no hope of better terms, he showed me his pet love of a jewel; and I thought of what Lorna was to me, as I cut it out (with the hinge of my knife severing the snakes of gold), and placed it in his careful. hand. Another moment, and he was gone, and away through Gwenny's postern; and God knows what became of him.

Now as to Carver, the thing was this—so far as I could ascertain, from the valiant miners; no two of whom told the same story; any more than one of them told it twice. The band of Doones, which sallied forth for the robbery of the pretended convoy, was met by Simon Carfax, according to arrangement, at the ruined house called the "Warren," in that part of Bagworthy Forest, where the river Exe (as yet a very small stream) runs through it. The Warren, as all our people know, had belonged to a fine old gentleman, whom every one called "The Squire;" who had retreated from active life to pass the rest of his days in fishing, and shooting, and helping his neighbours. For he was a man of some substance; and no poor man ever left the Warren, without a bag of good victuals, and a few shillings put in his pocket. However this poor Squire never made a greater mistake, than in hoping to end his life peacefully upon the banks of a trout-stream, and in the green forest of Bagworthy. For as he came home from the brook at dusk, with his fly-rod over his shoulder, the Doones fell upon him, and murdered him, and then sacked his house, and burned it.

Now this had made honest people timid about going

past the "Warren" at night; for, of course, it was said that the old Squire "walked," upon certain nights of the moon, in and out the trunks of trees, on the green path from the river. On his shoulder he bore a fishing-rod, and his book of trout-flies in one hand, and on his back a wicker-creel; and now and then he would burst out laughing to think of his coming so near the Doones.

And now that one turns to consider it, this seems a strangely righteous thing, that the scene of one of the greatest crimes even by Doones committed should, after twenty years, become the scene of vengeance falling (like hail from heaven) upon them. For although the "Warren" lies well away to the westward of the mine; and the gold, under escort to Bristowe, or London, would have gone in the other direction; Captain Carfax finding this place best suited for working of his design, had persuaded the Doones, that for reasons of Government, the ore must go first to Barnstaple for inspection, or something of that sort. And as every one knows that our Government sends all things westward when eastward bound, this had won the more faith for Simon, as being according to nature.

Now Simon, having met these flowers of the flock o villainy, where the rising moonlight flowed through the weir-work of the wood, begged them to dismount; and led them with an air of mystery into the Squire's ruined hall, black with fire, and green with weeds.

"Captain, I have found a thing," he said to Carver Doone himself, "which may help to pass the hour, ere the lump of gold comes by. The smugglers are a

noble race; but a miner's eyes are a match for them.
There lies a puncheon of rare spirit, with the Dutch-
man's brand upon it, hidden behind the broken hearth.
Set a man to watch outside; and let us see what this
be like."

With one accord they agreed to this; and Carver
pledged Master Carfax, and all the Doones grew
merry. But Simon being bound, as he said, to see to
their strict sobriety, drew a bucket of water from the
well into which they had thrown the dead owner, and
begged them to mingle it with their drink; which some
of them did, and some refused.

But the water from that well was poured, while they
were carousing, into the priming-pan of every gun of
theirs; even as Simon had promised to do with the
guns of the men they were come to kill. Then just as
the giant Carver arose, with a glass of pure hollands
in his hand, and by the light of the torch they had
struck, proposed the good health of the Squire's ghost,
—in the broken doorway stood a press of men, with
pointed muskets, covering every drunken Doone. How
it fared upon that I know not, having none to tell me ;
for each man wrought, neither thought of telling, nor
whether he might be alive to tell. The Doones rushed
to their guns at once, and pointed them, and pulled at
them; but the Squire's well had drowned their fire:
and then they knew that they were betrayed; but
resolved to fight like men for it. Upon fighting I can
never dwell: it breeds such savage delight in me;
of which I would fain have less. Enough that all

the Doones fought bravely; and like men (though bad ones) died in the hall of the man they had murdered.   And with them died poor young De Whichehalse; who in spite of all his good father's prayers, had cast in his lot with the robbers.  Carver Doone alone escaped.  Partly through his fearful strength, and his yet more fearful face; but mainly perhaps through his perfect coolness, and his mode of taking things.

I am happy to say that no more than eight of the gallant miners were killed in that combat, or died of their wounds afterwards; and adding to these the eight we had lost in our assault on the valley (and two of them excellent warehousemen) it cost no more than sixteen lives to be rid of nearly forty Doones, each of whom would most likely have killed three men in the course of a year or two.   Therefore, as I said at the time, a great work was done very reasonably: here were nigh upon forty Doones destroyed (in the valley, and up at the "Warren") despite their extraordinary strength, and high skill in gunnery: whereas of us ignorant rustics, there were only sixteen to be counted dead—though others might be lamed, or so—and of those sixteen, only two had left wives, and their wives did not happen to care for them.

Yet for Lorna's sake, I was vexed at the bold escape of Carver.   Not that I sought for Carver's life, any more than I did for the Counsellor's; but that for us it was no light thing, to have a man of such

power, and resource, and desperation, left at large and
furious, like a famished wolf round the sheepfold. Yet
greatly as I blamed the yeomen, who were posted on
their horses, just out of shot from the Doone-gate, for
the very purpose of intercepting those who escaped the
miners, I could not get them to admit that any blame
attached to them.

But lo, he had dashed through the whole of them,
with his horse at full gallop; and was nearly out of
shot before they began to think of shooting him. Then
it appears from what a boy said—for boys manage to
be everywhere—that Captain Carver rode through the
Doone-gate, and so to the head of the valley. There,
of course, he beheld all the houses, and his own among
the number, flaming with a handsome blaze, and
throwing a fine light around, such as he often had
revelled in, when of other people's property. But he
swore the deadliest of all oaths, and seeing himself to
be vanquished (so far as the luck of the moment went),
spurred his great black horse away, and passed into
the darkness.

## CHAPTER XXI.

THINGS at this time so befell me, that I cannot tell one half; but am like a boy who has left his lesson, (to the master's very footfall) unready, except with false excuses. And as this makes no good work ; so I lament upon my lingering, in the times when I might have got through a good page, but went astray after trifles. However, every man must do according to his intellect : and looking at the easy manner of my constitution, I think that most men will regard me with pity and good will for trying, more than with contempt and wrath for having tried unworthily. Even as in the wrestling ring, whatever man did his very best, and made an honest conflict, I always laid him down with softness, easing off his dusty fall.

But the thing which next betided me was not a fall of any sort; but rather a most glorious rise to the summit of all fortune. For in good truth it was no less than the return of Lorna—my Lorna, my own darling ; in wonderful health and spirits, and as glad as a bird to get back again. It would have done any one good for a twelvemonth, to behold her face and doings,

and her beaming eyes and smile, (not to mention blushes
also at my salutation) when this Queen of every heart
ran about our rooms again.  She did love this, and she
must see that, and where was her old friend the cat?
All the house was full of brightness, as if the sun had
come over the hill, and Lorna were his mirror.

My mother sate in an ancient chair, and wiped her
cheeks, and looked at her; and even Lizzie's eyes must
dance to the freshness and joy of her beauty.  As for
me, you might call me mad; for I ran out and flung
my best hat on the barn, and kissed mother Fry, till
she made at me with the sugar-nippers.

What a quantity of things Lorna had to tell us!
And yet how often we stopped her mouth—at least
mother, I mean, and Lizzie—and she quite as often
would stop her own, running up in her joy to some one
of us!  And then there arose the eating business—
which people now call "refreshment," in these dandi-
fied days of our language—for how was it possible
that our Lorna could have come all that way, and to
her own Exmoor, without being terribly hungry?

"Oh, I do love it all so much," said Lorna, now for
the fiftieth time, and not meaning only the victuals:
"the scent of the gorse on the moors drove me wild,
and the primroses under the hedges.  I am sure I was
meant for a farmer's—I mean for a farmhouse life,
dear Lizzie"—for Lizzie was looking saucily—"just
as you were meant for a soldier's bride, and for writing
despatches of victory.  And now, since you will not ask
me, dear mother, in the excellence of your manners,

and even John has not the impudence, in spite of all his coat of arms—I must tell you a thing, which I vowed to keep until to-morrow morning; but my resolution fails me. I am my own mistress—what think you of that, mother? I am my own mistress!"

"Then you shall not be so, long:" cried I; for mother seemed not to understand her, and sought about for her glasses.: "darling, you shall be mistress of me; and I will be your master."

"A frank announcement of your intent, and beyond doubt, a true one; but surely unusual at this stage, and a little premature, John. However, what must be, must be." And with tears springing out of smiles, she fell on my breast, and cried a bit.

When I came to smoke a pipe over it (after the rest were gone to bed), I could hardly believe in my good luck. For here was I, without any merit, except of bodily power, and the absence of any falsehood (which surely is no commendation) so placed that the noblest man in England might envy me and be vexed with me. For the noblest lady in all the land, and the purest, and the sweetest, hung upon my heart, as if there was none to equal it.

I dwelled upon this matter, long and very severely, while I smoked a new tobacco, brought by my own Lorna for me, and next to herself most delicious; and as the smoke curled away, I thought, "Surely this is too fine to last; for a man who never deserved it."

Seeing no way out of this, I resolved to place my faith in God; and so went to bed and dreamed of it.

And having no presence of mind to pray for anything, under the circumstances, I thought it best to fall asleep, and trust myself to the future. Yet ere I fell asleep, the roof above me swarmed with angels, having Lorna under it.

In the morning Lorna was ready to tell her story, and we to hearken; and she wore a dress of most simple stuff; and yet perfectly wonderful, by means of the shape, and her figure. Lizzie was wild with jealousy, as might be expected, (though never would Annie have been so, but have praised it, and craved for the pattern) and mother, not understanding it, looked forth, to be taught about it. For it was strange to note that lately my dear mother had lost her quickness; and was never quite brisk, unless the question were about myself. She had seen a great deal of trouble ; and grief begins to close on people, as their power of life declines. We said that she was hard of hearing ; but my own opinion was, that seeing me inclined for marriage made her think of my father, and so perhaps, a little too much, to dwell upon the courting of thirty years agone. Anyhow, she was the very best of mothers; and would smile and command herself; and be (or try to believe herself) as happy as could be, in the doings of the younger folk, and her own skill in detecting them. Yet, with the wisdom of age, renouncing any opinion upon the matter ; since none could see the end of it.

But Lorna in her bright young beauty, and her knowledge of my heart, was not to be checked by any thoughts of haply coming evil. In the morning she

was up, even sooner than I was, and through all the
corners of the hens, remembering every one of them.
I caught her and saluted her with such warmth (being
now none to look at us), that she vowed she would never
come out again ; and yet she came the next morning !

These things ought not to be chronicled. Yet I am
of such nature, that finding many parts of life adverse
to our wishes, I must now and then draw pleasure from
the blessed portions. And what portion can be more
blessed than with youth, and health, and strength, to
be loved by a virtuous maid, and to love her with all
one's heart? Neither was my pride diminished, when
I found what she had done, only from her love of me.

Earl Brandir's ancient steward, in whose charge she
had travelled, with a proper escort, looked upon her as
a lovely maniac ; and the mixture of pity and admiration, wherewith he regarded her, was a strange thing to
observe ; especially after he had seen our simple house
and manners. On the other hand Lorna considered him
a worthy but foolish old gentleman ; to whom true happiness meant no more than money and high position.

These two last she had been ready to abandon
wholly, and had in part escaped from them, as the
enemies of her happiness. And she took advantage of
the times, in a truly clever manner. For that happened
to be a time — as indeed all times hitherto (so far
as my knowledge extends) have, somehow or other,
happened to be — when everybody was only too glad to
take money for doing anything. And the greatest
money-taker in the kingdom, (next to the King and

Queen, of course, who had due pre-eminence, and had taught the maids of honour) was generally acknowledged to be the Lord Chief-Justice Jeffreys.

Upon his return from the Bloody Assizes, with triumph and great glory, after hanging every man who was too poor to help it, he pleased His Gracious Majesty so purely with the description of their delightful agonies, that the King exclaimed, "This man alone is worthy to be at the head of the law." Accordingly in his hand was placed the great seal of England.

So it came to pass that Lorna's destiny hung upon Lord Jeffreys; for, at this time Earl Brandir died, being taken with gout in the heart, soon after I left London. Lorna was very sorry for him; but as he had never been able to hear one tone of her sweet silvery voice, it is not to be supposed that she wept without consolation. She grieved for him as we ought to grieve for any good man going; and yet with a comforting sense of the benefit which the blessed exchange must bring to him.

Now the Lady Lorna Dugal appeared to Lord Chancellor Jeffreys so exceeding wealthy a ward that the lock would pay for turning. Therefore he came, of his own accord, to visit her, and to treat with her; having heard (for the man was as big a gossip as never cared for anybody, yet loved to know all about everybody) that this wealthy and beautiful maiden would not listen to any young lord, having pledged her faith to the plain John Ridd.

Thereupon our Lorna managed so to hold out

golden hopes to the Lord High Chancellor; that
he, being not more than three parts drunk, saw his
way to a heap of money. And there and then (for
he was not the man to dally long about anything) upon
surety of a certain round sum—the amount of which I
will not mention, because of his kindness towards me—
he gave to his fair ward permission under sign and
seal, to marry that loyal knight, John Ridd; upon condition only that the King's consent should be obtained.

His Majesty, well-disposed towards me for my previous service, and regarding me as a good Catholic,
being moved moreover by the Queen, who desired
to please Lorna, consented without much hesitation,
upon the understanding that Lorna when she became
of full age, and the mistress of her property (which
was still under guardianship) should pay a heavy fine
to the Crown, and devote a fixed portion of her estate
to the promotion of the holy Catholic faith, in a manner
to be dictated by the King himself. Inasmuch, however, as King James was driven out of his kingdom
before this arrangement could take effect; and another
king succeeded, who desired not the promotion of the
Catholic religion, neither hankered after subsidies
(whether French or English), that agreement was pronounced invalid, improper, and contemptible. However
there was no getting back the money once paid to
Lord Chancellor Jeffreys.

But what thought we of money at this present
moment; or of position, or anything else, except indeed
one another? Lorna told me, with the sweetest smile,

that if I were minded to take her at all, I must take
her without anything; inasmuch as she meant, upon
coming of age, to make over the residue of her estates
to the next of kin, as being unfit for a farmer's wife.
And I replied with the greatest warmth and a readiness
to worship her, that this was exactly what I longed for,
but had never dared to propose it. But dear mother
looked most exceeding grave; and said that to be sure
her opinion could not be expected to count for much,
but she really hoped that in three years' time, we
should both be a little wiser, and have more regard
for our interests, and perhaps those of others by that
time; and Master Snowe having daughters only, and
nobody coming to marry them, if anything happened to
the good old man—and who could tell in three years'
time what might happen to all or any of us—why
perhaps his farm would be for sale, and perhaps Lady
Lorna's estates in Scotland would fetch enough money
to buy it, and so throw the two farms into one, and save
all the trouble about the brook, as my poor father had
longed to do many and many a time, but not having a
title could not do all quite as he wanted. And then
if we young people grew tired of the old mother, as
seemed only too likely and was according to nature;
why we could send her over there, and Lizzie to keep
her company.

When mother had finished, and wiped her eyes,
Lorna, who had been blushing rosily at some portions
of this great speech, flung her fair arms around
mother's neck, and kissed her very heartily, and

scolded her (as she well deserved) for her want of
confidence in us. My mother replied that if anybody
could deserve her John, it was Lorna; but that she
could not hold with the rashness of giving up money
so easily; while her next of kin would be John him
self; and who could tell what others, by the time she
was one and twenty?

Hereupon, I felt that after all my mother had common sense on her side; for if Master Snowe's farm
should be for sale, it would be far more to the purpose
than my coat of arms, to get it; for there was a
different pasture there, just suited for change of diet
to our sheep as well as large cattle. And beside
this, even with all Annie's skill (and of course yet
more now she was gone), their butter would always
command in the market, from one to three farthings
a pound more than we could get for ours. And few
things vexed us more than this. Whereas, if we got
possession of the farm, we might, without breach of the
market-laws, or any harm done to any one (the price
being but a prejudice) sell all our butter as Snowe
butter, and do good to all our customers.

Thinking thus, yet remembering that Farmer
Nicholas might hold out for another score of years—
as I heartily hoped he might—or that one, if not all,
of his comely daughters might marry a good young
farmer (or farmers, if the case were so)—or that, even
without that, the farm might never be put up for sale;
I begged my Lorna to do as she liked; or rather to
wait and think of it; for as yet she could do nothing.

## CHAPTER XXII.

EVERYTHING was settled smoothly, and without any fear or fuss, that Lorna might find end of troubles, and myself of eager waiting, with the help of Parson Bowden, and the good wishes of two counties. I could scarce believe my fortune, when I looked upon her beauty, gentleness, and sweetness, mingled with enough of humour, and warm woman's feeling, never to be dull or tiring; never themselves to be weary.

For she might be called a woman now; although a very young one, and as full of playful ways, or perhaps I may say ten times as full, as if she had known no trouble. To wit, the spirit of bright childhood, having been so curbed and straitened, ere its time was over, now broke forth, enriched and varied with the garb of conscious maidenhood. And the sense of steadfast love, and eager love enfolding her, coloured with so many tinges all her looks, and words, and thoughts, that to me it was the noblest vision even to think about her.

But this was far too bright to last, without bitter

break, and the plunging of happiness in horror,
and of passionate joy in agony.  My darling in her
softest moments, when she was alone with me, when
the spark of defiant eyes was veiled beneath dark
lashes, and the challenge of gay beauty passed into
sweetest invitation ; at such times of her purest love
and warmest faith in me, a deep abiding fear would
flutter in her bounding heart, as of deadly fate's
approach.  She would cling to me, and nestle to me,
being scared of coyishness, and lay one arm around my
neck, and ask if I could do without her.

Hence, as all emotions haply, of those who are
more to us than ourselves, find within us stronger echo,
and more perfect answer, so I could not be regardless
of some hidden evil ; and my dark misgivings deepened
as the time drew nearer.  I kept a steadfast watch on
Lorna, neglecting a field of beans entirely, as well as
a litter of young pigs, and a cow somewhat given to
jaundice.  And I let Jem Slocombe go to sleep in the
tallat, all one afternoon, and Bill Dadds draw off
a bucket of cider, without so much as a " by your
leave."  For these men knew that my knighthood, and
my coat of arms, and (most of all) my love, were
greatly against good farming ; the sense of our country
being—and perhaps it may be sensible—that a man
who sticks up to be anything, must allow himself
to be cheated.

But I never did stick up, nor would, though all the
parish bade me ; and I whistled the same tunes to my
horses, and held my plough-tree, just the same as

if no King, nor Queen, had ever come to spoil my tune
or hand, For this thing, nearly all the men around
our parts upbraided me : but the women praised me ;
and for the most part these are right, when themselves
are not concerned.

However humble I might be, no one knowing anything of our part of the country, would for a moment
doubt that now here was a great to-do and talk of
John Ridd, and his wedding.   The fierce fight with
the Doones so lately, and my leading of the combat
(though I fought not more than need be), and the
vanishing of Sir Counsellor, and the galloping madness
of Carver, and the religious fear of the women that
this last was gone to hell—for he himself had declared
that his aim, while he cut through the yeomanry—also
their remorse, that he should have been made to
go thither, with all his children left behind—these
things, I say (if ever I can again contrive to say
anything), had led to the broadest excitement about
my wedding of Lorna.   We heard that people meant
to come from more than thirty miles around, upon
excuse of seeing my stature and Lorna's beauty ;
but in good truth out of sheer curiosity, and the love
of meddling.

Our clerk had given notice, that not a man should
come inside the door of his church, without shilling-
fee ; and women (as sure to see twice as much) must
every one pay two shillings.   I thought this wrong ;
and as churchwarden, begged that the money might
be paid into mine own hands, when taken.   But the

clerk said that was against all law; and he had orders
from the parson to pay it to him, without any delay.
So as I always obey the parson, when I care not much
about a thing, I let them have it their own way;
though feeling inclined to believe, sometimes, that I
ought to have some of the money.

Dear mother arranged all the ins and outs of
the way in which it was to be done; and Annie and
Lizzie, and all the Snowes, and even Ruth Huckaback
(who was there, after great persuasion), made such a
sweeping of dresses that I scarcely knew where to
place my feet, and longed for a staff, to put by their
gowns. Then Lorna came out of a pew half-way, in
a manner which quite astonished me, and took my
left hand in her right, and I prayed God that it were
done with.

My darling looked so glorious, that I was afraid of
glancing at her, yet took in all her beauty. She was
in a fright, no doubt; but nobody should see it;
whereas I said (to myself at least) "I will go through
it, like a grave-digger."

Lorna's dress was of pure white, clouded with faint
lavender (for the sake of the old Earl Brandir), and as
simple as need be, except for perfect loveliness. I
was afraid to look at her, as I said before, except
when each of us said "I will;" and then each
dwelled upon the other.

It is impossible for any, who have not loved as
I have, to conceive my joy and pride, when after ring
and all was done, and the parson had blessed us,

Lorna turned to look at me with her glances of subtle fun subdued by this great act.

Her eyes, which none on earth may ever equal, or compare with, told me such a depth of comfort, yet awaiting further commune, that I was almost amazed, thoroughly, as I knew them. Darling eyes, the sweetest eyes, the loveliest, the most loving eyes— the sound of a shot rang through the church, and those eyes were filled with death.

Lorna fell across my knees when I was going to kiss her, as the bridegroom is allowed to do, and encouraged, if he needs it; a flood of blood came out upon the yellow wood of the altar steps; and at my feet lay Lorna, trying to tell me some last message out of her faithful eyes. I lifted her up, and petted her, and coaxed her; but it was no good; the only sign of life remaining was a spirt of bright red blood.

Some men know what things befall them in the supreme time of their life—far above the time of death—but to me comes back as a hazy dream, without any knowledge in it, what I did, or felt, or thought, with my wife's arms flagging, flagging, around my neck, as I raised her up, and softly put them there. She sighed a long sigh on my breast, for her last farewell to life, and then she grew so cold, and cold, that I asked the time of year.

It was now Whit-Tuesday, and the lilacs all in blossom; and why I thought of the time of year, with the young death in my arms, God, or his angels, may decide, having so strangely given us. Enough that so

I did, and looked; and our white lilacs were beautiful. Then I laid my wife in my mother's arms, and begging that no one would make a noise, went forth for my revenge.

Of course, I knew who had done it. There was but one man in the world, or at any rate in our part of it, who could have done such a thing—such a thing. I used no harsher word about it, while I leaped upon our best horse, with bridle but no saddle, and set the head of Kickums towards the course now pointed out to me. Who showed me the course, I cannot tell. I only know that I took it. And the men fell back before me.

Weapon of no sort had I. Unarmed, and wondering at my strange attire (with a bridal vest, wrought by our Annie, and red with the blood of the bride), I went forth just to find out this; whether in this world there be, or be not God of justice.

With my vicious horse at a furious speed, I came upon Black Barrow Down, directed by some shout of men, which seemed to me but a whisper. And there, about a furlong before me, rode a man on a great black horse, and I knew that the man was Carver Doone.

"Your life, or mine," I said to myself; "as the will of God may be. But we two live not upon this earth, one more hour, together."

I knew the strength of this great man; and I knew that he was armed with a gun—if he had time to load again, after shooting my Lorna,—or at any rate with pistols, and a horseman's sword as well. Nevertheless, I had no more doubt of killing the man before me, than a cook has of spitting a headless fowl.

Sometimes seeing no ground beneath me, and sometimes heeding every leaf, and the crossing of the grass-blades, I followed over the long moor, reckless whether seen or not. But only once, the other man turned round and looked back again, and then I was beside a rock, with a reedy swamp behind me.

Although he was so far before me, and riding as hard as ride he might, I saw that he had something on the horse in front of him; something which needed care, and stopped him from looking backward. In the whirling of my wits, I fancied first that this was Lorna; until the scene I had been through fell across hot brain and heart, like the drop at the close of a tragedy. Rushing there through crag and quag, at utmost speed of a maddened horse, I saw, as of another's fate, calmly (as on canvass laid), the brutal deed, the piteous anguish, and the cold despair.

The man turned up the gully leading from the moor to Cloven-Rocks, through which John Fry had tracked Uncle Ben, as of old related. But as Carver entered it, he turned round, and beheld me not a hundred yards behind; and I saw that he was bearing his child, little Ensie, before him. Ensie also descried me, and stretched his hands and cried to me; for the face of his father frightened him.

Carver Doone, with a vile oath, thrust spurs into his flagging horse, and laid one hand on a pistol-stock,

whence I knew that his slung carbine had received no
bullet, since the one that had pierced Lorna. And a
cry of triumph rose from the black depths of my heart.
What cared I for pistols? I had no spurs, neither was
my horse one to need the rowel, I rather held him in
than urged him, for he was fresh as ever; and I knew
that the black steed in front, if he breasted the steep
ascent, where the track divided, must be in our reach
at once.

His rider knew this; and, having no room in the
rocky channel to turn and fire, drew rein at the cross-
ways sharply, and plunged into the black ravine leading
to the Wizard's Slough. "Is it so?" I said to myself,
with brain and head cold as iron: "though the foul
fiend come from the slough, to save thee; thou shalt
carve it, Carver."

I followed my enemy carefully, steadily, even lei-
surely; for I had him, as in a pitfall; whence no escape
might be. He thought that I feared to approach him,
for he knew not where he was: and his low disdainful
laugh came back. "Laugh he who wins," thought I.

A gnarled and half starved oak, as stubborn as my
own resolve, and smitten by some storm of old, hung
from the crag above me. Rising from my horse's back,
although I had no stirrups, I caught a limb, and tore
it (like a mere wheat-awn) from the socket. Men
show the rent even now, with wonder; none with more
wonder than myself.

Carver Doone turned the corner suddenly on the
black and bottomless bog; with a start of fear he

reined back his horse, and I thought he would have
turned upon me.    But instead of that, he again rode
on ; hoping to find a way round the side.

Now there is a way between cliff and slough, for those
who know the ground thoroughly, or have time enough
to search it : but for him there was no road, and he lost
some time in seeking it.    Upon this he made up his
mind ; and wheeling, fired, and then rode at me.

His bullet struck me somewhere, but I took no heed
of that.   Fearing only his escape, I laid my horse across
the way, and with the limb of the oak struck full on the
forehead his charging steed.   ' Ere the slash of the
sword came nigh me, man and horse rolled over, and
well nigh bore my own horse down, with the power of
their onset.

Carver Doone was somewhat stunned, and could not
arise for a moment.    Meanwhile I leaped on the
ground, and awaited ; smoothing my hair back, and
baring my arms, as though in the ring for wrestling.
Then the little boy ran to me, clasped my leg, and
looked up at me : and the terror in his eyes made me
almost fear myself.

" Ensie dear," I said quite gently, grieving that he
should see his wicked father killed ; " run up yonder
round the corner, and try to find a pretty bunch of blue-
bells for the lady." The child obeyed me, hanging back,
and looking back, and then laughing, while I prepared
for business.    There and then, I might have killed
mine enemy with a single blow, while he lay uncon-
scious : but it would have been foul play.    .

With a sullen and black scowl, the Carver gathered his mighty limbs, and arose, and looked round for his weapons; but I had put them well away. Then he came to me, and gazed; being wont to frighten thus young men.

"I would not harm you, lad;" he said, with a lofty style of sneering: "I have punished you enough, for most of your impertinence. For the rest I forgive you; because you have been good and gracious to my little son. Go, and be contented."

For answer, I smote him on the cheek; lightly, and not to hurt him; but to make his blood leap up. I would not sully my tongue by speaking to a man like this.

There was a level space of sward, between us and the slough. With the courtesy derived from London, and the processions I had seen, to this place I led him. And that he might breathe himself, and have every fibre cool, and every muscle ready, my hold upon his coat I loosed, and left him to begin with me, whenever he thought proper.

I think he felt that his time was come. I think he knew from my knitted muscles, and the firm arch of my breast, and the way in which I stood: but most of all from my stern blue eyes; that he had found his master. At any rate a paleness came, an ashy paleness on his cheeks, and the vast calves of his legs bowed in; as if he were out of training.

Seeing this, villain as he was, I offered him first chance. I stretched forth my left hand, as I do to a weaker antagonist, and I let him have the hug of me. But in this I was too generous; having forgotten my pistol-wound, and the cracking of one of my short lower ribs. Carver Doone caught me round the waist, with such a grip as never yet had been laid upon me.

I heard my rib go; I grasped his arm, and tore the muscle out of it * (as the string comes out of an orange); then I took him by the throat, which is not allowed in wrestling; but he had snatched at mine; and now, was no time of dalliance. In vain he tugged, and strained, and writhed, dashed his bleeding fist into my face, and flung himself on me with gnashing jaws. Beneath the iron of my strength—for God that day was with me—I had him helpless in two minutes; and his fiery eyes lolled out.

" I will not harm thee any more;" I cried, so far as I could for panting, the work being very furious: " Carver Doone, thou art beaten : own it, and thank God for it ; and go thy way, and repent thyself."

It was all too late. Even if he had yielded in his ravening frenzy—for his beard was like a mad dog's jowl—even if he would have owned that, for the first time in his life, he had found his master; it was all too late.

The black bog had him by the feet; the sucking of the ground drew on him, like the thirsty lips of death. In our fury, we had heeded neither wet nor dry; nor

---

* A far more terrible clutch than this, is handed down, to weaker ages, of the great John Ridd.—ED. L. D.

thought of earth beneath us. I myself might scarcely leap, with the last spring of o'er-laboured legs, from the engulfing grave of slime. He fell back, with his swarthy breast (from which my gripe had rent all clothing) like a hummock of bog-oak, standing out the quagmire; and then he tossed his arms to heaven, and they were black to the elbow, and the glare of his eyes was ghastly. I could only gaze and pant; for my strength was no more than an infant's, from the fury and the horror. Scarcely could I turn away, while, joint by joint, he sank from sight.

## CHAPTER XXIII.

WHEN the little boy came back with the blue-bells, which he had managed to find—as children always do find flowers, when older eyes see none—the only sign of his father left was a dark brown bubble, upon a new-formed patch of blackness. But to the centre of its pulpy gorge the greedy slough was heaving, and sullenly grinding its weltering jaws among the flags and the sedges.

With pain, and ache, both of mind and body, and shame at my own fury, I heavily mounted my horse again, and looked down at the innocent Ensie. Would this playful, loving child grow up like his cruel father, and end a godless life of hatred with a death of violence? He lifted his noble forehead towards me, as if to answer " Nay, I will not: "' but the words he spoke were these:

" Don,"—for he never could say " John "—" oh Don, I am so glad that nasty naughty man is gone away. Take me home, Don. Take me home."

It has been said of the wicked, " not even their own

children love them." And I could easily believe that
Carver Doone's cold-hearted ways had scared from him
even his favourite child. No man would I call truly
wicked, unless his heart be cold.

It hurt me, more than I can tell, even through
all other grief, to take into my arms the child of the
man just slain by me. The feeling was a foolish one,
and a wrong one, as the thing had been—for I would
fain have saved that man, after he was conquered—
nevertheless my arms went coldly round that little
fellow; neither would they have gone at all, if there
had been any help for it. But I could not leave him
there, till some one else might fetch him; on account
of the cruel slough, and the ravens which had come
hovering over the dead horse; neither could I, with my
wound, tie him on my horse and walk.

For now I had spent a great deal of blood, and was
rather faint and weary. And it was lucky for me that
Kickums had lost spirit, like his master, and went
home as mildly as a lamb. For, when we came
towards the farm, I seemed to be riding in a dream
almost; and the voices both of men and women (who
had hurried forth upon my track) as they met me,
seemed to wander from a distant muffling cloud.
Only the thought of Lorna's death, like a heavy knell,
was tolling in the belfry of my brain.

When we came to the stable-door, I rather fell from
my horse than got off; and John Fry, with a look of
wonder, took Kickums' head, and led him in. Into
the old farm-house I tottered, like a weanling child,

with mother in her common clothes, helping me along, yet fearing, except by stealth, to look at me.

"I have killed him," was all I said: "even as he killed Lorna. Now let me see my wife, mother. She belongs to me none the less, though dead."

"You cannot see her now, dear John," said Ruth Huckaback, coming forward; since no one else had the courage. "Annie is with her now, John."

"What has that to do with it? Let me see my dead one; and pray myself to die."

All the women fell away, and whispered, and looked at me, with side glances, and some sobbing: for my face was hard as flint. Ruth alone stood by me, and dropped her eyes, and trembled. Then one little hand of hers stole into my great shaking palm, and the other was laid on my tattered coat; yet with her clothes she shunned my blood, while she whispered gently—

"John, she is not your dead one. She may even be your living one yet, your wife, your home, and your happiness. But you must not see her now."

"Is there any chance for her? For me, I mean; for me, I mean?"

"God in heaven knows, dear John. But the sight of you, and in this sad plight, would be certain death to her. Now come first, and be healed yourself."

I obeyed her, like a child, whispering only as I went, for none but myself knew her goodness—"Almighty God will bless you, darling, for the good you are doing now."

Tenfold, ay and a thousandfold, I prayed and I
believed it, when I came to know the truth.  If it had
not been for this little maid, Lorna must have died at
once, as in my arms she lay for dead, from the dastard
and murderous cruelty.  But the moment I left her
Ruth came forward, and took the command of every
one, in right of her firmness and readiness.

She made them bear her home at once upon the
door of the pulpit, with the cushion under the drooping
head.  With her own little hands she cut off, as
tenderly as a pear is peeled, the bridal-dress so steeped
and stained, and then with her dainty transparent
fingers (no larger than a pencil) she probed the vile
wound in the side, and fetched the reeking bullet
forth ; and then with the coldest water staunched the
flowing of the life-blood.  All this while, my darling
lay insensible, and white as death ; and all the women
around declared that she was dead, and needed nothing
but her maiden shroud.

But Ruth still sponged the poor side and forehead,
and watched the long eyelashes flat upon the marble
cheek ; and laid her pure face on the faint heart,
and bade them fetch her Spanish wine.  Then she
parted the pearly teeth (feebly clenched on the
hovering breath), and poured in wine from a christening
spoon, and raised the graceful neck and breast, and
stroked the delicate throat, and waited ; and then
poured in a little more.

Annie all the while looked on, with horror and
amazement, counting herself no second-rate nurse, and

this as against all theory. But the quiet lifting of Ruth's hand, and one glance from her dark bright eyes, told Annie just to stand away, and not intercept the air so. And at the very moment when all the rest had settled that Ruth was a simple idiot, but could not harm the dead much, a little flutter in the throat, followed by a short low sigh, made them pause, and look, and hope.

For hours, however, and days, she lay at the very verge of death, kept alive by nothing but the care, the skill, the tenderness, and perpetual watchfulness of Ruth. Luckily Annie was not there very often, so as to meddle; for kind and clever nurse as she was, she must have done more harm than good. But my broken rib, which was set by a doctor, who chanced to be at the wedding, was allotted to Annie's care; and great inflammation ensuing, it was quite enough to content her. This doctor had pronounced poor Lorna dead; wherefore Ruth refused most firmly to have aught to do with him. She took the whole case on herself; and with God's help she bore it through.

Now whether it were the light and brightness of my Lorna's nature; or the freedom from anxiety—for she knew not of my hurt;—or, as some people said, her birthright among wounds and violence, or her manner of not drinking beer—I leave that doctor to determine, who pronounced her dead. But any how, one thing is certain; sure as the stars of hope above us; Lorna recovered, long ere I did.

For the grief was on me still, of having lost my love

and lover, at the moment she was mine. With the power of fate upon me, and the black cauldron of the wizard's death boiling in my heated brain, I had no faith in the tales they told. I believed that Lorna was in the churchyard, while these rogues were lying to me. For, with strength of blood like mine, and power of heart behind it, a broken bone must burn itself.

Mine went hard with fires of pain, being of such size and thickness; and I was ashamed of him for breaking by reason of a pistol-ball, and the mere hug of a man. And it fetched me down in conceit of strength; so that I was careful afterwards.

All this was a lesson to me. All this made me very humble; illness being a thing, as yet, altogether unknown to me. Not that I cried small, or skulked, or feared the death which some foretold; shaking their heads about mortification, and a green appearance. Only that I seemed quite fit to go to heaven, and Lorna. For in my sick distracted mind (stirred with many tossings), like the bead in a spread of frog-spawn carried by the current, hung the black and central essence of my future life. A life without Lorna; a tadpole life. All stupid head; and no body.

Many men may like such life; anchorites, fakirs, high-priests, and so on. But to my mind, it is not the native thing God meant for us. My dearest mother was a show, with crying and with fretting. The Doones, as she thought, were born to destroy us. Scarce had she come to some liveliness (though sprinkled with tears, every now and then) after her

great bereavement, and ten years' time to dwell on it—
when lo, here was her husband's son, the pet child of
her own good John, murdered like his father! Well,
the ways of God were wonderful!

So they were, and so they are; and so they ever will
be. Let us debate them, as we will; our ways are
His, and much the same; only second-hand from
Him. And I expected something from Him, even in
my worst of times; knowing that I had done my best.

This is not edifying talk—as our Non-conformist
parson says, when he can get no more to drink—therefore let me only tell what became of Lorna. One day,
I was sitting in my bed-room; for I could not get down
stairs, and there was no one strong enough to carry
me, even if I would have allowed it.

Though it cost me sore trouble and weariness, I had
put on all my Sunday clothes, out of respect for the
docter, who was coming to bleed me again (as he
always did, twice a week) and it struck me that he
had seemed hurt in his mind, because I wore my worst
clothes to be bled in—for lie in bed I would not, after
six o'clock; and even that was great laziness.

I looked at my right hand, whose grasp had been
like that of a blacksmith's vice; and it seemed to
myself impossible that this could be John Ridd's. The
great frame of the hand was there, as well as the
muscles, standing forth like the guttering of a candle,
and the broad blue veins, going up the back, and
crossing every finger. But as for colour, even Lorna's
could scarcely have been whiter: and as for strength,

little Ensie Doone might have come and held it fast. I laughed as I tried in vain to lift the basin set for bleeding me.

Then I thought of all the lovely things going on out of doors just now, concerning which the drowsy song of the bees came to me. These must be among the thyme, by the sound of their great content. Therefore the roses must be in blossom, and the woodbine, and clove-gilly-flower; the cherries on the wall must be turning red, the yellow Sally must be on the brook, wheat must be callow with quavering bloom, and the early meadows swathed with hay.

Yet here was I, a helpless creature, quite unfit to stir among them, gifted with no sight, no scent of all the changes that move our love, and lead our hearts, from month to month, along the quiet path of life. And what was worse, I had no hope of caring ever for them more.

Presently a little knock sounded through my gloomy room; and supposing it to be the doctor, I tried to rise, and make my bow. But to my surprise it was little Ruth, who had never once come to visit me, since I was placed under the doctor's hands. Ruth was dressed so gaily, with rosettes, and flowers, and what not, that I was sorry for her bad manners; and thought she was come to conquer me, now that Lorna was done with.

Ruth ran towards me with sparkling eyes, being rather short of sight; then suddenly she stopped, and I saw entire amazement in her face.

"Can you receive visitors, Cousin Ridd—why, they

never told me of this!" she cried: "I knew that you were weak, dear John; but not that you were dying. Whatever is that basin for?"

"I have no intention of dying, Ruth: and I like not to talk about it. But that basin, if you must know, is for the doctor's purpose."

"What, do you mean bleeding you? You poor weak cousin! Is it possible that he does that still?"

"Twice a week for the last six weeks, dear. Nothing else has kept me alive."

"Nothing else has killed you, nearly. There!" and she set her little boot across the basin, and crushed it. "Not another drop shall they have from you. Is Annie such a fool as that? And Lizzie, like a zany, at her books! And killing their brother, between them!"

I was surprised to see Ruth excited; her character being so calm and quiet. And I tried to soothe her with my feeble hand, as now she knelt before me.

"Dear cousin, the doctor must know best. Annie says so, every day. Else what has he been brought up for?"

"Brought up for slaying, and murdering. Twenty doctors killed King Charles, in spite of all the women. Will you leave it to me, John? I have a little will of my own: and I am not afraid of doctors. Will you leave it to me, dear John? I have saved your Lorna's life. And now I will save yours; which is a far, far, easier business."

"You have saved my Lorna's life! What do you mean, by talking so?"

"Only what I say, Cousin John. Though perhaps I over-prize my work. But at any rate, she says so."

"I do not understand," I said, falling back with bewilderment: "all women are such liars."

"Have you ever known me tell a lie?" cried Ruth in great indignation—more feigned, I doubt, than real— "your mother may tell a story, now and then, when she feels it right; and so may both your sisters. But so you cannot do, John Ridd; and no more than you, can I do it."

If ever there was virtuous truth in the eyes of any woman, it now was in Ruth Huckaback's: and my brain began very slowly to move, the heart being almost torpid, from perpetual loss of blood. "I do not understand," was all I could say for a very long time.

"Will you understand, if I show you Lorna? I have feared to do it, for the sake of you both. But now Lorna is well enough; if you think that you are, Cousin John. Surely you will understand, when you see your wife."

Following her, to the very utmost of my mind and heart, I felt that all she said was truth; and yet I could not make it out. And in her last few words there was such a power of sadness rising through the cover of gaiety, that I said to myself, half in a dream, "Ruth is very beautiful."

Before I had time to listen much for the approach of footsteps, Ruth came back, and behind her Lorna; coy as if of her bridegroom; and hanging back with her

VOL. III.                                                        z

beauty. Ruth banged the door, and ran away; and
Lorna stood before me.

But she did not stand for an instant; when she saw
what I was like. At the risk of all thick bandages,
and upsetting a dozen medicine bottles, and scattering
leeches right and left, she managed to get into my
arms, although they could not hold her. She laid her
panting warm young breast on the place where they
meant to bleed me, and she set my pale face up; and
she would not look at me, having greater faith in
kissing.

I felt my life come back, and warm; I felt my trust
in women flow; I felt the joy of living now, and the
power of doing it. It is not a moment to describe;
who feels can never tell of it. But the rush of Lorna's
tears, and the challenge of my bride's lips, and the
throbbing of my wife's heart (now at last at home on
mine), made me feel that the world was good, and not
a thing to be weary of.

Little more have I to tell. The doctor was turned
out at once; and slowly came back my former strength,
with a darling wife, and good victuals. As for Lorna,
she never tired of sitting and watching me eat and eat.
And such is her heart that she never tires of being
with me here and there, among the beautiful places,
and talking with her arm around me—so far at least
as it can go, though half of mine may go round her—
of the many fears, and troubles, dangers and dis-
couragements, and worst of all the bitter partings,
which we used to have, somehow.

There is no need for my farming harder than
becomes a man of weight. Lorna has great stores of
money, though we never draw it out, except for some
poor neighbour; unless I find her a sumptuous dress,
out of her own perquisites. And this she always looks
upon as a wondrous gift from me; and kisses me much
when she puts it on, and walks like the noble woman she
is. And yet I may never behold it again: for she gets
back to her simple clothes, and I love her the better in
them. I believe that she gives half the grandeur away,
and keeps the other half for the children.

As for poor Tom Faggus, every one knows his
bitter adventures, when his pardon was recalled,
because of his journey to Sedgemoor. Not a child in
the country, I doubt, but knows far more than I do of
Tom's most desperate doings. The law had ruined
him once, he said; and then he had been too much for
the law: and now that a quiet life was his object, here
the base thing came after him. And such was his
dread of this evil spirit, that being caught upon Barnstaple Bridge, with soldiers at either end of it (yet
doubtful about approaching him), he set his strawberry
mare, sweet Winnie, at the left-hand parapet, with a
whisper into her dove-coloured ear. Without a moment's doubt she leaped it, into the foaming tide, and
swam, and landed according to orders. Also his
flight from a public-house (where a trap was set for
him, but Winnie came and broke down the door, and
put two men under, and trod on them), is as well known
as any ballad. It was reported for awhile, that poor

z 2

Tom had been caught at last, by means of his fondness
for liquor, and was hanged before Taunton Gaol: but
luckily we knew better.  With a good wife, and a
wonderful horse, and all the country attached to him,
he kept the law at a wholesome distance; until it
became too much for its master; and a new king
arose.  Upon this, Tom sued his pardon afresh; and
Jeremy Stickles, who suited the times, was glad to
help him in getting it, as well as a compensation.
Thereafter the good and respectable Tom lived a
godly (though not always sober) life; and brought
up his children to honesty, as the first of all quali-
fications.

My dear mother was as happy, as possibly need be,
with us; having no cause for jealousy, as others
arose around her.   And everybody was well-pleased,
when Lizzie came in, one day, and tossed her book-
shelf over, and declared that she would have Captain
Bloxham, and nobody should prevent her.   For that
he alone, of all the men she had ever met with, knew
good writing, when he saw it; and could spell a
word when told.   As he had now succeeded to
Captain Stickles' position—(Stickles going up the
tree)—and had the power of collecting, and of
keeping, what he liked, there was nothing to be
said against it: and we hoped that he would pay her
out.

I sent little Ensie to Blundell's school, at my own
cost and charges; having changed his name, for fear of
what any one might do to him.  I called him Ensie

Jones; and I think that he will be a credit to us. For the bold adventurous nature of the Doones broke out on him; and we got him a commission, and after many scrapes of spirit, he did great things in the Low Countries. He looks upon me as his father; and without my leave will not lay claim to the heritage and title of the Doones, which clearly belong to him.

Ruth Huckaback is not married yet; although upon Uncle Reuben's death she came into all his property; except, indeed, 2000*l*., which Uncle Ben, in his dryest manner, bequeathed "to Sir John Ridd, the worshipful knight, for greasing of the testator's boots." And he left almost a mint of money, not from the mine, but from the shop, and the good use of usury. For the mine had brought in just what it cost; when the vein of gold ended suddenly; leaving all concerned much older, and some, I fear, much poorer; but no one utterly ruined, as is the case with most of them. Ruth herself was his true mine; as upon death-bed he found. I know a man even worthy of her: and though she is not very young; he loves her, as I love Lorna. It is my firm conviction, that in the end he will win her: and I do not mean to dance again, except at dear Ruth's wedding; if the floor be strong enough.

Of Lorna, of my lifelong darling, of my more and more loved wife, I will not talk; for it is not seemly that a man should exalt his pride. Year by year her beauty grows, with the growth of goodness, kindness, and true happiness—above all with loving. For change, she makes a joke of this, and plays with it, and laughs at it ; and then, when my slow nature marvels, back she comes to the earnest thing. And if I wish to pay her out for something very dreadful—as may happen once or twice, when we become too gladsome—I bring her to forgotten sadness, and to me for cure of it, by the two words " Lorna Doone."

FINIS.

LONDON: PRINTED BY W. CLOWES AND SONS, STAMFORD STREET AND CHARING CROSS.